1982

The First One Hundred Justices

JOHN JAY, THE FIRST CHIEF JUSTICE
From the collection of the Library of Congress

The First
One Hundred Justices

*Statistical Studies
on the Supreme Court of the United States*

BY
ALBERT P. BLAUSTEIN
AND
ROY M. MERSKY

ARCHON BOOKS
1978

© The Shoe String Press, Inc. 1978

First published 1978 as an Archon Book,

an imprint of THE SHOE STRING PRESS, INC.

Hamden, Connecticut 06514

Library of Congress Cataloging in Publication Data

Blaustein, Albert P   1921-
    The first one hundred justices.

    Bibliography: p.
    Includes index.
        1. United States. Supreme Court—Statistics. 2. Judges—
United States—Biography. I. Mersky, Roy M. joint author.
II. Title.
KF8741.A152B6   347′.73′2634   77-23543
ISBN 0-208-01290-7

Printed in the United States of America

Contents

Appendix

Selected Bibliography
[With Adrienne de Vergie, Jenni Parrish, and
Daniel W. Martin]
page 151

Index

Acknowledgement
The authors are grateful to Jessie L. Matthews for her skill in preparing the index and for her dedication to the entire project.

One

A Biography of the Supreme Court

The First One Hundred

The date was January 7, 1972. William Hubbs Rehnquist, who earlier that same day had taken his judicial oath, now assumed his seat on the far left of the Supreme Court bench as was proper for the new junior member of that august tribunal. It was an historical occasion, albeit an unheralded one.

For this event marked a centenary in the history of the United States Supreme Court. No, not the Court's one hundredth anniversary or birthday. That was properly celebrated on September 26, 1889, one hundred years after the date of John Jay's commission as the nation's first Supreme Court justice. What happened on January 7, 1972, was that Mr. Justice Rehnquist became the one hundredth man to see service on the nation's highest judicial body.

But the swearing-in ceremony had been number one hundred and four, rather than an even one hundred. On fifteen previous occasions, men had taken the oath as chief justice and history had recorded eighty-nine oath-takings for the post of associate justice. And fifteen plus eighty-nine does total one hundred and four. Yet Rehnquist was indeed number one hundred, since four members of the Court had been sworn in twice—first as an associate justice and subsequently as chief justice of the United States.

This chapter is the story of those first one hundred justices. It is a statistical story, a sort of composite biography. It does not include the presidential appointees who did not see judicial service. Their story is told in chapter four.

After the name of each justice mentioned in this biographical sketch is a number within parentheses, which marks the chronological order of appointment from Jay (1) to Rehnquist (100). It also provides a quick key to the tables found in the appendix to this volume.

The 1789 Judiciary Act set up a six-member Supreme Court. The first six justices, whose names are followed by numbers (1) to (6) in table 1, were the first of the ten appointed by President George Washington. The seats they occupied are numbered 1 to 10 in table 2, with the seat of the chief justice designated as 1. Thus, Thomas Johnson (7), the seventh justice to sit on the Court, was the second occupant of seat 2.

In 1807, the Court was enlarged to seven members, with Thomas Todd (16), the sixteenth justice, as the first occupant of seat 7. Court membership was increased to nine in 1837. John Catron (26) was the first appointee to occupy seat 8 and John McKinley (27) was the first justice to occupy seat 9. The Court has been a nine-member body since that time, save for the period 1863–1869. Stephen J. Field (38), with judicial service from 1863 to 1897, was the tenth justice at the time of his appointment. His successor on the bench, Joseph McKenna (57), could be classified as the occupant of either seat 8 or seat 10. The latter designation has been used here.

For the four justices who have served both as associate justice and as chief justice, only the first "associate justice number" has been used because this number marks the chronological order of his first appointment to the Court.

Thus John Rutledge remains (2). Edward D. White is always (55), Charles Evans Hughes is (62), and Harlan F. Stone is (73).

The Chief Justices

It is often surprising to foreigners that of the fifteen justices appointed to seat 1, eleven were named directly to that office. As noted, only four had previously served as associate justices. And of those four, only E. D. White (55) and Stone (73) were promoted while on the bench.

White served as an associate justice from 1894 to 1910, and then as chief justice from 1910 to 1921. Stone served as an associate justice from 1925 to 1941 and then as chief justice from 1941 to 1946. But the judicial service of Rutledge and Hughes was not consecutive. Rutledge, the second justice appointed to the bench, was later named as its second chief justice. His service from 1789 to 1791 ended with his resignation to accept the chief justiceship of South Carolina. President Washington nominated Rutledge as chief justice on July 1, 1795, followed by a swearing-in ceremony on August 12. But his service as chief justice was brief, for the Senate formally rejected his appointment on December 15, 1795. Appointed as associate justice in 1910, Hughes resigned in 1916 to become the Republican candidate for the presidency. Defeated by Woodrow Wilson, he went back into active legal practice until named by President Herbert Hoover as chief justice in 1930.

The record for longevity as chief justice goes to John Marshall (13), who served in the post for thirty-four years. But he was neither the youngest member named to the chief justiceship nor the oldest at the time his service came to an end. These records are held by Chief Justice John Jay (1), only forty-four at the time of his appointment, and Chief Justice Roger B. Taney (24), who was eighty-seven when he died in office.

Marshall (13) at age forty-five was the only chief justice other than John Jay (1) who was appointed while still in his forties. Seven others were named between their fiftieth and fifty-ninth birthdays. Oldest of the fifteen at the time of their appointments were Chief Justices Stone (73), aged sixty-eight, and Chief Justice Hughes (62), aged sixty-seven. Others who had passed the sixty-year-mark were Edward D. White (55), aged sixty-five; William H. Taft (69), aged sixty-three; Earl Warren (88), aged sixty-two; and Warren Burger (97), aged sixty-one.

Youngest at the time they left the Supreme Court bench were the two (the only two) chief justices who resigned from that office. Jay (1) was forty-nine and Oliver Ellsworth (10) was fifty-five. Rutledge (2) was only fifty-six at the time he was rejected for the post. Here is the breakdown on age at termination of office and reasons for termination:

Justice	Age at Termination	Reason for Termination
Taney (24)	87	death
Marshall (13)	79 (10 months)	death
Hughes (62)	79 (2 months)	retired
Warren (88)	78	retired
Fuller (50)	77	death
Douglas (79)	77	retired
White (55)	75	death
Stone (73)	73	death
Taft (69)	72	retired
Waite (43)	71	death
Chase (39)	65	death
Vinson (85)	63	death
Rutledge (2)	56	rejected
Ellsworth (10)	55	resigned
Jay (1)	49	resigned

The Presidents

Of the thirty-six presidents in the period covered by this study through Nixon—thirty-four made one hundred and thirty-eight nominations to the Supreme Court; no appointments were made by William Henry Harrison and Zachary Taylor. But only thirty-three presidents made the one hundred and four appointments which resulted in swearing-in ceremonies of the first one hundred men who served on the Court. (As noted, four of the men who served on the Court were sworn in twice, once as associate justice and once as chief justice.) Andrew Johnson made but one appointment and then saw Congress remove the vacancy by reducing the size of the Court.

The story of the thirty-four appointments which did not result in Supreme Court service (thirty-eight minus four) is told in chapter four. Here the focus is on the thirty-three presidents who made the one hundred and four appointments.

Washington, who of course had the most vacancies to fill, named the largest number to the Court: eleven, twice selecting Rutledge (2). Franklin D. Roosevelt made nine appointments from 1937 to 1943, although his four terms in office extended from 1933 to his death in 1945. Presidents Jackson (1829–1837) and Taft (1909–1913) each named six justices, and Lincoln (1861–1865) and Eisenhower (1953–1961) each named five.

Six presidents made four appointments: Grant (1869–1877), Benjamin Harrison (1889–1893), Cleveland (1885–1889) (1893–1897), Harding (1921–1923), Truman (1945–1953), and Nixon (1969–1974). Cleveland selected two justices during his first term, Lucius Q. C. Lamar (49) and Melville W. Fuller (50), and two during his second term, Edward D. White (55) and Rufus W. Peckham (56).

Thus six presidents made forty-two appointments and six presidents made four appointments each for a total of twenty-four more. The remaining thirty-eight appointments (forty-two plus twenty-four plus thirty-eight equals one hundred and four swearing-in ceremonies) were made by twenty-one presidents. Five presidents named three justices, seven named two, and eight named one.

Washington appointed Rutledge as chief justice six years after he had made him an associate justice. White (55) was appointed an associate justice by Cleveland in 1894 and then promoted by Taft in 1910. Hughes (62) was selected for an associate justiceship by Taft, also in 1910, and then chosen as chief justice by Hoover in 1930. Stone (73) was originally named by Coolidge in 1925 and then elevated by Franklin Roosevelt in 1941.

Of the present nine-member Court, four are Nixon appointees: Rehnquist (100), Powell (99), Blackmun (98), and Burger (97). Only one Johnson nominee is still on the Court, Thurgood Marshall (96), and only one Kennedy nominee still serves, Byron White (93). There are two justices designated by Eisenhower: Brennan (90) and Stewart (92). The newest member of the present Court is the successor of William O. Douglas (79) (the longest serving member of the Court, who retired on November 12, 1975). John Paul Stevens (101) was nominated by President Gerald R. Ford and sworn in on December 19, 1975.

The Politics

All the thirty-three appointing presidents and the one hundred and four appointees were members of one of five political parties.

Party	Number of Presidents	Number of Judicial Appointments
Republican	14	45
Democratic	11	36
Democratic- Republican	4	7
Federalist	2	14
Whig	2	2
Total	33	104

The two Federalist presidents (Washington and John Adams) only named Federalists to the Court, and the four Democratic-Republicans (Jefferson, Madison, Monroe, and J. Q. Adams) only selected Democratic-Republican justices.

However, the succeeding presidents did not confine nominations to their own parties.

Whig President Millard Fillmore appointed Whig Benjamin R. Curtis (32) to the Court, but Whig President John Tyler named a Democrat, Samuel Nelson (49). And the fourteen Republican presidents who made forty-two appointments hardly acted on the basis of political considerations—at least not consistently. For the political make-up of the 100 justices comes out this way:

Democrats	42
Republicans	37
Federalists	13
Democratic-Republicans	7
Whig	1
	100

President William Howard Taft (1909–1913), later Chief Justice Taft (61) (1921–1930), is the Republican chief executive most responsible for adding to the Democratic total. Of his six nominees, three were Democrats: Chief Justice White (55), Horace H. Lurton (61), and Joseph R. Lamar (64).

Among the other Republican presidents who named Democrats to the Supreme Court were:

Republican President	Democratic Nominee	Total Appointments
Lincoln	Field (38)	5
B. Harrison	Jackson (54)	4
Harding	Butler (71)	4
Hoover	Cardozo (75)	3
Eisenhower	Brennan (90)	5

On the other hand, Democrat Franklin D. Roosevelt promoted Republican Harlan F. Stone (73) to the chief justiceship and Democrat Harry Truman named his old friend, Republican Harold H. Burton (84), as the first of his four Supreme Court appointees. Andrew Jackson might almost be listed among the Democrats who named a non-

Democrat to the Court. A firm believer in the spoils system, Jackson made six appointments of six Democrats: John McLean (21) was, at least, nominally a Jacksonian at the time of his nomination. But, it is almost impossible to pin a party designation on maverick McLean. Postmaster General during the Democratic-Republican administrations of Monroe and J. Q. Adams, he was retained in that office when Jackson became president. Named to the Supreme Court in 1829, he was to be a presidential candidate four times for four parties during his thirty-two years on the bench: in 1832 as an Anti-Mason, in 1836 as an Independent, in 1842 as both a Whig and a Free-Soiler, and in 1856 as a Republican.

Since Supreme Court justices have life tenure, their political views may be felt long after the electorate has shown its preferences for other parties. Chief Justice Marshall (13), a Federalist appointed in the final days of the administration of Federalist John Adams in 1801, served through four Democratic-Republican administrations and then through more than half the tenure of Democratic President Jackson. Justice Story (17), a Democratic-Republican named by President Madison in 1811, also held office during Whig and Democratic administrations, more than fifteen years after the last Democratic-Republican president had left office.

The First One Hundred Justices

Occupational Backgrounds. While neither the Constitution nor acts of Congress have ever required a legal background for membership on the Supreme Court, all of the first one hundred justices have been lawyers. But only fifty-eight of the one hundred justices elevated to the nation's highest court had had any prior judicial experience at all—and only twenty-two of the fifty-eight had served more than ten years on a state or federal bench.

At the time of their appointment to the Supreme Court,

sixty were *not* holding judicial office. Here is the break-down, taken from table 1.

Private Law Practice	25	State Governorships	3
Federal Bench	20	House of Representatives	2
State Bench	20	U. S. Solicitors General	2
U. S. Attorneys General	7	U. S. "Assistant" Attorneys General	2
Other Cabinet Posts	7	Law School Professorships	2
U. S. Senate	6	Miscellaneous	4

The four in the "miscellaneous" category were Douglas (79), then chairman of the Securities and Exchange Commission; Duvall (17), who was U. S. comptroller of the treasury; Jay (1), secretary of foreign affairs under the Articles of Confederation; and Iredell (6), who had been serving as "digester" of statutes in North Carolina—a post which carried the duties of organizing and revising state legislation. Before his appointment as "digester," however, Iredell had served as a state judge and as state attorney general.

In addition to the forty who were judges at the time of their appointments (as detailed in table 5) at least another dozen Supreme Court justices had had *significant* prior judicial experience. Former President Taft was a Yale law professor at the time he became Chief Justice Taft (69), but he had previously been a judge of the U. S. Court of Appeals, Sixth Circuit. Other ex-federal appeal judges were Joseph McKenna (57) of the Ninth Circuit, Chief Justice Vinson (85) of the District of Columbia Circuit, and Thurgood Marshall (96) of the Second Circuit.

Smith Thompson (19) of New York and John Catron (26) of Tennessee had both served as their state's chief judges; and associate justiceships on state supreme courts had been held by McLean (21) of Ohio, Strong (40) of Pennsylvania, Chief Justice White (55) of Louisiana, and J. R. Lamar (64) of Georgia. Other important ex-state judges—not in judicial office at the time of appointment—were Iredell (6), Ellsworth (10), Wayne (23), Woodbury (30), and Matthews (46).

Charles Evans Hughes (62) was governor of New York before his appointment as associate justice and a member of the Permanent Court of International Justice at the time of his designation to the chief justiceship.

It has long been a matter of debate whether previous judicial experience should be a prerequisite for Supreme Court office. Certainly President Eisenhower thought so, appointing Harlan (89), Whittaker (91), and Stewart (92) to federal courts of appeals before naming them to the Supreme Court. And yet experience in judicial office has been no guide to Supreme Court performance. Eight of the fifteen chief justices, including Chief Justice Marshall (13), Taney (24), and Warren (88), had their first judicial experience on the Supreme Court.

Is public service a valid prerequisite? Holding significant nonjudicial posts *at the time* of their appointments (which certainly provided valuable background for Supreme Court office) were eleven former officials of the Department of Justice. These included seven ex-attorneys general: McKenna (57), Moody (60), McReynolds (66), Stone (73), Murphy (80), Jackson (82), and Clark (86); two ex-solicitors general: Reed (77) and Thurgood Marshall (96); and two "assistant" attorneys general: Deputy Attorney General Byron R. White (93) and William Rehnquist (100), assistant attorney general in charge of the Office of Legal Counsel. There were many other veterans of Department of Justice service who held different positions at the time of their appointments.

Although Warren (88) had never served as a judge before his designation as chief justice, he had been in the public service as a county district attorney, as governor of California, and as a vice-presidential candidate.

It would be difficult indeed to single out any member of the Supreme Court who had not had important prior public service. It is true that twenty-five of the justices were in private practice at the time of appointments. But from James Wilson (4) through Lewis F. Powell, Jr. (99) all had held official posts. Wilson, for example, was a delegate to the Federal Convention of 1787, where his role in the deliberations on the American Constitution has been described as second only to that of James Madison. Powell, in addition to his work in Virginia, was a member of the National Commission on Law Enforcement and Administration from 1965 to 1967 and a member of the Blue Ribbon Defense Panel to Study the Defense Department from 1969 to 1970.

Nor could any one of the Court's fifteen ex-law professors be classified as a purely private person, or as a typical resident of the ivory towers of academe. The only ones who were teaching at the time of their appointments were long-time presidential adviser Frankfurter (78) at Harvard Law School and former President Taft (69) at Yale Law School.

Here is a breakdown on the fifteen law professors, five of whom were or became law school deans and six of whom served on the Supreme Court together:

The ex-deans were Lurton (61) at Vanderbilt, Taft (69) at Cincinnati (before his election as president), Stone (73) at Columbia, Rutledge (83), at both Washington University in St. Louis and Iowa, and Roberts (74), a professor at the University of Pennsylvania before his appointment to the bench and dean at the same school after his retirement.

When ex-dean Rutledge (83) joined the Court in 1943, there were six ex-law professors on the bench at the same time. The others were Stone (73), Roberts (74), Frankfurter (78), Douglas (79) (both Columbia and Yale), and Murphy (80) (University of Detroit).

Strong (40) taught law at Columbian College which later became George Washington University; Holmes (58) was at Harvard; Hughes (62) was at Cornell for two years; McReynolds (66) was at Vanderbilt; Fortas (95) was at Yale; and Blackmun (98) taught at the William Mitchell College of Law and the University of Minnesota. And finally, Mr. Justice Story (18), the youngest appointee in the history of the Court, served as the first professor of law at Harvard College *during* his service on the bench from 1811 to 1845.

But, as noted on table 1, all but Frankfurter (78) and Taft (69) had left academic work and were in other posts at the time of their selection for the Court, including those who had spent most of their legal careers in the classroom. Columbia's Dean Stone (73), for example, was attorney general of the United States and Douglas (79) had left Yale to become chairman of the Securities and Exchange Commission.

The tables do not show the occasional nonconforming background, such as that of Miller (36) who received his medical degree in 1838 and practiced as a country doctor in the back hills of Kentucky before going into the law. They do show that Salmon P. Chase (39) was a Republican from Ohio and that he was secretary of the treasury when Abraham Lincoln appointed him to the chief justiceship in 1864. But the charts do not tell us how this eighth of eleven children, fatherless at nine, became a leader in the cause of black liberation (known as the "attorney general for runaway slaves"), and how he was both a senator and a governor (Ohio) and, for more than two decades, a leading presidential candidate.

Legal Education. While all of the first one hundred justices have been lawyers, it was not until March 25, 1957, that all nine members of the Supreme Court were law school graduates. It was on that date that Charles Evans Whittaker (91), LL.B., University of Kansas, was sworn into office, replacing the retired Stanley F. Reed (77), who had attended both Columbia Law School and the University of Virginia but who had never received his degree. Since that date, every member of the Court has held the LL.B. degree or its equivalent, the J.D.

It should come as no surprise that the vast majority of the justices did not have law degrees. There were no law schools at all during the first seventy-five years of the nation's existence—not as we know law schools today. Even after the establishment of the LL.B. program at some of the major universities, the overwhelming majority of the bar was trained under the apprenticeship system until after World War I.

Bushrod Washington (11), for example, studied law as an apprentice at the office of James Wilson (4). (All expenses were paid by the student's wealthy uncle, President George Washington.) The last justice who never even attended a law school was James F. Byrnes (81), who left school at fourteen to become a court reporter and who managed to study law on his own and in law offices at the same time.

Because the nature of the legal education changed so radically in the late nineteenth century, the statistical data on law schools were compiled only for the members of the Court appointed after 1900.

Holmes (58) was the first Supreme Court appointee of the twentieth century and the first with a "modern" law degree. His was a Harvard LL.B., class of 1866. Of the forty-three named to the Supreme Court since 1900, thirty had law degrees. With the exception of Reed (77), Byrnes (81), and Jackson (82), all of the twenty-five named to the Court since President Roosevelt's appointment of Hugo Black (76) (LL.B., Alabama, '06), had received law degrees. And Jackson had attended Albany Law School for more than a year.

The second recipient of a law degree was Horace Lurton (61), who was appointed to the Court in 1909; he received his LL.B. from Cumberland University in 1867. McReynolds (66) had a University of Virginia LL.B., Van Devanter (63) and Taft (69) graduated from Cincinnati, and both Brandeis (67) and Sanford (72) had Harvard law degrees. Stone (73) graduated from Columbia in 1898, but ex-Columbia law students Hughes (62) and Cardozo (75), as well as Reed (77), never received their LL.B. degrees. Roberts (74) was awarded his law degree by the University of Pennsylvania in 1898.

Here is the breakdown on the twenty-five appointees numbering 76 through 100:

No.	Justice	University	LL.B. Degree Year
100	Rehnquist	Stanford	1952
99	Powell	Washington & Lee	1931
		Harvard	1932 (LL.M.)
98	Blackmun	Harvard	1932
97	Burger	St. Paul	1931
96	Marshall	Howard	1933
95	Fortas	Yale	1946
94	Goldberg	Northwestern	1930
93	White	Yale	1940
92	Stewart	Yale	1941
91	Whittaker	U. of Kansas	1925
90	Brennan	Harvard	1931
89	Harlan	N. Y. Law School	1924
88	Warren	U. of California	1912
		U. of California	1914 (J.D.)
87	Minton	Indiana University	1915
		Yale	1916 (LL.M.)
86	Clark	U. of Texas	1922
85	Vinson	Centre College	1912
84	Burton	Harvard	1912
83	Rutledge	U. of Colorado	1922
82	Jackson	Albany	(attended)
81	Byrnes	———	——
80	Murphy	U. of Michigan	1914
79	Douglas	Columbia	1925
78	Frankfurter	Harvard	1906
77	Reed	U. of Virginia	(attended)
		Columbia	(attended)
76	Black	U. of Alabama	1906

Harvard, Yale, and Columbia have had the greatest number of alumni on the bench. Eight former justices were students at Harvard, with six of the eight earning degrees there: Holmes (58), Brandeis (67), Sanford (72), Frankfurter

(78), Burton (84), and Brennan (90). Justices Fuller (50) and Moody (60) attended Harvard but did not graduate.

Three of the four Yale graduates served together on the Court: Stewart (92), White (93), and Fortas (95) were colleagues from 1965 until 1969. The fourth Yale graduate, Minton (87), was awarded his LL.M. there in 1916.

Family Data: Husbands and Fathers. While the Supreme Court membership has its share of "rags to riches" examples, it has had more than its share of those "to the manor born" and even to the profession born. Twenty-seven of the one hundred had judges in their family—and twelve of those twenty-seven had judges as fathers.

The twelve judges' sons were Cushing (3), Moore (12), Waite (43), L. Q. C. Lamar (49), E. D. White (55), Peckham (56), Day (59), Pitney (65), Clarke (68), Taft (69), Cardozo (75), and Stewart (92). The other fifteen with relatives who were judges were Marshall (13), Livingston (15), Todd (16), Thompson (19), Barbour (25), Campbell (33), Harlan (44), Gray (47), Fuller (50), Brewer (51), Shiras (53), Holmes (58), Moody (60), J. R. Lamar (64), and Harlan (89).

Ninety-three of the first one hundred justices were married to a total of one hundred and twenty-three wives, with four of the justices having had more than two wives: Douglas (79) married four times and Livingston (15), Curtis (32), and Chase (39) each married three times. Seven of the justices never married: Baldwin (23), Blatchford (48), Moody (60), McReynolds (66), Clarke (68), Cardozo (75), and Murphy (80) were all bachelors.

The statistics on fatherhood reveal the one hundred to have been an unusually productive group, with nearly one-fifth of the justices fathering five or more offspring. Two had ten children, one had nine, five had eight, and eight justices had seven sons and daughters.

The fifteen chief justices had eighty-four children:

Jay	7	Fuller	8
Rutledge	10	White	4
Ellsworth	9	Taft	3
Marshall	10	Hughes	4
Taney	7	Stone	2
Chase	6	Vinson	2
Waite	5	Warren	5
Burger	2		

The more prolific associate justices include William Johnson (14), Thomas Todd (16), and Stanley Matthews (46), each of whom had eight children; James Wilson (4), Joseph Story (18), Smith Thompson (19), John McLean (21), Philip Barbour (25), and William Strong (40), each of whom had seven, and the first John M. Harlan (44) who fathered six—bringing the total number of children of these ten associate justices to eighty-two.

Religion. Eighty-nine of the first one hundred justices have been Protestants of the following denominations:

Episcopalian	26	Congregationalist	3
Presbyterian	17	Disciples of Christ	2
Unitarian	6	Lutheran	1
Baptist	5	Quaker	1
Methodist	4	Unspecified Protestant	24

Six of the remaining eleven were Catholics and five were Jews.

In 1836 Chief Justice Roger B. Taney (24), a member of the Catholic aristocracy of Maryland, was the first non-Protestant to be named to the Court. The second Catholic, E. D. White (55) of Louisiana, who was appointed fifty-eight years later, also became chief justice. From White's appointment in 1894 until 1949, there was always at least one Catholic on the Supreme Court bench: Joseph McKenna, the son of a poverty-stricken Irish immigrant who became a power in California politics, served from 1898 to 1925;

Pierce Butler (71) from 1922 to 1939; and Frank Murphy (80) from 1940 to 1949. The "Catholic seat" was vacant from 1949 until the appointment of William Brennan (89) in 1956.

There was a "Jewish seat" on the Supreme Court from the appointment of Brandeis (67) in 1916 until Abe Fortas (95) resigned in 1969. All of the Jewish justices except Brandeis (67) occupied seat 3. (See table 2.) Cardozo (75) was named to the Court in 1932 to fill the vacancy caused by the resignation of Holmes (58). Frankfurter (78) succeeded Cardozo (75) in 1939 and was succeeded in turn by Goldberg (94) in 1962. Fortas replaced Goldberg in 1965.

Geography. In the selection of Supreme Court justices, some presidents have sought an "equitable" geographical distribution as a tool of political gamesmanship. But despite such objectives, the first one hundred justices represented only thirty-one states. New York has had thirteen justices on the Court but twenty-two of the states have had three or less. Here is the breakdown:

New York	13	Iowa	2
Ohio	10	Louisiana	2
Massachusetts	8	Michigan	2
Pennsylvania	6	North Carolina	2
Tennessee	6	Arizona	1
Virginia	6	Colorado	1
Kentucky	5	Indiana	1
Maryland	4	Kansas	1
New Jersey	4	Maine	1
Alabama	3	Mississippi	1
California	3	Missouri	1
Connecticut	2	New Hampshire	1
Georgia	3	Texas	1
Illinois	3	Utah	1
Minnesota	3	Wyoming	1
South Carolina	3		

From the appointment of South Carolina's John Rutledge (2) in 1789 until the retirement of Hugo L. Black (76) in 1971 (excepting the Reconstruction Decade of 1866–1876) there has always been a Southerner on the Supreme Court. President Nixon acted in accordance with this tradition when he successively nominated Southerners Clement T. Haynsworth of South Carolina and George Harrold Carswell of Florida to succeed Black. Both failed of confirmation, however, and the next appointment went to Minnesota's Harry A. Blackmun (98). But, the next appointee was a Southerner, Lewis F. Powell (99) of Virginia.

Until 1867, seat 6 was a "Southern" seat (See table 2.) Seat 3 was a New England province until the appointment of Cardozo (75) in 1932. It had been held successively by Cushing (3) of Massachusetts, Story (18) of Massachusetts, Woodbury (30) of New Hampshire, Curtis (32) of Massachusetts, Clifford (34) of Maine, Gray (47) of Massachusetts, and Holmes (58) of Massachusetts. But when New York's Cardozo (75) was replaced in seat 3 it was by Frankfurter (78) of Massachusetts.

Six of the justices were born abroad. Iredell (6) and Sutherland (70) were born in England, Wilson (4) was born in Scotland, and Paterson (8) was born in Ireland. Turkey was the birthplace of Brewer (51) and Austria-Hungary the birthplace of Frankfurter (78).

Age. Statistical data on the ages of the first one hundred justices have been compiled in three categories:

(1) age at time of taking office;
(2) age at leaving bench;
(3) age at death.

The mean age at the time of taking office was 53.4 years, and the median age was slightly higher at 55. But had the statistics been gathered for only the first twenty-three justices, named from 1789 to 1835, the mean would have been

49.6 years and the median only 48. And for the period beginning in 1939, the mean was only 51.8 years, with the median at 53.

It was in the middle era of the Court's history, from 1836 to 1939, that the "average" justice began his Supreme Court tenure in his mid-fifties.

Only four justices were named to the Court before their fortieth birthdays: Joseph Story (18) was the youngest, but both he and William Johnson (14) were appointed at age thirty-two. Bushrod Washington (11) was thirty-six and James Iredell (6) was thirty-eight.

Between 1836 and 1938, only eight justices were less than fifty at the time of appointment. Three were Lincoln appointees: Miller (36) and Field (38), at age forty-six, and Davis (37) at age forty-seven. Curtis (32) and Campbell (73) were both forty-one, the first Harlan (44) was forty-four years old, and both E. D. White (55) and Hughes (62) were forty-eight at the time of their first appointments as associate justices.

More than one-third (eight of twenty-three) of the justices appointed since 1939 were younger than fifty when they joined the Court. Douglas (79) had just passed his fortieth birthday. Here is the list.

Douglas (79)	40	Clark (86)	49
Murphy (80)	49	Stewart (92)	43
Jackson (82)	49	White (93)	44
Rutledge (83)	48	Rehnquist (100)	47

Oldest at the time of their appointments were Chief Justices Stone (73) at age sixty-eight, Hughes (62) at age sixty-seven, and E. D. White (55) at age sixty-five. But all three were much younger when named as associate justices: Stone (73) was fifty-two, and Hughes (62) and White (55) were forty-eight. Chief Justices Taft (69), Warren (88), and Burger (97) were sixty-three, sixty-two, and sixty-one respectively. [John Jay (1) was only forty-four when he became the first chief justice and Marshall (13) was only forty-five.]

Of the ninety-three associate justice appointments, only thirteen have gone to men who were older than sixty. The oldest were Lurton (61) at sixty-five and Powell (99) at sixty-four.

Since Supreme Court appointments carry life tenure, the age at leaving the bench is expectedly high. The mean age is 68.2 years and the median age is 70.

Eight justices served past their eightieth birthdays: Holmes (58) retired at ninety, Taney (24) died in office at eighty-seven, Black (76) retired at eighty-five, Brandeis (67) and Duvall (17) both retired at eighty-two, McKenna (57) and Field (38) retired at eighty-one and Nelson (29) retired at eighty.

On the other hand, five justices left the Court before age fifty. Iredell (6) died in office at only forty-eight. The other four resigned: Curtis (32) at forty-seven, Moore (12) at forty-eight, and Chief Justice Jay (1) and Campbell (33) at forty-nine.

Iredell (6) was the only one of the first one hundred justices to die before he was fifty and only seven died in their fifties. Twenty-one died past their eightieth birthdays, four of them older than ninety: Holmes (58) died at ninety-three, Shiras (53) and Byrnes (81) died at ninety-two and Duvall (17) died at ninety-one.

Length of Service. On October 29, 1973, Douglas (79) became the longest-sitting justice in Supreme Court history, breaking the previous record set by Field (38) of thirty-four years, six months and eleven days on the bench. Justice Douglas was to continue as a member of the Court until November 12, 1975, for a total of thirty-six years, six months and twenty-six days.

Supreme Court service has been marked by longevity. Nine of the first one hundred justices served on the Court for more than thirty years and twenty-three others had more than twenty years on the bench.

Those with more than thirty years on the Court, listed according to longevity, were:

	Years		Years
Douglas (79)	36	Story (18)	33
Field (38)	34	Wayne (23)	32
Marshall (13)	34	McLean (21)	31
Black (76)	34	Washington (11)	30
Harlan (44)	34	Johnson (14)	30

All of Marshall's (13) service was as chief justice.

Holmes (58), who took his judicial oath in late 1902, retired in early 1932 with just over twenty-nine years on the bench. Taney (24) was on the Court for twenty-eight years, with the second longest term of office of the fifteen chief justices.

Those with the shortest tenure on the bench were John Rutledge (2) with just over a year as associate justice and just four months as chief justice, Thomas Johnson (7) who served fourteen months, and James F. Byrnes (81) who was a member of the Court for just under sixteen months.

Length of service is also indicated by the number of justices who have occupied each of the ten seats on the Court. As shown on table 2, there have been fifteen chief justices, i.e., the occupants of seat 1. Fifteen justices have also occupied seat 4, while the figure is twelve for seats 2, 3 and 7. There have been eleven justices in both seats 5 and 6, nine in seat 9, six in seat 10 and only one, as previously explained, in seat 8.

Leaving the Court. Tabulations prepared just prior to the resignation of Douglas (79) indicated a total of ninety-five instances that Supreme Court service had been terminated. For, as previously noted, there had been one hundred and four appointments. And one hundred and four, minus nine for nine incumbents, equals ninety-five.

Of those ninety-five, death terminated the services of forty-eight justices. There were twenty-four retirements, sixteen resignations, four who left the Court under disability legislation, and two whose service as an associate justice was ended so that they could be promoted to chief justice.

Chief Justice Rutledge (2) was the only one whose service was terminated by a rejection—nearly five years after the resignation of Associate Justice Rutledge (2).

Post-Judicial Careers. Supreme Court work is so important, so interesting, and so prestigious that comparatively few justices have resigned from the bench while still able to perform judicial duties. On the contrary, there has sometimes been the problem of convincing a justice that he should resign or retire when he could no longer meet the demands of office.

But of the sixteen justices who resigned (as opposed to retiring), only two did so to pursue more leisurely pursuits in their later years. Duvall (17) was eighty-two when he terminated his service and went on to live past his ninety-second birthday. John H. Clarke (68) resigned in 1922 at age sixty-five after five years of service, saying, "For a long time I have promised what I think is my better self that at that age I would free myself as much as possible from imperative duties that I may have time to read many books which I have not had time to read in a busy life; to travel and to serve my neighbors and some public causes." He died twenty-three years later in 1945.

Roberts (74) resigned at age seventy, but hardly to a life of leisure; he accepted the deanship at the law school of the University of Pennsylvania.

Possibly because the Supreme Court was less prestigious in its early history, the resignations were more frequent. Rutledge (2) resigned as an associate justice without ever sitting, in order to accept the chief justiceship of South Carolina; Jay (1) stepped down as chief justice to become governor of New York; and Ellsworth (10), the second chief justice, left the Court to become United States commissioner to France.

Three associate justices resigned while still in their forties. In the case of Moore (12) it was because of ill health when he was only forty-eight. But Curtis (32) left at age forty-seven after only six years of service to return to private practice in Massachusetts. He was President Andrew Johnson's chief counsel at the latter's impeachment trial. Campbell (33), who had also been named to the Supreme Court at age forty-one, resigned in 1861 after eight years on the bench. A native of Georgia who had practiced law in Alabama, Campbell (33) returned to the South after the outbreak of hostilities. He later held office in the Confederate government.

Administrator of the estate of President Lincoln, David Davis (37) resigned in 1877 to accept a Senate seat. Hughes (62) resigned in 1916, three days after he was nominated by the Republican party as its presidential candidate to oppose Woodrow Wilson.

In more recent times, Byrnes (81) resigned after only sixteen months on the Court to assume the post of chairman of the newly-created Economic Stabilization Board. He later became President Truman's secretary of state and still later governor of South Carolina. Goldberg (94) resigned at President Johnson's urgings after only three years of service to take the post as ambassador to the United Nations. The last of the sixteen to leave the Court by way of resignation was Abe Fortas (95); he stepped down under pressure when it was disclosed that he had contracted with a foundation to collect $20,000 per year for the remainder of his life and for the life of his wife if she outlived him.

So much for the first one hundred justices—as statistics. But how able were they as judges?

Two

RATING THE JUSTICES

The Best and the Worst

How good have our Supreme Court justices been? Who have been the great ones, the giants who tower over the others? Who have been the justices considered near great, but who just missed reaching the heights? Which of the justices were mediocre, which below average, and which outright failures?

What qualities or traits condition superb achievement on America's highest judicial tribunal? Were these attributes visible or predictable before the great justices were selected? And what are the limitations, the defects, the liabilities that plagued some of the justices and consigned them to no particular credit or to classification as less than adequate or to discredit as judicial failures?

How has the existing selection system for Supreme Court justices worked? What caliber of judge has the prevailing recruitment process yielded? How can this recruiting process

---

Claire Rocco and R. Lawrence Siegel made substantial contributions to this chapter.

Portions of this chapter appeared in *Life* Magazine on October 15, 1971, and in the *American Bar Association Journal* in November 1972.

be modified to assure the choice of capable Supreme Court justices and the elimination of mediocre performers or potential disasters?

The Supreme Court is a unique court because it possesses both the conventional legal authority common to tribunals of law and considerable political authority. This dual power, that of law and politics, has not only made the United States Supreme Court the most renowned of supreme courts throughout the world but has also transformed the panel into one of the most influential and respected governmental entities in the American constitutional system.

A justice of the Supreme Court is an appointed official. He is nominated by the president and subject to majority confirmation by the Senate. The president need not and normally does not disclose to the nation why he is making a particular nomination. Once the justice is confirmed and assumes his seat on the Court, he is not accountable to anyone; not to the president who appointed him nor to any succeeding president nor to the Senate which confirmed him nor to the people. He is appointed for life and is subject to removal only by impeachment. Of the first one hundred justices on the Supreme Court only one justice was impeached,[1] but at trial he was acquitted of the charges against him. Clearly then, Americans have a large stake in the selection process by which Supreme Court justices are chosen.

There are no known criteria, tests, or guidelines for appointment to the Supreme Court. In the absence of such standards, Americans have often been curious about how the existing method of selecting Supreme Court justices operates in practice. While the Supreme Court as an institution is esteemed and the individual justices held in high regard, the public is not familiar with the names and records of many justices. There is widespread ignorance concerning who have been the best and the worst among the justices and why individual justices are so classified.

---

1. Samuel Chase (9) charged Jefferson, both before and after his election as president, with "seditious attacks on the principles of the Constitution." This served as the basis of impeachment by the House of Representatives. Chase was acquitted by the Senate on March 1, 1805 by a scant four-vote margin.

Some answers to these questions have come from sixty-five experts (see table 4) members of the academic community, students of the Supreme Court, who undertook to furnish their answers in response to a poll conducted by the author of this book in 1970. The survey was taken shortly after the so-called Warren era on the Court came to its close with the retirement of Chief Justice Earl Warren (88) in June, 1969, and during the opening phases of Chief Justice Warren Burger's (97) tenure. The "judges of the justices" in this poll consisted of leading professors of constitutional law, American history, and politics, including several law school deans. Each was grounded in the proceedings of the Supreme Court from its beginnings when John Jay (1), the first chief justice, presided over the Court's initial session in February, 1790, then meeting in the Wall Street area of Manhattan.

Those polled were well qualified for the job of rating the justices. Their roster included specialists in many of the areas with which the Court must deal. Although the tribunal has attracted much of its public notice in this century via its rulings on civil liberties and civil rights, it is also called upon to hear and decide cases involving other aspects of American social, political, and economic life and activity. Futhermore, on occasion it is difficult to tell whether a particular dispute presents a civil liberties or civil rights question or rather an issue in economics, sociology, or applied politics. Regardless of an issue's complexity or profound implications, however, the justices facing it are required to make a decision. Tocqueville spotted this feature of American life in the 1830s and 1840s, observing that "scarcely any political question arises in the United States that is not resolved, sooner or later, into a judicial question." What Toqueville found a century and a third ago is still true today, and the determination of these issues often has a lasting impact upon the American people.

The breadth and scope of the business of the Supreme Court are staggering. Much of a Supreme Court justice's labor is expended on resolving constitutional problems: issues involving the interpretation and application of language contained in the Constitution of the United States or in the constitutions of the fifty states, or in statutes enacted by Congress, state legislatures, or local municipalities. Thus, a Supreme Court member must be judged for competence in many fields: corporation law, consumer problems, environmental law, criminal law, conflict of laws, public utilities, antitrust law and fair trade practices, bankruptcy and creditor proceedings, taxation, labor-management law, contracts, sales, insurance, admiralty and international law, problems arising out of congressional hearings, state legislative bodies, administration of educational institutions and religious organizations, problems in separation of church and state, family law, partnerships, copyrights, trademarks and patents, naturalization and deportation, libel, contempt, election, nomination, primary and office-seating disputes, zoning or cooperative problems, controversies between states or between a state and the federal government or between a private citizen and a city or a state or the national government and, as in the Nixon proceedings, disputes between a special prosecutor and the president. Further, since change is a constant in America, and inevitably human activity in new areas evolves into disputes, the fields of law must always expand in response to the needs of the times. Thus the already formidable dimensions of law with which·a justice must cope are always subject to additions.

The 1970 Justices' Poll

The experts who agreed to rate the justices in 1970 were issued a ballot which listed all the justices in chronological order. Originally the pollees were invited to grade each of the justices from Chief Justice John Jay (1), the first appointee of President George Washington, to Chief Justice Warren Burger (97), the first Nixon appointee. However, the ballots cast definitely showed that it was much too early in 1970 (his freshman year on the Court) to rate Chief Justice Burger. As a result, the pollsters dropped Burger from the tabulations. Thus the poll rates every justice from Jay up to but excluding the four Nixon appointees: Chief Justice Burger (97) and

Associate Justices Harry A. Blackmun (98), Lewis F. Powell, Jr. (99), and William H. Rehnquist (100). It also excludes the most recent addition to the Supreme Court, John P. Stevens (101). The poll thus embraces ninety-six justices, from John Jay (1) to Thurgood Marshall (96).

On the ballots each justice was coupled or grouped with the name of the president who appointed him. For example, the ten justices whom President Washington named to the Court were listed under his name and he, like the other presidents who succeeded in placing their nominees on the Supreme Court, was in turn identified by his own political affiliation, state, and years in office. Thus, Justice James Wilson (4), one of the Washington appointments, was grouped under Washington, who was described on the ballot as "Federalist, from Virginia, 1789-1797." And Wilson, as the fourth justice appointed by Washington, appeared as "4 James Wilson, 1788-1798." The same pattern was used for every other justice, except for those four who were initially associate justices and later became chief justices: John Rutledge (2), Edward D. White (55), Charles Evans Hughes (62), and Harlan F. Stone (73). Each of these was listed once under the name of the president who first named him to the Court. Thus, Edward D. White's name was placed under President Cleveland, Democrat from New York, who first appointed him as an associate justice; White's name appeared this way on the ballot:

55 Edward White
1894-1910
1910-1921 (Appointed chief justice by President Taft)

Neither criteria, yardsticks, nor measuring rods were provided the experts to assist in making their appraisals; there are really no accepted criteria for measuring Supreme Court competence. Nor is there any established touchstone for gauging the attributes that earn a member of the Supreme Court the highest accolade, or the lowest rank, or an in-between standing.

The instructions on each ballot were quite simple. The

raters were requested to grade all the justices in a continuum from A to E: A for great, B for near great, C for average, D for below average, and E for failure. (As academicians, the raters were familiar with the use of the grading scale.) They were free to utilize their own tests or canons. Space was provided on the ballots to add explanatory remarks and many of the graders did so. Of the ninety-six Supreme Court justices being evaluated, the experts chose twelve as great, fifteen as near great, fifty-five as average, six as below average, and eight as failures. In sum, they gave passing grades to eighty-two of the ninety-six justices or more than eighty-five percent of those evaluated. Fourteen of the justices, about fifteen percent, were adjudged as something less than average.

Here is the list of the Supreme Court justices, classified according to the five categories and listed in chronological order of service under each category. The dates represent the years in which each justice served on the Court.

The Twelve Greats

John Marshall (13)	1801–1835
Joseph Story (18)	1811–1845
Roger B. Taney (24)	1836–1864
John M. Harlan (44)	1877–1911
Oliver W. Holmes, Jr. (58)	1902–1932
Charles E. Hughes (62)	1910–1916 and 1930–1941
Louis D. Brandeis (67)	1916–1939
Harlan F. Stone (73)	1925–1946
Benjamin N. Cardozo (75)	1932–1938
Hugo L. Black (76)	1937–1971
Felix Frankfurter (78)	1939–1962
Earl Warren (88)	1953–1969

The Fifteen Near-Greats

William Johnson (14)	1804–1834
Benjamin R. Curtis (32)	1851–1857
Samuel F. Miller (36)	1862–1890

Stephen J. Field (38)	1863–1897
Joseph P. Bradley (41)	1870–1892
Morrison R. Waite (43)	1874–1888
Edward D. White (55)	1911–1921
William H. Taft (69)	1921–1930
George Sutherland (70)	1922–1938
William O. Douglas (79)	1939–1975
Robert H. Jackson (82)	1941–1954
Wiley B. Rutledge	1943–1949
John Harlan II (89)	1955–1971
William J. Brennan, Jr. (90)	1956–
Abe Fortas (95)	1965–1969

The Fifty-Five Classified as Average

John Jay (1)	1789–1795
John Rutledge (2)	1789–1791; 1795
William Cushing (3)	1789–1810
James Wilson (4)	1789–1798
John Blair (5)	1789–1796
James Iredell (6)	1790–1799
William Paterson (8)	1793–1806
Samuel Chase (9)	1796–1811
Oliver Ellsworth (10)	1796–1799
Bushrod Washington (11)	1798–1829
Brockholst Livingston (15)	1806–1823
Thomas Todd (16)	1807–1826
Gabriel Duvall (17)	1812–1835
Smith Thompson (19)	1823–1843
John McLean (21)	1829–1861
Henry Baldwin (22)	1830–1844
James M. Wayne (23)	1835–1867
John Catron (26)	1837–1865
John McKinley (27)	1837–1852
Peter V. Daniel (28)	1841–1860
Samuel Nelson (29)	1845–1872
Levi Woodbury (30)	1845–1851
Robert C. Grier (31)	1846–1870
John Campbell (33)	1853–1861

Nathan Clifford (34)	1858–1881
Noah H. Swayne (35)	1862–1881
David Davis (37)	1862–1877
Salmon P. Chase (39)	1864–1873
William Strong (40)	1808–1895
Ward Hunt (42)	1873–1882
Stanley Matthews (46)	1881–1889
Horace Gray (47)	1882–1902
Samuel Blatchford (48)	1882–1893
Lucius Q. C. Lamar (49)	1888–1893
Melville W. Fuller (50)	1888–1910
David J. Brewer (51)	1890–1910
Henry B. Brown (52)	1891–1906
George Shiras, Jr. (53)	1892–1903
Rufus W. Peckham (56)	1896–1909
Joseph McKenna (57)	1898–1925
William R. Day (59)	1903–1922
William H. Moody (60)	1906–1910
Horace H. Lurton (61)	1910–1914
Joseph R. Lamar (64)	1911–1916
Mahlon Pitney (65)	1912–1922
John H. Clarke (68)	1916–1922
Edward T. Sanford (72)	1923–1930
Owen J. Roberts (74)	1930–1945
Stanley F. Reed (77)	1935–1957
Frank Murphy (80)	1940–1949
Tom C. Clark (86)	1949–1967
Potter Stewart (92)	1958–
Byron R. White (93)	1962–
Arthur J. Goldberg (94)	1962–1965
Thurgood Marshall (96)	1967–

The Six Classified as Below Average

Thomas Johnson (7)	1791–1793
Alfred Moore (12)	1799–1804
Robert Trimble (20)	1826–1828
Philip P. Barbour (25)	1836–1841
William B. Woods (45)	1881–1887
Howell E. Jackson (54)	1893–1895

The Eight Failures

Willis Van Devanter (63)	1911=1937
James C. McReynolds (66)	1914=1941
Pierce Butler (71)	1922=1939
James F. Byrnes (81)	1941=1942
Harold H. Burton (84)	1945=1958
Fred M. Vinson (85)	1946=1953
Sherman Minton (87)	1949=1956
Charles Whittaker (91)	1957=1962

The Twelve Great Justices

The twelve justices receiving the accolade of "great" command special attention. This was not a rating readily given, and many would argue that there are other justices who should have been installed in this particular judicial Olympus. Only one, Chief Justice John Marshall (13), received the ranking of great from every one of the professors. This was expected since Marshall is commonly acclaimed as the most important of all American jurists. Closely trailing Marshall was Louis D. Brandeis (67) and Oliver Wendell Holmes, Jr. (58), with Brandeis receiving sixty-two votes in the "great" category and Holmes receiving sixty-one. None of the other nine greats was close to this trio in the ballot results; Hugo L. Black (76) was in fourth place with forty-two votes as great.

But not all of the professor-critics agreed on the top twelve. Holmes, Black, and Felix Frankfurter (78), for example, all received at least one "average" vote. And one of the raters graded Frankfurter with a surprising "failure." Was this because Frankfurter overemphasized judicial self-restraint? Was Black given some bad ratings because of excessive judicial activism? Some of the marginal notes would so indicate. Other marginal notes (plus commentaries on the poll) suggest that top ratings should have gone to Stephen J. Field (38), William O. Douglas (79), and Robert H. Jackson (82).

Comments on the Twelve Greats

Former Congressman and former Secretary of State John Marshall (13) deserves first place because of his special role in making the Supreme Court "supreme" in fact as well as name. At the time of his appointment, in 1801, the Court was considered the one branch of government which had failed in its purpose. Under Marshall, it emerged as an equal partner. In 1803, in *Marbury* v. *Madison*, he wrote the first opinion holding that an act of Congress was unconstitutional. It was this decision, more than any other, which made the Supreme Court a coordinate partner with the legislative and executive branches, thereby achieving the balance of power sought by the framers of the Constitution. In the next thirty-two years, the Marshall Court decided cases involving almost every aspect of the still new Constitution, providing the basic judicial gloss as to its meaning.

Joseph Story (18) is considerably less well known by the general public, primarily because he served with Marshall for most of the thirty-three years of his tenure and was overshadowed by his chief justice. Yet many students of the Court consider Story its greatest scholar, a virtuoso who contributed to equity jurisprudence, substantially created American law on copyrights and patents, stamped his mark on property, trusts, partnership and insurance law, and helped formulate America's commercial and maritime law.

The selection of Roger B. Taney (24) reflects the judgment of the experts that a jurist with outstanding skill and competence should not be rated on the basis of the negative view which history has affixed to one of his decisions. In Taney's case, his overall excellence has proved sufficient to negate the effect of his opinion in the 1856 *Dred Scott* decision, the case which denied full citizenship rights to blacks, and in so doing helped trigger the Civil War, and incidentally damaged the Court's prestige. Taney is considered among the best of the chief justices, with a career which surprised many, including Daniel Webster. At the time of Taney's appointment by President Jackson, Senator Webster had reacted with horror: "The Supreme Court is gone." But Taney, the Catholic son of slave-owning Marylanders and a strong believer in states' rights, proved willing to deny the states the power to obstruct federal processes, thus enhancing the stature which the Court had achieved under Marshall.

John M. Harlan (44), grandfather of the near-great justice of the same name (89) who retired in 1971, is best remembered for his dissent in *Plessy* v. *Ferguson*. In response to this 1896 decision which upheld the constitutional validity of separate seating for blacks and whites on buses and trains, Harlan asserted that the "Constitution is color-blind." In his thirty-four years as the acknowledged workhorse of the Court, Harlan was transformed from a man steeped in the slave-owning tradition into a sometimes harsh and outspoken advocate of civil rights for blacks. Attacked on his past record, he once replied: "Let it be said that I am right rather than consistent."

The two almost unanimous choices for the category of great, Oliver Wendell Holmes, Jr. (58) and Louis D. Brandeis (67), were both early twentieth-century appointees to the Court. They served together on the bench for more than sixteen years and voted together in numerous decisions in which they expressed the minority position. Holmes, in fact, is remembered as "the Great Dissenter," although he actually sided with the majority in most of his decisions. Supreme Court history indicates that there were other justices who dissented far more often (see chapter five). The scion of an aristocratic family and son of a famous author, Holmes argued consistently that the law must protect the common man. He shared the bench with justices who were determined to prevent federal and state governments from regulating private enterprise and his dissents, though lucid and saltily skeptical, generally failed to sway his conservative colleagues at the time. His liberal, humanistic interpretation of the Constitution, however, did influence a later generation of jurists and many of his minority opinions have since been adopted by a majority of the Court.

Louis Brandeis (67), a member of a well-known Jewish

family, was a successful and wealthy activist attorney before his appointment by President Wilson in 1916. As a Supreme Court justice, he maintained his early reputation as "the poor man's lawyer." He fought against trusts, monopolies, and some of the other powerful business interests of his day. Even more than Holmes, he often expressed minority opinions with such insight and brilliance that they paved the way for later majority decisions. The experts polled admired Brandeis as a solid "lawyer's lawyer" as well as a protector of human liberties.

Like Marshall, Charles Evans Hughes (62) is noted for his outstanding qualities of leadership as a chief justice. He had been a corporation lawyer and a law professor at Cornell before he was elected governor of New York in 1906 at the age of forty-four. Named to the Court by President Taft, he resigned to make an almost-successful run for the presidency against Woodrow Wilson. Continuing in public life, he became President Harding's secretary of state. Later, as President Hoover's sixty-seven-year-old nominee for chief justice, Hughes had to weather a fierce Senate storm over excessive conservatism on the Court. He returned to the bench to produce a notable series of opinions that sustained the cause of civil rights against encroachment by the states. An experienced politician, Hughes is credited with having outmaneuvered President Roosevelt's attempt in the mid-1930s to "pack" the Court. His most famous remark is one which some say he later regretted: "We are under a Constitution, but the Constitution is what the judges say it is."

Harlan F. Stone (73), another chief justice, is considered outstanding for the creativity of his opinions and his zeal for social justice, rather than for his administrative abilities as chief. His career spanned two distinct eras of constitutional debate. In his early years on the Court he was associated with Brandeis and Holmes as one of three great dissenters. Later, as chief justice, he wrote majority opinions questioning the power of the popular majority to control individual conscience and expression. He stated clearly the limits of judicial review: "While unconstitutional exercise of power by executive and legislative branches of the Government is subject to judicial restraint, the only check upon our own exercise of power is our own sense of restraint."

Justice Benjamin Cardozo (75) provoked wide disagreement among the raters as to his greatness as a Supreme Court justice, although the total vote clearly places him among the Supreme Court's top dozen. The question is whether the lofty esteem in which Cardozo is held (and that esteem is virtually unanimous) can fairly be attributed to a tenure on the Court of a scant six years. As a liberal on what was then a conservative Court, he did help prepare the way for the judicial developments which were to come. But he is certainly not famous for the scope and breadth of significant or numerous Supreme Court determinations. His reputation as one of the greatest judges of common law was gained as chief judge of the New York Court of Appeals, where he was famed both for his role in continuously reshaping legal doctrine to modern needs and for the grace and power of his legal writings. Fate unfortunately denied him the opportunity to exploit fully his talents on the Supreme Court; he died after serving only six years.

At the time President Roosevelt appointed him to the Supreme Court, Felix Frankfurter (78) was generally considered a liberal by his fellow law professors at Harvard. Once on the Court, however, he generally adhered to the philosophy of judicial restraint while his brothers on the bench were engaged in creating the most activist era in modern Supreme Court history. He tended to probe each case for a fine legal point on which it might turn, often basing his opinions on comparatively minute technicalities. Although he did not repudiate the power of the judicial branch to strike down legislation, he used it sparingly, noting that "A merely private judgment that the time has come for a shift of opinion regarding law does not justify such a shift." It is because of this preoccupation with judicial restraint that one of the graders rated him a failure. That professor considered Frankfurter "consistently overrated," declaring that he had used his brilliance to restrict the development of law.

Hugo Black (76), last of the greats to leave the Court,

had the fourth longest tenure on the bench, almost thirty-four years. He was probably the most influential of the strong figures on the Court over the past thirty years. But his tenure had a bad beginning. A Senator from Alabama, Black had been one of the most dedicated New Dealers in Congress and became the first of President Roosevelt's nine high court appointments. His appointment to the Court, however, became suddenly controversial when, within days of his selection, it was revealed that he had once been a member of the Ku Klux Klan. Primarily a self-educated man, Black was respected for his ability to cut to the core of intellectual problems and not be sidetracked by apparent erudition. A man of intense moral commitment, he was revered as a defender of personal liberties, freedom of speech, and the rights of "the weak, the helpless and the outnumbered." He considered himself a strict constructionist and explained his approach to the Constitution in these words: "I believe the Court has no power to add to or subtract from the procedures set forth by the Founders . . . . I shall not at any time surrender my belief that the document itself should be our guide, not our own concept of what is fair, decent and right."

Although Earl Warren (88) became the fourteenth chief justice without any prior judicial experience (he had been an attorney general and governor of California), he soon took philosophic as well as administrative control of the Court. He is rated outstanding more for his ability to pull the Court together and give it a sense of direction than for his written opinions. In his first year on the bench, he spoke for the unanimous Court in *Brown* v. *Board of Education* declaring state-sanctioned racial segregation in the public schools unconstitutional. Within a short time the Court so sharply reflected his views that it became known as "the Warren Court." Presiding over one of the Court's most creative and controversial periods, Warren's leadership resulted in decisions that meant new rights and freedoms for black citizens, "one man, one vote" apportionment, and a new judicial watchfulness over police procedures.

The Fifteen Near-Great Justices

The careers of several justices rated as near great have been obscured by historical circumstances. The accomplishments of William Johnson (14), for example, were consistently overshadowed by the presence of John Marshall on the same Court at the same time. Johnson often objected to being bossed by Marshall and protested against what he regarded as Marshall's excessive concern for property values at the expense of human values. Unlike Johnson, who sat on the Court for thirty years, another near great, Benjamin R. Curtis (32), did not like the routine of being a justice and resigned after only six years, in part because of his dislike of Chief Justice Roger Taney and Taney's behavior during the decision making in the *Dred Scott* case. Despite his brief tenure on the Court, Curtis merited the rating of near great because of his brilliance in admiralty and commercial law and his courage in casting one of the two dissenting votes in the *Dred Scott* case.

Three of the justices who served during the Court's middle period in the late nineteenth century, Samuel Miller (36), Stephen Field (38), and Joseph Bradley (41), might have been rated as great if they had served in a more active judicial era. Intellectually, they dominated the post-Civil War Court, sharing the spotlight for a number of years with the first John M. Harlan (44), ranked as great by the experts. Another trio of near-greats were Chief Justices Morrison R. Waite (43), Edward D. White (55), and William H. Taft (69) (who served nearly nine years as chief justice after one term as president). All received high marks for leadership and administrative ability.

George Sutherland (70) was chosen as a near-great even though his personal popularity has been dimmed by his leadership of the conservative bloc that obstructed so much of President Roosevelt's New Deal legislation. His three close judicial allies—Willis Van Devanter (63), James C. McReynolds (66), and Pierce Butler (71)—were all ranked as failures in the survey. Yet Sutherland earns general respect.

Even though he often played the obstructionist role, he did so as a learned judge and legal craftsman. And his opinion in the Scottsboro case marked the beginning of the Supreme Court's modernization of criminal justice.

Near-great Robert H. Jackson (82), who stepped down from the bench to serve as chief prosecutor at the Nuremberg Trials, was respected by all for his technical proficiency in the law. Wiley B. Rutledge (83), on the other hand, was better known for his opinions in the field of civil rights. He was a prodigious worker, writing one hundred and seventy opinions in six years. The second John Harlan (89), a Wall Street lawyer, was rated a cut below his grandfather but was still considered a superb technician in the Frankfurter tradition.

Of the twentieth-century justices rated as near great, the experts expressed the opinion that Abe Fortas (95) had had the best chance to achieve greatness. It is ironic that Fortas (who never sought the office and repeatedly declined its offer by President Johnson) was forced to resign after only four years on the bench and nomination for the chief justiceship because of a question of ethics. Controversy also surrounds the rating of William O. Douglas (79). The experts' opinions vary from "courageous pioneer" to "his opinions are sloppily written." William J. Brennan, Jr. (90), the only incumbent on the list of near greats, was the author of several of the most important opinions in the Warren years. Today he is considered the major spokesman in the Warren tradition and one who might have been ranked higher if his legal writing were more precise.

The Justices Rated Average and Below

It is interesting, and perhaps disturbing, to note that of the ninety-six justices in the ratings, fifty-five (or more than fifty-seven percent) were only average. There are four chief justices in this group: John Rutledge (2), Oliver Ellsworth (10), Salmon P. Chase (39), and Melville Fuller (50).

In categorizing six justices as below average and eight as failures, the experts made a distinction between judges who are unknown and unimportant and those who must be viewed negatively. All of the below-average justices served in the nineteenth century and their tenures on the Court were all relatively brief, ranging from two to six years. Alfred Moore (12), for example, served a five-year tenure before resigning in an unimportant judicial period, and is written off by the critic as "unbelievably unimportant" but not as a failure.

James C. McReynolds (66) and Charles E. Whittaker (91) share the dubious distinction of being voted at the bottom of the list of failures. McReynolds suffers from the general distaste of all Supreme Court observers regarding his pettiness and prejudices. It is commonly accepted legal gossip that President Wilson appointed the crotchety, cantankerous McReynolds to the Court because he could not stand working with him as attorney general and wanted him out of the way. During his twenty-seven years on the bench, McReynolds failed to write his share of opinions and was hypercritical of the opinions of others. In his five years on the Court, ex–Kansas City politician Whittaker cast the deciding vote in forty-one crucial decisions, each time standing on the side that would deny civil rights or the extension of personal liberty. A Whittaker biographer says of him: "He was neither a judicial thinker nor a legal technician. None of his opinions showed any new insights. They were pedestrian."

Three of those rated failures were in the four-member anti–New Deal bloc headed by Sutherland (70): Willis Van Devanter (63), Pierce Butler (71), and McReynolds (66).

James F. Byrnes (81), a Roosevelt appointee who also saw service as assistant to the president, as secretary of state, and as governor of South Carolina, was a man of talent who contributed little of his ability to the Supreme Court. He wrote only sixteen majority opinions during his less than one year on the bench and never wrote an individual dissenting or concurring opinion.

Eras of Judicial Performance

The history of the Supreme Court, in terms of successful judicial performance, can be broken down into several distinct eras. The twentieth century has been the age of the best and the worst, the time for the greats and the failures. The period from the end of the Civil War to the present, an interval spanning the last century of the Court's existence, has been the time of the near-great justice. The average justices have been in evidence throughout the Court's entire history, but chiefly in the nineteenth century. The below-average justices are crowded into three relatively brief intervals, the late eighteenth century and the early and latter parts of the nineteenth century.

Nine of the dozen greats were on the bench during the past one hundred years: John Harlan I (44), Holmes (58), Hughes (62), Brandeis (67), Stone (73), Cardozo (75), Black (76), Frankfurter (78), and Warren (88). Only one of this group, Harlan (44), had served prior to this period and his lengthy tenure extended into the first ten years of this century (1877–1910). Just three of the great justices, John Marshall (13), Story (18), and Taney (24) were on the Court before 1870. Note that none of this threesome sat during the Court's infancy from 1790 to 1800. Marshall (13), who served from 1801 to 1835, was the first of the great justices.

All eight failures served in relatively recent times. Three of them were members of the well-known "Four Horsemen," the implacable foes of Roosevelt's New Deal legislative program of the early 1930s. Of the five other failures, three were Truman appointees (Chief Justice Fred M. Vinson (85) and Justices Sherman Minton (87) and Harold Burton (84). Presidents Roosevelt and Eisenhower, whose appointees generally received high ratings, nevertheless each contributed a failure: Roosevelt had appointed James F. Byrnes (81) and Eisenhower had appointed Justice Charles E. Whittaker (91).

Most of the near greats were members of two strong benches: the Court of the post-Reconstruction years with Morrison R. Waite (43) as chief justice and the Court headed by Chief Justice Warren (88) in the 1950s and 1960s. The Waite Court, whose years can be fixed as 1874–1888, witnessed remarkable performances by Justices Stephen Field (38), Samuel Miller (36), Joseph P. Bradley (41), and the Chief Justice himself. In addition to its three greats—Chief Justice Warren (88) and Justices Black (76) and Frankfurter (78)— the Warren Court boasted five near greats: William O. Douglas (79), Robert H. Jackson (82), John Harlan II (89), William J. Brennan, Jr. (90), and Abe Fortas (95). Three other near greats sat during the second and third decades of this century: Chief Justices White (55) and Taft (69) and Justices Sutherland (70) and Wiley B. Rutledge (83). Only two of the near greats served before the Civil War: William Johnson (14), 1804–1834, and Benjamin R. Curtis (32), 1851–1857.

With the exception of Cardozo (75), who died at age sixty-eight after only six years on the bench, the great justices have a remarkable record of longevity on the Supreme Court. Long service by itself is, of course, not a hallmark of greatness or even of competence. Some of the Court's mediocre justices also had lengthy tenures. But long service gives a great justice a longer period to display his greatness and to make more of a contribution to judicial history. The Court careers of five of the great justices—Marshall (13), Story (18), Harlan I (44), Holmes (58), and Black (76)—each spanned more than thirty years, and Taney (24), Brandeis (67), Stone (73), and Frankfurter (78) labored on the Court for more than twenty-two years each.

The Mark of Greatness on the Supreme Court

From the votes, together with the supplementary remarks of the raters, comes some appreciation of the standards which were invoked to measure greatness, near greatness, mediocrity, below-average stature and failure. In their evaluations, the experts found that success on the Supreme Court was the result of several qualities in combination: scholarship; legal learning and analytical powers; craftsmanship and technique;

wide general knowledge and learning; character, moral integrity and impartiality; diligence and industry; the ability to express oneself with clarity, logic, and compelling force; openness to change; courage to take unpopular positions; dedication to the Court as an institution and to the office of Supreme Court justice; ability to carry a proportionate share of the Court's responsibility in opinion writing; and finally, the quality of statesmanship. This last is the indispensable attribute. Greatness as a Supreme Court justice demands an understanding of the nature of the American governmental system as a continuing experiment in democracy and an understanding of the special role of the Court in conducting that experiment.

All of the justices categorized as great had made important (and readily recognized) seminal contributions to the development of the law. The near greats were, for the most part, outstanding justices who had some one flaw or limitation which denied them preeminent status among their brethren. The average justices were usually well versed in legal craftsmanship and legal statesmanship, but that was all. These justices failed to put an indelible stamp on the law and to make their presence felt either in their own time or later. The below-average category seemed designed for the justices deficient either in legal scholarship, analysis, output, statesmanship, or in two or more of these qualities. The justices branded as failures were either unproductive or somehow constituted a disturbing element on the Court; they were generally outclassed and overmatched by the totality of the tribunal's function.

These ratings are useful in reflecting *what* the justices have done; they do not explain *why*. Is there a relationship between background factors and judicial performance? What is the impact of social background determinants and experiences on the quality of judicial performance?

Three

SELECTION OF CAPABLE JUSTICES

Factors to Consider

By Thomas G. Walker and William E. Hulbary

It is difficult to underestimate the importance of those who assume positions on the United States Supreme Court. The decisions they render have numerous and far-reaching consequences for the country; the rulings they hand down have a profound impact on the politics, laws, and moral life of the nation. Consequently, it is important for the nation to select the best possible individuals to sit on the Court. Indeed, it is especially important because those recruited to positions on the Supreme Court serve for life, virtually immune from removal from office. A justice appointed in the 1970s may well be influencing our laws and customs long well after the year 2000. When a poorly qualified person is selected for the Court and serves for a period of more than a quarter-century, the nation may suffer in uncountable ways. While we cannot hope to choose a Marshall or a Brandeis for

The authors are grateful to Thomas G. Walker of the Department of Political Science at Emory University and William E. Hulbary of the Department of Political Science at the University of South Florida for contributing this chapter.

every Court vacancy, we certainly should avoid the elevation of those who will not carry their weight.

With each nomination to the Supreme Court the president is making a prediction. Regardless of the criteria he employs in determining his appointments, the president attempts to nominate individuals who will be productive and positive members of the Court. Similarly, when the Senate deliberates on the president's nomination, it attempts to use its confirmation power to eliminate those who, like Nixon's appointee, George Harrold Carswell, lack the capacity to become contributing members of the nation's highest tribunal. Historically, persons involved in the Supreme Court selection process have chosen rather well. However, it appears most difficult to predict with a great deal of accuracy the level of competence which will be exhibited by a person who is nominated for the Court. There is always a degree of uncertainty. No foolproof formula exists for selecting the best possible jurists.

In earlier chapters of this book the individuals who have graced the Supreme Court have been examined in terms of their personal characteristics (age, professional experience, longevity) as well as their levels of ability as rated by a group of experts. In this chapter we will explore the relationship between the two. We will attempt to discover if individuals with certain characteristics make better justices than other persons. If there is any demonstrable relationship between a justice's background and his subsequent performance on the Court, then our understanding of the Supreme Court selection process would be enhanced and we may even be able to predict with greater confidence how well a person will perform if he is appointed to the nation's highest bench.

Analyzing Personal Characteristics and Judicial Ability

In order to examine the relationships between certain personal characteristics and judicial ability, we began with the ability ratings discussed in Chapter Two. Each of the justices who served on the Court from 1789 to 1969 (John Jay through Thurgood Marshall) was given a numerical score based upon his rated ability level. "Greats" were assigned the score of 5, "near greats" received a score of 4, "average" justices were given a 3, "below average" judges a 2, and the Court's "failures" were assigned a 1. Designating numerical values for each level of judicial ability allows us to compute "average ability scores" for various subgroups of justices. By doing so we are able to compare the ability ratings of justices with certain characteristics against justices with different traits. For example, we can compare justices with prior judicial experience with those who did not have prior judicial experience. Such a comparison permits us to evaluate a frequently expressed claim—that those justices with experience on the lower courts are more capable Supreme Court justices than those without lower court experience. By conducting an analysis such as this over a wide range of background factors we can determine whether the presence of certain characteristics in a justice's past indicates a tendency to demonstrate a given level of performance on the Court.

The average ability score for the first ninety-six justices was 3.18, indicating that the typical justice performed at a slightly above-average level. We confined our analysis to the first ninety-six justices on the grounds that Justices Burger, Blackmun, Powell, Rehnquist, and Stevens have not yet been on the Court a sufficient period of time to establish an accurate record of performance.

For each of the justices studied we compiled information on a large number of background characteristics.[2] These characteristics can be loosely grouped into three broad categories: family background factors, personal traits, and career

---

2. Information on the backgrounds of the justices used in this study was made available by the Inter-University Consortium for Political Research. The data were originally collected by Professor John R. Schmidhauser. Neither the original collector of the information nor the Consortium bears any responsibility for the analysis and interpretations presented here. The background information has been updated by the authors where necessary.

experiences. If certain individual characteristics are associated with levels of judicial ability, we should see evidence
of it in the following pages.

Family Background and Judicial Ability. It was evident
from the discussion in chapter one that United States Supreme
Court justices are not typical of the population as a whole.
They are different from the average ctizen in terms of several
factors: rather than coming from a wide range of socio-
economic backgrounds, Supreme Court justices have come
for the most part from prominent, well-to-do families. Relatively few individuals from humble family origins have
achieved a position on the bench. When we compared the
eighty-one justices whose backgrounds indicated roots in
more affluent and prestigious families against those fifteen
justices with lower socio-economic origins, we obtained the
following results:

Family Status	Number of Justices	Average Ability Score
High Socio-economic Status	81	3.22
Low Socio-economic Status	15	2.93

At best we can say that slight differences appear. The justices who came from higher class families achieved a level of
performance which was slightly higher than average; whereas, the justices from lower socio-economic origins performed
at a slightly below-average level of judicial quality. The
differences, however, are not so great as to allow us to make
any sweeping generalizations regarding the influence of
family origins on subsequent judicial ability.

Another indication of a justice's family origins is the
occupation through which the family gained its livelihood.
A family's values and life styles are often closely related to
the father's means of making a living. For this reason we

examined the justices and their later ability levels according to paternal occupation. The results offer some interesting differences:

Father's Occupation	Number of Justices	Average Ability Score
Farming	29	2.90
Business	16	3.47
Professional	41	3.22
Labor	5	3.80
Other/Unknown	2	2.50

First, over the long history of the Court a majority of the justices have had fathers engaged in business or the professions. A good number have also been raised in farming families, but the bulk of these justices were appointed during the earlier years of the nation's history when farming was the country's primary occupation. Relatively few justices have come from working class families. These differences quite probably are due not only to the relative advantage of business and professional people in terms of economic assets, but also because business and professional people tend to place a higher value on intellectual activities and transfer this importance to their children.

The second major finding obvious from the paternal occupation analysis is that there appears to be a relationship between the father's occupational category and the justice's subsequent performance. The business and professional categories are associated with above-average performance. So, too, are those justices who have come from working class families, but their number is small and any generalization should be viewed as extremely tentative. Justices from agricultural backgrounds, however, perform at a below-average level.

We also examined the role politics played in the early learning of the justices, studying whether or not the justice's fathers engaged in political activity. We thought that justices who grew up in a political environment might well perform differently than justices who acquired their initial political experiences later in life. The evidence shows that more of the members of the Supreme Court have come from politically active families:

Father's Political Activity	Number of Justices	Average Ability Score
Politically Active	55	3.07
Politically Inactive	41	3.32

By learning about politics early in life an individual will often place a high value on politics and begin his own political career earlier than those individuals who do not come from politically active families. In addition, individuals raised in families of which members are participants in the governmental process often make early political contacts which aid them in their careers. While persons with politically active fathers tend to have a higher probability of being appointed to the Supreme Court, such a background does not appear to affect the level of performance once on the Court. In fact, those justices who have come from politically inactive families have slightly higher levels of performance. The differences, however, are not large.

Finally, we analyzed the justices who have served on the Supreme Court in terms of whether their families had a tradition of judicial service. It is interesting that more than a quarter of the justices have been raised in families in which a close relative had served in a judicial capacity. It appears that judges tend to beget judges and that a child at an early age may learn to aspire to become a member of the judiciary. The ability levels of those individuals from judicial families were also slightly higher than persons coming from families without such a tradition of service. Once again, however, the differences are quite small.

Family Judicial Service	Number of Justices	Average Ability Score
Judicial Tradition in Family	25	3.36
No Judicial Tradition in Family	71	3.11

Based upon what we have found it does not appear likely that the antecedents of judicial ability can be found in a justice's family origins. Admittedly, the factors which we examined were rather crude indicators and it is possible that other family traits, more subtle and less observable, have an impact on a person's subsequent professional performance. Nonetheless, among those factors examined here none clearly distinguish the superior justices from their less-qualified counterparts.

Personal Traits and Judicial Ability. There is at least some reason to suspect that if a person's background characteristics affect his subsequent behavior, there may be a greater likelihood of finding such relationships among an individual's personal traits than his family origins. Obviously family characteristics are quite remote from what a justice may do forty or fifty years after he leaves the home of his parents. The impact of his family may be weakened over the years. But an individual's personal traits are both more specific to his own development as well as more proximate to the performance we are interested in understanding. We, therefore, examined several personal characteristics of the justices of the Supreme Court—characteristics ranging from where they were raised to their educational experiences.

First, we examined the type of environment in which the justice was born and raised. An often-articulated theory states that the values and way of life in America's rural areas tend to produce strong individuals with high levels of patriotism. Similarly, American culture tends to idealize life in small towns, which are often identified as the cradle of American democracy, while urban environments are rarely discussed in terms such as these. Among the ninety-six men who have served on the Supreme Court a substantial number have come from each of the three environments, but small town origins appear to be the most prominent.

Early Childhood Environment	Number of Justices	Average Ability Score
Rural Areas	21	3.10
Small Towns	41	3.07
Urban Areas	34	3.35

Contrary to popular images, those justices who have been raised in an urban environment performed at a higher average level than those raised in either small town or rural areas. The differences are not so great as to prompt us to propose that presidents ignore less densely populated areas in making future appointments, but modest differences do appear to be associated with the conditions under which the judges were raised.

Perhaps closely related to the environment in which a justice was raised is the region of the country in which he spent most of his life. Cultural differences often have been associated with the various regions, having been even more pronounced in the past than they are at the present time. It is possible that we find that judges coming from certain areas perform at levels superior to those raised in other sections of the country. We categorized each of the justices according to the region from which he was appointed and compared average ability ratings on the basis of such regional groupings.

Region	Number of Justices	Average Ability Score
East	36	3.60
West	6	3.33
South and Border	35	2.97
Midwest	20	2.75

The eastern and southern states have dominated the appointments to the Supreme Court followed closely by the justices who have come from the midwestern region. The West clearly trails other regions in the number of representatives on the Court. These differences, of course, are due primarily to the way in which the nation developed. Presidents have been quite responsive to geographical demands and have been quick to appoint individuals to the Supreme Court to represent the later developing sections of the country.

However, more than any other factor discussed up to this point, region seems to have an impact on the level of judicial performance. Justices who have come from the eastern region have produced records superior to those of justices from the other regions. The South and Midwest particularly have tended to produce justices of less than average caliber. The superiority of the East is probably due to the fact that the northeastern United States has always been the center of the nation's best law firms and institutions of legal education. Therefore, when the president wishes to fill an "Eastern seat" on the Court he has a great many qualified attorneys from which to choose. The pool of potentially excellent judges is simply greater in the East than in any other region.

We also inquired into the justice's ethnic origins. All of the ninety-six Supreme Court justices appointed before 1970, save Thurgood Marshall, could trace their ancestry to European beginnings. The overwhelming majority of Court members had backgrounds steeped in the traditions of the British Commonwealth countries. A smaller number have had roots extending to countries in continental Europe. It is this final category of judges who demonstrated the highest average ability score. The solidly above-average performance of these judges is particularly impressive when compared to the justices of Scottish or Irish descent who as a group had a below-average mean ability score.

Ethnic Group	Number of Justices	Average Ability Score
English/Welsh	55	3.22
Scottish/Irish	27	2.89
Continental European	13	3.60
African	1	3.00

Religious affiliation is another personal trait which may have a good deal of influence on personal development, values, and attitudes. Historically, politics has been at least partially dependent upon religious interests. Appointments to political positions, including the Supreme Court, have often been made to placate certain religious groups or to insure representation for the various religious communities in the United States. Most of the justices who have served on the Supreme Court have been members of the Protestant faith and most frequently affiliated with "high church" Protestant denominations such as Episcopalian, Congregational, Presbyterian, and Unitarian sects. "Low church" Protestant members (for example, Baptist, Lutheran, and Methodist) have accounted for the second largest number of justices appointed to the Court. In addition to the majority Protestant members, there have been six Catholics and five Jews who have served on the nation's highest Court. As can be seen in the figures below there is a substantial relationship between religious affiliation and judicial performance:

Religious Affiliation	Number of Justices	Average Ability Score
High Protestant	59	3.13
Low Protestant	15	2.93
Catholic	6	3.33
Jewish	5	4.40
Other	3	3.00

The high church Protestants generally performed at a level approximating the average for the entire history of the Court. The low church Protestants, however, performed at a relatively low level. The most remarkable results concern the representatives of the "minority" religious faiths. The Catholic justices have performed at a level above that of either of the Protestant groups and the Jewish members of the Court earned a phenomenally high 4.40 average ability score. This should be no surprise if we recall the Jewish members of the Court—Brandeis, Cardozo, Frankfurter, Goldberg, and Fortas—all of whom made important contributions to the development of United States jurisprudence.

Given the fact that Supreme Court duties require intellectual ability and legal scholarship, we might expect a justice's performance to be related to the quality of his educational experiences. Therefore, we examined the justices' pre-legal and legal educations. The majority of members of the Supreme Court have enjoyed excellent educational opportunities. Largely due to the relatively high socioeconomic status of their families, Supreme Court justices have attended institutions of pre-legal education which had high academic standings. By studying at such prestige institutions the future justices undoubtedly made important political and professional contacts, received superior educations, and obtained a boost in the building of their early careers. As well as helping them attain their high station, it also aided their performance when serving on the Court.

Pre-Legal Education	Number of Justices	Average Ability Score
Tutor	12	2.83
School of Average Standing	28	3.00
School of High Standing	56	3.34

In the past there was much greater diversity in the legal educations of men who have become members of the Court, ranging from those justices who taught themselves to those who attended prestigious institutions. This reflects the growth and development of legal education over the last 200 years. Our evidence indicates that the quality of legal education is in fact associated with the quality of service on the bench. Those justices who received the best legal education of the day have performed at a superior level.

Legal Education	Number of Justices	Average Ability Score
Self Taught	2	3.50
Apprenticeship from Prominent Attorney	32	3.13

Apprenticeship from		
Average Attorney	11	2.73
Law School of		
High Standing	38	3.45
Law School of		
Average Standing	13	2.85

Justices who were trained at universities of high standing or educated by attorneys of high reputation earned average ability scores in excess of 3.00; in contrast, Supreme Court judges who studied at average law schools or under average attorneys performed at below-average levels.

As expected, the personal traits of the ninety-six justices who have served on the Court were more closely related to their subsequent contributions on the bench than were the family origin characteristics. The studies of regional, ethnic, religious, and education factors produced some evidence that justices with certain personal characteristics tend to perform at particular levels of quality.

Career Experiences and Judicial Ability. Among those background characteristics which a justice brings with him to the Court, the most proximate to his service are those relating to his career. We would expect these to have an influence on the way the justice conducts himself on the bench. Since service on the Court requires dealing with political and legal questions of substantial importance, we examined aspects of the justices' careers which were both political and legal in nature.

We first studied the political party affiliation of the justices. Party membership often affects the careers of those involved in public service. It not only shapes or reinforces a person's views and attitudes on political matters, but it also influences the political contacts he will make and the political opportunities made available to him. As noted in chapter one, presidents usually confine their choices for the bench to potential nominees of the same political persuasion. We categorized each of the ninety-six justices according to his party affiliation in order to determine whether certain political movements have produced judges with superior records of achievement. The results showed that political party affiliation did not sharply distinguish the justices according to ability.

Political Party Membership	Number of Justices	Average Ability Score
Federalists	13	3.00
Democratic-Republicans	7	3.29
Whig	1	4.00
Republican	33	3.27
Democrat	42	3.10

The average ability scores of the various political parties are closely grouped. None of the parties can lay claim to producing the most superior justices, nor does any party significantly lag behind others in terms of the representatives they have sent to the Supreme Court.

Almost all of the nation's Supreme Court justices have devoted a considerable proportion of their pre-Court lives to public service. Usually this has taken the form of holding public office of various kinds. The backgrounds of the justices reveal a diversified list of positions held. We divided the ninety-six justices according to the type of public service in which they were engaged prior to their Court appointments. We were particularly interested in comparing justices whose political careers were primarily in state government with those who were primarily active in politics at the federal level. The majority of the justices had careers chiefly in the federal level of government, although over one-third were primarily state officials. If one were to break down this information historically he would find that in the earlier years of the nation, state politics was the most frequent avenue to a Supreme Court appointment. Over the years, however, experience at the federal level has increasingly become the more frequent road to the Court. If we are interested in judicial performance, the level of a potential nominee's political activity appears to be an unimportant criterion. The average performance of those justices who were primarily state politicians is only slightly higher than the average ability of those who spent the bulk of their political careers in the United States government.

Level of Political Activity	Number of Justices	Average Ability Score
State Government	35	3.23
Federal Government	54	3.13
Other/Non-Political	7	3.29

While there is no formal requirement that Supreme Court justices be attorneys, all of the members of the Supreme Court have been members of the bar and all have practiced law in some form during their pre-Court years. We were interested in whether a justice's legal career could be linked with his subsequent Supreme Court performance. For this reason we classified each of the justices according to the way he spent the greatest part of his legal career. The bulk of the justices practiced law only minimally. They were usually engaged in law as a means of being active in politics. For them law was a natural path to political office rather than an end in itself. However, about a third of the justices could be classified primarily as corporate lawyers and a lesser number practiced as teachers in law schools. While there were only four justices who could be classified as primarily academic lawyers, the average performance score of this group was clearly superior to the other categories. It appears that if a person is able to distinguish himself in legal scholarship within a university, the same talents will serve him well while on the Court.

Type of Law Practice	Number of Justices	Average Ability Score
Lawyer/Politician	55	3.07
Corporate Lawyer	31	3.23
Academic Lawyer	4	4.50
Other	6	3.00

66   ONE HUNDRED JUSTICESONE HUNDRED JUSTICES

We now come to one of the most controversial relationships between career experiences and judicial performance—
the question of judicial experience (See table 5.) Many
individuals have argued that Congress should impose the
requirement that nominees for the Supreme Court first serve
on the lower state or federal courts. To these critics of the
current judicial selection procedures, candidates for the
Court should have substantial judicial experience: they argue
that it is unwise to elevate someone to the nation's highest
tribunal who has never before sat on the bench. Opponents,
such as Justice Frankfurter, have responded that there is no
tangible evidence that prior judicial experience makes a
person better qualified to sit on the Supreme Court. Quite
the contrary, Frankfurter argued, some of history's most
outstanding justices have come to the Court without any
previous experience as judges. Given the long standing
nature of this debate, we were extremely curious to see how
the ninety-six justices would compare on the basis of their
prior judicial experience. We divided the justices into three
categories: those with no prior bench service, those with some
judicial experience, and those who had extensive records of
prior judicial service. The results clearly supported the
position that previous training as a judge has no bearing on
the ability of a justice to carry out his responsibilities on the
Supreme Court. In fact, the group of justices with the
highest performance scores were those who had no judicial
service prior to assuming a position on the Court.

Judicial Experience	Number of Justices	Average Ability Score
None	37	3.43
Some	21	3.00
Extensive	38	3.03

Next, we examined the justices grouped according to
their age at appointment. Presidents have often been quite
vocal about using age as a criterion for the selection of
Supreme Court justices. For the most part, presidents have

preferred their nominees to be in the mid- to late-fifties. A person in this age group, so the rationale goes, is experienced enough to have developed stable political values and to have achieved a public record which reflects those values, and yet is young enough to have a reasonable life expectancy on the Court. Presidents have shied away from those potential nominees of advanced years for fear the impact the justice would have would be extremely short lived. Younger persons have similarly been rejected by many presidents on the grounds that their values and attitudes might not yet be firmly anchored. Given the importance placed on age, we analyzed the justices' ability scores based upon three groupings: justices appointed under the age of fifty-one, between their fifty-first and sixtieth years, and after their sixtieth birthday. The results were surprising:

Age at Appointment	Number of Justices	Average Ability Score
Under 51 years	23	3.45
51–60 years	53	2.94
Over 60 years	10	3.50

The preference for justices in their fifties is clearly demonstrated. More than half of the justices in the Court's history attained their positions at this stage of their lives. However, more than one-third of the justices fell into the category of being considered either too old or too young. What is interesting is that the justices who were appointed between their fifty-first and sixtieth years earned ability scores inferior to those of both the older and younger groups. It appears possible that the common presidential practice of choosing justices in their middle years works against the selection of superior jurists.

Finally, we looked at the justices' lengths of tenure. On this factor we found interesting, although not surprising, results. The table below clearly suggests that quality of performance increases as length of tenure increases. The longer a justice serves the greater likelihood that he will make

significant contributions to the Court. It obviously takes
a substantial length of time for a justice to begin making
positive contributions. Based upon our evidence it seems
that a major line of demarcation occurs with the fifteenth
year of service. Justices in the tenure categories in excess
of fifteen years produced records of above-average performance; in contrast, justices who served less than fifteen years
earned below-average mean ratings. In fact, the ratings for
the justices who served less than five years were the lowest
average ability scores of any group of justices found in our
study.

Tenure on Court	Number of Justices	Average Ability Score
Less than 5 years	9	2.44
5–14 years	40	2.98
15–24 years	27	3.30
25 or more years	20	3.75

The career experiences of the justices add several useful
pieces of information to our knowledge of performance on the
Supreme Court. Two of the factors we examined are important because they are *unrelated* to judicial ability; neither
party affiliation nor prior judicial experience appeared to
influence the performance levels of the justices. Clearly, no
political persuasion holds a monopoly over the production
of superior justices; nor does the training of individuals in
lower court judgeships appear to give them a head start in
becoming outstanding jurists. Two other factors are especially interesting because of the manner in which they
are related to judicial ability. The relationship between
judicial ability and age at appointment seems to question
conventional wisdom and the traditional preconceptions of a
number of presidents. Those justices appointed when they
are between fifty-one and sixty years of age—judged by
many to be the ideal age for a Court appointee—tend to be
less able Supreme Court justices than those who are either
younger or older when appointed. Equally interesting is
the relationship between tenure on the Court and judicial

performance; the longer the period of service, the greater is the probability that a justice will make a positive contribution. Indeed, it appears that a maturing process of fifteen years or more on the Court is typically necessary before an individual begins to gain above-average ratings.

Conclusion

We have studied the backgrounds of the men who have served on the United States Supreme Court in order to determine if certain characteristics are associated with specific levels of judicial performance. Our analysis has not uncovered any one trait which clearly distinguishes the capable from the incapable. Nonetheless, certain patterns tend to emerge. On one hand, if we were to develop a profile of an individual with a strong likelihood of becoming an excellent jurist, he would be a person raised in a northeastern urban area as a member of a business-oriented family. His ethnic roots could be traced back to the European continent and he would be Jewish. He would have received his education from high-quality institutions and would have experience in the academic community as a legal scholar. He would have been appointed to the Court at a relatively early age, without prior judicial experience, and serve in that institution for more than twenty-five years. On the other hand, if we were to describe the background of a typical Supreme Court "failure," he would be a man from the midwestern United States, raised in a small town and from a family engaged in farming. His ethnic origins would be Scottish or Irish and he would be affiliated with a "low church" Protestant denomination. He would have attended mediocre educational institutions and his career would have been closely tied to partisan political acitivities. His appointment to the Court would have occurred during his mid-fifties and he would serve less than five years. These, of course, are general profiles. There are exceptions to every broad generalization, as attested to by the fact that McReynolds served more than a quarter-century and Cardozo but six years. Yet McReynolds is universally rated a "failure" and Cardozo a "great."

Some of the specific background factors studied are worthy of special attention. Interestingly, the prior judicial experience factor produced results in direct contradiction to the arguments of proponents of lower court apprenticeships. While the differences were not great, justices without lower court experience outperformed those who had previous training. While the specific explanation for the direction of these differences may be difficult to establish, it is clear that the supporters of lower court experience requirement are left with a shallow case.

The length of tenure factor is also of particular significance, largely because of the rather dramatic differences which emerged. Of the twelve "great" justices only Cardozo served less than ten years and only two others, Chief Justices Warren and Hughes, served less than two decades. While longevity does not insure greatness (e. g. McReynolds, Van Devanter, Washington, McLean, Wayne), it is reasonable to conclude that a justice will have difficulty establishing a record of excellence without spending a relatively long period on the Court.

Similarly, the age at appointment appears to be an important factor. While it may be difficult to explain with complete satisfaction, the historical facts are clear. A comparison of the "great" and "failure" categories is illustrative. Among the eight "failures," seven were appointed between their fifty-first and fifty-eighth years (the lone exception being James Byrnes who was sixty-two); but only three of the twelve "greats" (Stone, Black, and Frankfurter) were nominated during this period of their lives.

Our analysis does not provide an unerring formula for the selection of capable jurists. But it does illustrate some interesting relationships which have stood the test of almost two hundred years of Supreme Court history. Given some of the more substantial linkages between backgrounds and judicial ability, it is interesting to speculate upon the potentials of the five most recent appointees to the Court.

After examining their backgrounds we found that two of the five justices, Lewis Powell and William Rehnquist, possessed a number of characteristics which in the past have been associated with above-average performance. Both come from urban areas, received high quality pre-legal and legal educations, and had no previous judicial experience. Powell was appointed at a relatively old age and Rehnquist in a reasonably youthful period of his life. The only significant factors associated with low-level performances possessed by these two men are Powell's southern background and Rehnquist's practice as a politically oriented lawyer. If our analysis has relevance for the future, then history probably has reserved a place in the "average" category for Harry Blackmun and John Paul Stevens. Both possess the highly-rated characteristics of receiving excellent educations and both had been corporate lawyers with part-time law school professorship experience. However, Blackmun and Stevens share a midwestern background, prior judicial experience, and Protestant religious affiliations. In addition, Blackmun has a small town background and Stevens was appointed when fifty-five years old. Among the most recent five, Chief Justice Burger appears to have the most strikes against him. While his age at appointment (62) and ethnic background (Swiss/German) are similar to those justices who have served well in the past, his family origins (rural, farming), region (midwestern), religion (Protestant), education (University of Minnesota and St. Paul College of Law), and judicial experience (thirteen years) are factors which, over the history of the Court, have been associated with less than distinguished levels of performance.

Obviously there are a number of factors which influence the performance of a judge. Many of these are personal characteristics peculiar to the individual himself, factors which do not fall into the gross categories we have used in this chapter. However, there does appear to be a general association between a judge's background experiences and his demonstrated ability on the Court. This fact alone enhances our understanding of the judicial process and it is hoped, will encourage others to focus their research efforts on the question of selecting capable jurists.

Four

NOMINATED . . . BUT DID NOT SERVE

Although William Rehnquist is the one hundredth justice to serve on the Supreme Court of the United States, his nomination to that post was the one hundred thirty-eighth which an American president submitted to the Senate to "advise and consent" under the Constitution's Article II, Section 2, Clause 6. This is the story of those thirty-eight "additional" nominations—nominations which did not result in adding justices to the Supreme Court.

To the chronological list in Table 1 which numbers the first hundred justices from (1) to (100) we now add a chronological list of the 138 nominees. Numbers follow the names of all justice-nominees: the number in parentheses ( ) records the chronological order of service as a Supreme Court justice, and the number(s) in brackets [ ] records the chronological order of the nominations. Thus Rehnquist (100) [138] is the one hundredth justice to serve on the Supreme Court and the one hundred and thirty-eighth nominee to that office. Table 6 incorporates basic data on the 138 nominees.

The Statistics

Of the 138 nominations, 111 were confirmed by the Senate. Forgetting for the moment the twenty-seven nominations not confirmed, the number of Senate confirmations is still eleven more than the number of justices who have served on the Court. Of these eleven, three were the nominations of one-time associate justices who were being confirmed as chief justices: Edward D. White (55) [85] [92], Charles E. Hughes (62) [93] [105], and Harlan F. Stone (73) [104] [114]. Of the other eight, seven nominees declined the office despite confirmation, and one, Edwin Stanton, Lincoln's secretary of war, died four days after confirmation.

Nomination Confirmed By Senate
But Nominee Did Not Serve

Robert H. Harrison [4]
William Cushing (3) [3] [12]*
John Jay (1) [1] [17]*
Levi Lincoln [22]
John Quincy Adams [24]
William Smith [36]
Edwin Stanton [63]
Roscoe Conkling [75]

* nomination as chief justice

John Jay (1) [1] [17] declined a second appointment to the chief justiceship five years after resigning from that office, while William Cushing (3) [3] [12] elected to remain as associate justice despite his second nomination and confirmation.

The other twenty-seven nominations which failed to add a justice to the Supreme Court resulted from:

(1) the Senate's formal rejection of the nominee; or

(2) the Senate's failure to act on the nomination; or

(3) the Senate's postponement of hearings on the nomination and/or

(4) the president's withdrawal of the nomination.

These twenty-seven nominations actually involved only twenty-six nominees because Edward King [42] [43], twice nominated to the Supreme Court, twice was failed to be confirmed.

Nominations
Not Confirmed by the Senate

(1) Nomination Formally Rejected;
  John Rutledge (2) [2] [11]
  Alexander Wolcott [23]
  John C. Spencer [40]
  George C. Woodward [46]
  Jeremiah S. Black [55]
  Ebenezer R. Hoar [62]
  William B. Hornblower [83]
  Wheeler H. Peckham [84]
  John C. Parker [107]
  Clement F. Haynsworth [134]
  George Harrold Carswell [135]

                                        TOTAL   11

(2) Senate Failed to Act on Nomination
  John M. Read [45]
  Edward A. Bradford [50]
  William C. Micou [52]
  Henry Stanbery [61]
  Stanley Matthews (46) [72] [73]
  Homer Thornberry [132]

                                        TOTAL   6

(3) Senate Postponed Consideration of
  Nomination without Further Action
  John J. Crittenden [29]
  Roger B. Taney (24) [33] [34]

Edward King - *1844* [42] [43]
George E. Badger [51]

TOTAL *4*

(4) Nomination Withdrawn by President
    (a) Prior to Senate Action:
        William Paterson (8) [9] [10]
        George H. Williams [67]*
        Caleb Cushing [68]*
    (b) After Senate Postponed Consideration
        of Nomination:
        Reuben H. Walworth [41]
        Edward King - *1845* [42] [43]
        Abe Fortas (95) [129] [131]*

TOTAL *6*

* as chief justice

Multiple Nominees

The total of thirty-eight "additional" nominations involved only twenty-eight nominees who were not to become Supreme Court justices because eleven of these nominees were nominated twice; and of these "multiple nominees," ten saw service on the Court. (See table 7 for an outline summary of the multiple nominees.) Edward King [42] [43] was the only exception. His two nominations represented the only instance in Supreme Court history where a president failed to get his choice on the Court after a second try.

A distinguished Philadelphia lawyer, King was nominated by President Tyler in both June and December, 1844. The Whig-controlled Senate postponed consideration of the nomination both times. Since Tyler had decided not to become a candidate in the presidential elections of November, 1844, he was already a lame-duck President by June of that year. The Senate, believing that the Whigs would gain the presidency in November, denied confirmation to preserve the selection for the incoming chief executive.

Three of the ten multiple nominees received Senate consent after being nominated for a second time—all three having been denied confirmation after their first nominations. William Paterson (8) [9] [10] and Stanley Matthews (46) [72] [73] were confirmed as associate justices and Roger B. Taney (24) [33] [34] was confirmed as chief justice.

The second nominations of the other seven multiple nominees were nominations of former justices for the chief justiceship. Three nominees, Edward D. White (55) [85] [92], Charles E. Hughes (62) [93] [105], and Harlan F. Stone (73) [104] [114] were to serve as chief justices as well as associate justices. Two others, John Jay (1) [1] [7] and William Cushing (3) [3] [12], declined office even after Senate confirmation. But the other two failed to gain Senate approval as chief justice: John Rutledge (2) [2] [11] and Abe Fortas (95) [129] [131]. Rutledge, however, did serve as chief justice in 1795 under an appointment made by President Washington after Congress had recessed. When the Senate reconvened four months later, it refused confirmation primarily because Rutledge had opposed the Jay Treaty of 1794.

Making It the Second Time Around

While eight of the second nominations of the eleven multiple nominees were confirmed by the Senate, only three of these resulted in adding a member to the Supreme Court: William Paterson (8) [9] [10], Roger B. Taney (24) [33] [34], and Stanley Matthews (46) [72] [73]. As the careers of these three justices illustrate, the fact that a nominee is not confirmed is not necessarily indicative of either incompetence or unsuitability.

Paterson's initial rejection was due to a technicality. At the time he had been nominated by President Washington in 1793 to fill the vacancy created by the resignation of Justice Thomas Johnson (7) [8], he was an elected senator from New Jersey and had been in the Senate when the office of Supreme Court justice was created. Thus his nomination was invalidated by the Constitution's Article I, Section 6, Clause 2 which reads:

> No Senator or Representative shall, during the time for which he was elected, be appointed to any civil Office under the Authority of the United States, which shall have been created, or the Emoluments whereof shall have been encreased during such time; and no Person holding any Office under the United States, shall be a Member of either House during his Continuance in Office.

Advised of the problem, Washington withdrew the nomination on February 28, 1793, but resubmitted it four days later—after Paterson's term in the Senate duly expired on March 4. Paterson's second nomination was confirmed within twenty-four hours.

The initial Senate rejection of Roger B. Taney (24) [33] [34] was the result of political opposition to both Taney and President Andrew Jackson. Taney had served as secretary of the treasury under a Jackson recess appointment and in that post complied with Jackson's highly controversial order to remove all government deposits from the Bank of the United States. The Senate forced Taney's resignation from the Treasury by failing to confirm him in that post and Jackson vowed revenge. When Justice Gabriel Duvall (18) [26] resigned, Jackson nominated Taney to fill the vacancy. The Whig-dominated Senate first unsuccessfully attempted to decrease the number of seats on the Supreme Court, thereby removing the basis for the Taney nomination. Then came the death of Chief Justice John Marshall (13) [18] and Jackson's nomination of Taney as chief justice on December 28, 1835. The Senate thwarted this nomination by postponing consideration on March 3, 1836, the last day of its session. On March 4, however, the new Senate came into office with the balance of power shifted to the Jacksonian Democrats. The three months of bitter debate on the Senate floor ended on March 15 when Taney was confirmed (29–15) over the opposition of such influential Senate leaders as John C. Calhoun, Henry Clay, and Daniel Webster.

While opposition to Taney's nomination was directed at President Jackson as much as at Taney himself, the initial Senate rejection of Stanley Matthews (46) [72] [73] focused on his avowed association with corporate finance and railroad interests. Although the charge of nepotism was raised against President Hayes for nominating his college class-mate, fellow regimental officer, and close friend, the real issue was the charge that Matthews would be controlled by the business community. When Matthews was again nomi-nated to the Court (this time by President Garfield less than two months later), his nomination passed the Senate by only one vote (24-23).

While Justice Paterson's initial rejection can certainly be attributed to a constitutional technicality, the circum-stances surrounding the first nominations of Taney and Matthews involved significant political and economic con-flicts. Taney's loyalty to President Jackson aroused the enmity of the opposition-controlled Senate; the Senate re-action mirrored the power struggle between the Jacksonian Democrats and the Whig-Calhoun coalition. Taney's personal qualifications were ignored as the Court seat became a trophy for the victor. Justice Matthews' initial rejection reflected congressional concern with economics rather than an evaluation of juristic talent. The argument was whether Matthews' corporate and railroad ties would cause him to decide cases on behalf of big business. The closeness of the Senate vote on the second nomination (24-23) indicated that the doubts continued.

Nomination Confirmed, But Nominee Declined

There have been instances in which the Senate confirmed a nominee who then declined to accept appointment to the Supreme Court. All offered personal reasons for their deci-sion. The seven who declined apparently shared an under-standing of the responsibilities of the office and honest insight into their personal needs or deficiencies as potential justices. In some cases, they preferred another office.

Robert H. Harrison [4] was the first man to decline an appointment. Nominated by his close friend George Washington, he was chosen as Chancellor of Maryland (the equivalent of chief justice of that state's highest court) five days after the Senate confirmed his Supreme Court nomination. Preferring the state post as one of more substance and dignity, Harrison declined the Supreme Court nomination in spite of Washington's pleas.

John Quincy Adams [24] had already been both a senator and an important diplomat by the time of his nomination to the Supreme Court. Acceptable to both political parties, he was unanimously confirmed by the Senate on the very same day that it had received the nomination. But, citing both his lack of legal experience and his presidential ambitions, Adams declined. He was elected president thirteen years later in 1824.

John Jay (1) [1] [17] had resigned the chief justiceship in 1795 to become governor of New York. He then declined to accept his second appointment as chief justice in 1801. His refusal was based on congressional failure to act on his suggestion to relieve the justices from what he considered the onerous duty of sitting part-time on the circuit courts.

William Smith [36] was a close political ally of President Jackson who nominated him to the Court in 1837. But Smith preferred a life of active politics and wanted to work in support of Jacksonian Democracy. Recognizing the conflict between political life and the neutrality inherent in the post of Supreme Court justice, he declined the appointment.

Controversial New York Senator Roscoe Conkling [75] also declined a Supreme Court appointment to avoid the conflict between the Court and politics. In 1873 President Grant offered him the chief justiceship out of friendship, but Conkling declined the offer. Then, in 1882, President Arthur formally nominated him as associate justice. Weathering the storm of opposition directed at him by the press, Conkling was the beneficiary of the Senate tradition of never rejecting one of its own. However, while he was confirmed by a comfortable 39–12 margin, he finally decided to decline the post.

Both William Cushing (3) [3] [12] and Levi Lincoln [22] declined their appointments for personal reasons. Cushing was already an associate justice at the time he was nominated as chief justice. Pleading his "advanced" age of sixty-four, he declined the promotion to continue as associate justice, a post he retained until his death fourteen years later. Levi Lincoln was sixty-two at the time of his appointment and plagued by poor eyesight. Although pressed by President Madison to accept the appointment, Lincoln declined on the ground that his failing eyesight would not permit him to execute the duties of a Supreme Court justice.

Nomination Not Confirmed

While the official records show only eleven *formal* rejections, the twenty-seven nominations which the Senate has refused to confirm must all be considered as rejections in fact. Whether the Senate refused to take action on the nomination, or merely postponed consideration of the nomination, the effect has been the same: the president's choice has not been confirmed.

Senate rejections have been based upon one or more of the following factors: (1) opposition to the nominating president; (2) opposition based on the nominee's involvement in public issues; (3) perceived unsuitability or lack of qualifications of the nominee; (4) perceived political unreliability of the nominee; (5) "senatorial courtesy"; and (6) opposition to the record of the incumbent Court.

The initial rejection of Roger B. Taney (24) [33] [34], already discussed, provided a good example of reason (1). Yet it has been more often the case that the opposition-controlled Senate will reject a lame-duck president's nomination in order to preserve the post for the choice of the incoming opposition president. This treatment of lame-duck nominations has been responsible for at least nine of the "additional" nominations.

The first victim of this senatorial tactic was John J. Crittenden [29]. When, toward the end of his term, President John Quincy Adams nominated the Whig Crittenden, the Jacksonian Democratic majority in the Senate postponed consideration of the nomination in order to give incoming President Andrew Jackson the opportunity to select his own nominee. In 1844, the Senate rejected five of President Tyler's nominees (John C. Spencer [40], Reuben H. Walworth [41], Edward King [42] [43], and John M. Read [45]) based on the mistaken belief of the Whig majority that Whig leader Henry Clay would defeat Democrat James K. Polk in the next presidential election. Again, toward the end of Millard Fillmore's term in 1853 the Senate rejected Edward Bradford [50], George E. Badger [51], and William C. Micou [52] in order that incoming President Franklin Pierce might fill the vacancies with his own choices.

The most pronounced case of senatorial opposition to a nominee, based on its opposition to a nominating president, came in 1865 when Andrew Johnson named Henry Stanbery [61]. Johnson, impeached by the House under eleven largely spurious articles focusing on his dismissal of Edwin M. Stanton as secretary of war, had escaped conviction in the Senate by one vote. Animosity between the president and Congress ran high. Anxious to impede the president's every move, the Senate postponed consideration of the Stanbery nomination—and then went one step further. Congress passed a bill that reduced the size of the Supreme Court from ten members to nine, with an added proviso which would further reduce the Court to eight upon the next vacancy. Thus the Senate not only rejected Stanbery but prevented Johnson from making any further nominations.

Senate opposition to a nominee's political involvement forestalled confirmations of John Rutledge (2) [2] [11], Stanley Matthews (46) [72] [73], Alexander Wolcott [23], George Woodward [46], Ebenezer Hoar [62], John J. Parker [107], and George Harrold Carswell [135]. Rutledge, as already noted, had opposed the Senate-supported Jay Treaty of 1794, and Matthews' association with highly political corporate and railroad interests raised the issue of judicial impartiality.

Wolcott, although questioned extensively by the Senate on his legal qualifications, was rejected primarily on the basis of his vigorous enforcement of the embargo and non-intercourse acts while he was U.S. Collector of Customs in Connecticut. George Woodward was an admitted radical and, in the Senate's opinion, offensive to Irish-Americans because of some "native American" sentiments he had expressed in a public speech. Ebenezer Hoar was rejected for a host of political reasons: he opposed the political nature of circuit judge appointments, demanding that positions be filled by talented jurists rather than political allies; advocated civil service reform; and had supported Andrew Johnson during the latter's impeachment trial.

Political opposition based on "misunderstandings" surrounded Senate failure to confirm Circuit Judge John J. Parker [107] in 1930—the only nominee rejected by the Senate between 1894 and 1968. He was opposed by the American Federation of Labor (AFL), the NAACP, and the Senate for "anti-labor, racist tendencies." Labor opposed him because he had voted to sustain a lower court determination upholding a yellow dog contract—a contract under which employees agree not to join a labor union. But Parker had not expressed himself in favor of such a contract; his conclusion had been governed by a prior Supreme Court decision in a similar matter.

NAACP opposition was based on one of Judge Parker's campaign statements as the 1920 Republic candidate for the North Carolina governorship. To the Democratic taunt that he was too "liberal" on racial issues came this unfortunate rebuttal: "The participation of the Negro in politics is a source of danger to both races and is not desired by the wise men in either race or by the Republic Party of North Carolina." But this was by no means reflective of Parker's racial attitudes; he was in fact "liberal" on the subject. As Chief Judge of the Fourth Circuit he was to write some of the most significant opinions against racial segregation.

Nixon nominee George Harrold Carswell [135] was initially suspect on the basis of his civil rights record. This remained the principal reason for his formal Senate rejection, although Senate investigations had also disclosed dubious financial transactions and raised questions as to the nominee's legal capabilities.

The third factor, the nominee's suitability and qualifications, has been measured by such criteria as age and health, legal education and experience, and the nominee's record in and out of public office. Nominees whose capacity for high judicial office were deemed questionable included Carswell [135], Wolcott [23], Conkling [75], and George H. Williams [67]. Williams had been both a senator and the territorial governor of Oregon, but his record as an attorney and as President Grant's attorney general was charitably considered less than impressive. When Grant nominated Wiliams to succeed Chief Justice Salmon P. Chase (39) [60], the Senate was outraged that such a "mediocrity" had been chosen for so important a post. The nomination was also opposed by the organized bar, especially the New York Bar Association which wrote that Williams' nomination "disappoints the just expectation of the legal profession and does not deserve the approval of the people."[3] Even though Williams charged his critics with slander, he still asked Grant to withdraw his nomination.

While the age criterion has been used against a nominee, it has never been the key factor in the Senate's decision. For the most part, it has been only supportive of evaluations based on other criteria. For example, 74-year-old Caleb Cushing [68] was opposed primarily due to the fourth factor: political unreliability. Cushing had changed his political ideology at least once too often. He had been a Whig, a Tyler Whig, a Democrat, a Johnson Constitutional Conservative, and a Republican. The Senate did not want such a political chameleon on the Supreme Court. It was, however, easier for many senators to cite age as the reason for denying confirmation.

While the first four rejection factors all require some evaluation of the nominee, the fifth, "senatorial courtesy,"

---

3. The Association of the Bar of the City of New York. 3 Warren, *The Supreme Court in United States History*, 1923. p. 276.

is in a different category. Senatorial courtesy is the deference
of the Senate to the reasonable wishes of its individual members. In practical terms, this means that the Senate is quick
to confirm the nomination of one of its members and quick
to follow the views of the senators who represent the nominee's home state. If a president, over the objections of a
home state (or any influential) senator, persists in submitting
the nomination of an objectionable candidate, the offended
senator will invoke senatorial courtesy.

The rejections of William B. Hornblower [83] and
Wheeler H. Peckham [84] were the result of senatorial courtesy. In filling the vacancy left by the death of New Yorker
Samuel Blatchford (48) [76], President Grover Cleveland
desired to nominate another New Yorker. But as Cleveland
had ignored the suggestions of New York's influential Senator David B. Hill, the latter threatened to invoke senatorial
courtesy. Cleveland persisted in nominating Hornblower and
Peckham, and Senator Hill, true to his word, rallied his
colleagues to defeat both nominations by 24–30 and 32–41
margins respectively.

The 1894 Hornblower and Peckham rejections were to
be the last until Parker [107] was rejected thirty-six years
later. Prior to 1894, the Senate had refused to confirm twenty-
two out of eighty-four nominations—a rejection rate of more
than twenty-five percent. From 1895 to 1968, however, there
was only the one Parker rejection following forty-five nominations. But since 1968 there has been a series of rejections
based on the sixth factor: opposition to the record of the incumbent Court. It has been a delayed conservative reaction
(or backlash) to the judicial activism and liberal (or leftist)
philosophy of the Supreme Court under Earl Warren (88)
[122], who was confirmed as chief justice in 1953.

Two months after President Lyndon Johnson announced
his intention to "neither seek nor accept" the Democratic
Party nomination for the 1968 presidential elections, Chief
Justice Warren submitted his resignation. Johnson, now a
lame-duck president with a hostile Senate, nominated his
close friend, Associate Justice Abe Fortas (95) [129] [131] as

the new chief justice. From a purely legal-judicial point of view, the choice was a wise one. In less than four years on the Court Fortas had distinguished himself as a scholar and as a libertarian concerned with fundamental human rights. Yet in the summer of 1968, Republicans regarded the Fortas nomination as a continuation of the Warren Court. Hostile to the previous fifteen years of decisions on desegregation and busing, reapportionment and redistricting, criminal justice, separation of church and state and civil disobedience, many senators looked upon Fortas as the scapegoat on which to vent their accumulated hostility to the Warren Court.

But whatever chance Fortas might have had to secure Senate confirmation ended with Johnson's nomination of his old crony, Judge William Homer Thornberry [132] to fill the vacancy which would result from the Fortas promotion. While Thornberry was a solid public servant with fourteen years in the House of Representatives and commendable service as a federal judge, the Senate generally regarded his nomination as a combination of politics and cronyism. Subjected to the pressures of intense Senate scrutiny that were a product of the political times, Fortas asked Johnson to withdraw his nomination for the chief justiceship. Thornberry then was denied confirmation simply because there was no vacancy for which he could be confirmed.

Six months later, Fortas was under fire for revelations concerning his dealings with financier Louis Wolfson. With the integrity and prestige of the Court at issue, he resigned his position as associate justice.

Nixon Republicans now had their opportunity to see the appointment of less activist judges to the Court. Nine days after the Fortas resignation, President Nixon nominated Warren Earl Burger (97) [133] to replace Earl Warren. (Warren, commenting that "since they won't confirm Abe, they'll have me," had stayed his resignation for another full term.) Burger was confirmed as chief justice within two weeks. Then came Nixon's attempt to fill the Fortas vacancy.

Nixon's first choice was Chief Judge Clement F. Haynsworth [134] of the U. S. Court of Appeals for the Fourth

Circuit. But the Senate Judiciary Committee found evidence that Haynsworth possessed the same insensitivity to financial and conflict of interest improprieties that had led to the Fortas resignation. Nixon then chose Judge George Harrold Carswell [135], of dubious objectivity in civil rights matters. (While U. S. Attorney for Florida, he helped transfer a federally-funded, municipally-owned golf course to private hands in order to circumvent a Supreme Court ban on municipal segregation.) Again, the president's choice was rejected.

Many of the twenty-seven rejected nominees were as well qualified as the one hundred and one justices who did serve on the Supreme Court. The Senate rejections have resulted largely from the interplay of personalities and political times; had most of the rejected nominees been selected at a different time, or by a different president, Senate confirmation would have been readily forthcoming. Edward King, for example, might have been spared the ignominy of twice being rejected if the conflict between a lame-duck Democratic president and a Whig Senate had not existed. Had President Grover Cleveland not infuriated Senator David B. Hill, either Hornblower or Peckham might have served with distinction on the Supreme Court. And had Lyndon Johnson not nominated Homer Thornberry, Abe Fortas, and not Warren Burger, might be chief justice. More important, had Johnson not nominated Fortas, the inquisitorial spirit surrounding Supreme Court nominees might never have been aroused, and Nixon's nominee Haynsworth might well have been confirmed.

But the inquisitorial spirit of the Senate has been aroused. And in the post-Watergate era it will continue. The detente of the post–Hornblower-Peckham days is over, and the Senate can be expected to exercise with a renewed fervor this most important restraint on presidential power.

Five

COUNTING THE OPINIONS

The First 34,000 Decisions

Let's make a physical count of all of the judicial opinions of all of the first one hundred Supreme Court justices and see what we come up with. One could hardly say "no" to such a *fashionable* idea; it is undoubtedly an idea whose time has come. This is, after all, the era of the computer and the era of quantification. American economic history, we are told, "has undergone radical revision as a result of the application of mathematical and statistical methods." This, we are further told, "is part of a more ambitious effort to reconstruct the entire history of American economic development on a sound quantitative basis." In *Time on the Cross*,[4] authors Fogel and Engerman applied their quantitative methods to a reexamination of American slavery. Why not apply such methods to Supreme Court history?

Those engaged in such enterprises, say Fogel and Engerman, are called "new economic historians" or "Cliometric-

---

4. R. W. Fogel and Stanley L. Engerman. *Time on the Cross*. Boston: Little, Brown & Co., 1974. p. 6.

ians."[5]   So, as a self-appointed "amateur cliometrician," editor Mersky started counting judicial opinions. But long before he reached the end of the first 412 volumes of the United States Reports, covering nearly all of the first 191 Supreme Court terms over a period of 183 years, he turned the counting chores over to three then-librarians and research assistants at the University of Texas School of Law: David E. Brown, Susan Roberts, and Bardie C. Wolfe, Jr.

When these human computers reached a total of 21,428 opinions of the Court, plus 6,488 per curiam opinions, and enough concurring, dissenting and "other" opinions to total 34,153, they called it quits. Their tabulations, duly recorded on the tables 8, 9, 10, and 11 were turned over to editor Blaustein for comment and analysis. But he delayed any writing, editing, and analyzing until he obtained the assistance and guidance of Rutgers-Camden Law School students, Bertin Corsell-Emmons, Angela Tolleris, and Matthew Jodziewicz.

What follows are the quantities and preliminary quantitative analyses resulting from the efforts of all of these amateur cliometricians.

But first a caveat—or a note of qualification on all of this quantification. The editors have been looking at these figures for so long that they are not sure that they can see the forest for the trees. Nor are they entirely convinced that the revelations thus far culled from all of this quantification were worth all of that counting. Just because data have been amassed does not mean that anything can be learned from the effort. But it is worth a try. The editors urge other students of Supreme Court history (and of all judicial history) to join them in a continuing search for important conclusions which might result from quantification, and then recommend other possible areas of quantitative research or even recommend that such research be scrapped.

---

5. What *Clio*, the Muse of history, might have thought about all of this is beyond—far beyond—the scope of this chapter.

The Totals

With so much counting by so many non-computers, there are bound to be some minor discrepancies in some of the totals. But editor Mersky certifies that the count on the first 412 volumes of the official edition of the United States Supreme Court Reports totals 34,153 opinions. Here is the breakdown: totals and then average number of opinions per volume of the law reports.

Opinions of the Court	Per Curiam Opinions	Total Decisions
21,428	6,488	27,916
* 52.01	15.75	—

* averages by volume

Concurring Opinions	Dissenting Opinions	Other Opinions	Total Opinions
1,322	3,915	1,000	34,153
* 3.21	9.50	2.42	82.89

* averages by volume

This is detailed in table 8.

There have been 191 terms of Court in the 183 years of Supreme Court history involved in this count. Table 9 shows the *averages* by term as follows:

Opinions of the Court	Per Curiam Opinions	Concurring Opinions
114.59	34.70	7.07

Dissenting Opinions	Other Opinions	Total Opinions
20.94	5.35	182.63

The total opinion average from 1935 to 1972 is 224.84 opinions per term, as contrasted with the overall average of 182.63.

Table 10 has the tabulation broken down by justices. The 100 justices, with approximately 1,500 years of total service, rendered a total of 27,665 written opinions bearing their names. (To this must be added the 6,488 per curiam opinions to reach the total of 34,153.) In addition to the 34,153 opinions, there were 1,367 concurrences without opinion, and 3,915 dissents which were likewise without opinion.

Table 11 details the average number of opinions per justice per year in all of these categories.

A word of explanation on the "categories":

1. *Opinions of the Court.* Opinions written by one justice on behalf of the Court majority or, in some instances, a plurality of the bench. Such opinions are also known as majority opinions.

2. *Per Curiam Opinions.* Opinions, usually brief and often unanimous, setting forth the holding conclusion of the Court without naming any justice as author.

3. *Concurring Opinions.* Opinions by a justice agreeing with the majority result but giving different reasons for his conclusions.

4. *Dissenting Opinions.* Opinions explaining a justice's disagreement with the holding of the majority.

5. *Other Opinions or Mixed Opinions.* Seriatim opinions, judicial "asides", opinions which concur in part and dissent in part, and other opinions difficult to classify.[6] Some of the early opinions of the Supreme Court are specifically referred to as "other opinions."

Tabulations have also been made of concurrences and dissents without opinion. Concurrences without opinion include notations that a justice agreed with a majority judgment-conclusion but not necessarily in its reasoning; or that he joined in the concurring opinion written by another justice. Dissents without opinion include notations that a justice disagreed with a majority judgment-conclusion or joined in the written dissent of another justice.

---

6. See the *Passenger Cases*, 48 U.S. (7 How.) 283 (1849).

The Caseload-Workload

As everybody has come to know—and as the members of the Supreme Court constantly complain—the caseload is increasing all the time. But that is not reflected in the tabulations. Neither the number of opinions of the Court nor the number of per curiam opinions is on the increase. Nor is there any sudden outpouring of concurring and dissenting opinions. Quite the contrary.

The workload-overload has come in the form of making decisions on which cases should be decided. The justices must devote weeks of working time in reading petitions for *certiorari* (by far the most common method of bringing a case before the Supreme Court for review) and arguing about which petitions should be granted. Between 1935 and 1972, the number of cases brought before the Court each year showed a phenomenal increase: from 938 to 3,794.[7] Thus there has been less time to devote to the actual process of decision-making and the number of decided cases has been on the decrease.

The average number of decided cases per *term* has been 149.29, which means just over 150 cases per *year*—for there have been more terms than years in the records of the Supreme Court. The decided-cases figure has been determined by adding the number of opinions of the Court and the number of per curiam opinions and dividing by 191, i.e. the number of terms that the Supreme Court has sat. These 191 terms, however, encompass only 183 years of Supreme Court history. The usual Supreme Court term runs annually from October to June of the following year, but there have been eight additional terms, primarily in the Court's early history.

The average number of cases decided per term (or per year) from 1935 to 1972 was roughly 225, ranging from a high of 376 in 1967-68 to a low of 121 in 1953-54. From 1953-1968, encompassing the fifteen-year tenure of Chief

7. Gerhard Casper and Richard A. Posner, "A Study of the Supreme Court's Caseload," 3 J. Legal Studies 339, 340 (1974).

Justice Earl Warren (88), the yearly average stood at 266. But this dropped to an average of fewer than 200 decided cases per term under the chief justiceship of Warren Earl Burger (97), beginning in 1969.

This does not mean that the members of today's Court have been less diligent than their immediate predecessors. For, as pointed out, the present Court is forced to spend so much more time in deciding so many more petitions for *certiorari*. It has been suggested that they are spending too much time in the process.[8]

What these quantitative tabulations reveal (or apparently reveal) is that there is an outer limit on the quantity of work that can be done by nine justices during a single Court term, and that this limit has been reached. Or at least the limit has been reached for a judicial term which begins every October and ends every June. Whether judicial quality would be compromised by a greater caseload or a term which extends beyond nine months of decision-making is another question.

Congress long ago recognized the inability of the Supreme Court to decide every case that every litigant wanted to bring before it. This recognition resulted in the Judiciary Act of 1925[9] which granted the Court broad discretion over its jurisdiction by means of the *certiorari* process. But perhaps the caseload figures show that the 1925 solution is no longer adequate. If the number of *certiorari* petitions continues at the present rate for another decade it will reach the 7,500 figure. At that point the job of deciding which cases to decide will take up nearly all of the Court's time.[10]

Radical restructuring of the Supreme Court's procedural apparatus may now be necessary. Proposals have come forth. Best known are the 1972 recommendations made by a study group of the Federal Judicial Center, headed by Harvard

8. S. M. Hufstedler, "Comity and the Constitution: The Changing Role of the Federal Judiciary," 47 N.Y.U. L. Rev. 841, 850 (1972).

9. Act of February 13, 1925. 43 Stat. 936 (1925).

10. Supra, note 8.

Law School's Paul A. Freund.[11] Yet, despite the concurrence of Chief Justice Burger (97), the recommendations have yet to be acted upon.

A better understanding of the Supreme Court workload, which includes the writing of concurrences and dissents as well as majority opinions, is revealed in an examination of the statistics in a historical context.

The Court in History

Total Opinions and Opinions of The Court. The busiest period in Supreme Court history was the October 1967 term (October 1967 to June 1968) with a total of 548 opinions in all five categories. The next busiest workloads were in the 1968 and 1970 terms when the number of written opinions was 479 and 478 respectively. But these were not necessarily the years when the greatest number of cases were decided. There were, for example, only 109 opinions of the Court in the 1967 term, 5 less than the 191-term average of 114.59.

The number of opinions of the Court fell below the 200-figure only three times during the last quarter of the nineteenth century, when there were 198 opinions of the Court in the 1898 term, 184 in the 1897 term, and 173 in the 1898 term. There were record highs of 298 and 297 in the 1886 and 1890 terms. Majority opinions also totaled 200 or more in 16 of the next 25 years. But the 210 total of 1925 was followed by 199 in 1926 and was never to reach the 200 figure again.

What has made the five-category totals so high in the 1960s and 1970s has been the startling increase in per curiam opinions as well as the more publicized increase in concurring and dissenting opinions. The 1967 term was indeed the one in which the greatest number of cases was decided, for there

---

11. Federal Judicial Center. Report on the Caseload of the Supreme Court (1972) (The Freund Report). Discussion of these recommendations is beyond the scope of this statistical study.

were 267 per curiam opinions as well as 109 opinions of the Court included in the 548 total. And there were 220 per curiam opinions among the 479 in 1968. In 1970, however, the 478 total was largely the result of the record number of concurring opinions, for the number of per curiam opinions that year had dropped to 47.

The number of opinions of the Court ranged up and down the scale from zero to 94 in the first six decades of Supreme Court history. The 94 high of 1851, for example, was followed by 53 in 1852. The number went over 100 for the first time in 1859 with 115 opinions, falling to 64 in the following year. The next 17 years saw the total fluctuating between 41 in 1862 and 193 in 1873 until the 200 figure was first reached in the 1875 term.

Dividing Supreme Court activity into historic eras reveals a steady increase in decision-making. In the period which ended with the death of Chief Justice Marshall (13) in 1835 the Court decided an average of 31 cases per term. The figure more than doubled to 64 in the period from 1835 to 1868. Then it nearly quadrupled to 232 decisions per term in the period 1868 to 1900.

The low point in Supreme Court activity during the second half of the last century was in the Civil War period. The total number of majority opinions was 74, 41, 75, 55, and 70 respectively in the years covering the Court terms from December 1861 through December 1865. The total number of opinions for those 5 terms was 78, 49, 83, 65, and 82. The high total prior to the Civil War was 190, and the 1866 total was up to 138. This total was never to fall below the 100-mark again, nor was the total figure after 1873 ever to be less than 200 in a regular term of Court, except in 1953, when the number fell to 190.

There was no corresponding reduction in judicial activity during the two World Wars. In the 1911–1920 decade, for example, the average for the war years was actually slightly higher than during the non-war years. And the average number of total opinions in the four years of World War II was 300, as compared with a 260 average in the preceding four years and a 297 average in the first 4 post-war years.

Nor has there been any discernible increase or decrease of judicial activity or judicial workload based on national prosperity or depression.

Per Curiam Opionions. The average number of per curiam opinions per term is 34.70, with the greatest number (267) in the 1967 term. Such opinions, "usually brief and often unanimous setting forth the holding-conclusion of the Court without naming any justice as author," (See definitions on page 90.) made their first appearance in Volume 67 of the United States Reports in the October 1862 term. There was one. There were only six more in the next decade. The high in the 1800s was thirty-six in 1896, but there were ten in the 1899 term.

The number of per curiam opinions per term fluctuated in the next half-century between highs of 110, 116, and 115 in 1926, 1927, and 1928 and lows of 23 in 1903 and 1910. There were only 38 per curiam opinions in 1952 and 40 in 1945.

But the number was to increase radically during the Warren years and then fall just as radically during the Burger period. In 1955, the third year of Warren's chief justiceship, there were 138 per curiam opinions. There were 172 in 1957, 250 in 1962 and, as noted, 267 in 1967. The number fell slightly to 220 and 190 during the 1968 and 1969 terms and then dropped to 47, 42, and 44 in the first years of the Burger Court.

Concurring Opinions. Concurring opinions were unusual in the early history of the Court and uncommon until the beginning of World War II. While one such opinion is reported as early as 1797, there were no concurring opinions as late as the regular terms of 1924 and 1925. (One cannot count the short, special terms of June 1958.) The high point through 1940 was the 1856 term when fourteen concurring opinions were reported; there were eleven each in the years 1937 and 1938 and nine in 1873.

The number jumped from five in 1940 to seventeen in

1941 and then (in the next quarter-century) ranged from ten in 1949 to forty-two in 1964. But the 1967 term saw another jump to sixty-two, with a further jump to one hundred and fourteen in 1970. The figure dropped to sixty-eight in 1971 and was back in the forties in the 1972 term.

The Dissenting Voice (1). While dissenting opinions have been increasingly common, the increase in numbers alone has not been dramatic. Nor is there anything really startling in the number of dissents compared with the number of opinions of the Court in any one term.

The greatest number of dissents in any one term covered by this study was in 1972. The total was 128, the same number recorded for majority opinions. Of special note on the judicial workload are the statistics for the 1970 term: there were 127 dissenting opinions as compared with 120 opinions of the Court. But there are comparable figures for some earlier years as well. In eleven terms, dating back to 1946, the justices wrote eighty or more dissenting opinions. Here are the figures:

Date	Opinion of the Court	Dissenting Opinions
1946	140	80
1948	106	86
1952	109	90
1957	105	87
1960	110	91
1963	111	82
1967	109	101
1968	102	90
1970	120	127
1971	129	120
1972	128	128

Dissenting opinions have been known from the earliest days of Supreme Court history, but not so many of them. There was one dissent each in the 1790, 1796, and 1805 terms and then dissents in every term since 1808 with the exceptions of 1819, 1825, 1826, and 1841.

The 1845 term was the first in which the number of dissents was more than ten, but it was not until 1927 that the number reached thirty-two. And then came World War II and the sudden jump to forty-four, sixty-three, sixty-eight, and seventy-nine dissenting opinions for the terms beginning in 1941 through 1944. The figures continued to climb in the post-war years: up to ninety by 1952, a drop in the mid-fifties, ninety-one in 1960, one hundred and one in 1957, and then one hundred and twenty-eight in 1972.

The Dissenting Voice (2). Again the basic questions: To what extent does this quantitative conglomeration yield qualitative results? Do any of these totals add to knowledge about the Court? Does any of this come as a surprise?

It was never any secret that Chief Justice John Marshall (13) dominated the Court during his thirty-four year tenure from 1801 to 1835. What these statistics do is to measure the extent of that domination—graphically. There were 1,244 opinions of the Court during this period and Chief Justice Marshall wrote 508 of them, a surprising forty-one percent. So strong was his influence that there were but seventy dissenting opinions in all thirty-four years, and Marshall wrote only six of them. These dissents amounted to 5.6 percent of the total number of written opinions or one dissent for every 17.77 cases decided.

Of course the number and proportion of dissents was to increase at the end of the Marshall era. But was the increase significant? The years from 1835 to the end of the Civil War period were marked by dissension over the legal aspects of slavery. They were also the years when lawyers contested the expansion of the "police powers of the states."[12] And there was certainly a lack of unanimity at the bar over the "invention" of the "political question" doctrine in the

---

12. Louisville C. & C.R. Co. v. Letson, 43 U.S. (2 How.) 497 (1844).

case which arose out of Dorr's rebellion in Rhode Island.[13]
For the years 1835=1868 the proportion of dissents increased
to 9.6 percent of the total number of written opinions, or
one dissent for every nine cases. This was nearly a doubling
of the percentage of dissents during the Marshall years, but
it hardly indicates a divided Supreme Court.

The dissent ratio declined during the 1868–1900 period
when the figure fell to 6.6 percent or one out of every 13.3
opinions of the Court. And while the actual number of
dissents rose during the years 1900–1932, the percentage
again declined. With an average of 260 decisions per term,
only one in every seventeen opinions of the Court (5.3 percent) was accompanied by a dissent.

Dissents became commonplace during the presidency of
Franklin D. Roosevelt, and the percentage continues to increase. The average over the last four decades was 225 cases
decided per term, with an average of 328 total opinions in all
five categories. Dissents totaled 19.2 percent of all written
opinions.

The Judicial Opinion-Writer—Quantitatively

In their 1,500 years of Supreme Court service, the first
100 justices wrote 27,665 judicial opinions under their individual authorship, plus 6,488 per curiam opinions. Of
these 27,665 individual opinions, 21,428 were opinions of the
Court. There were 1,322 concurrences, 3,915 were dissents, and 1,000 were "other" or "mixed" opinions.

Thus the "average" justice, with an average tenure of 15
years, wrote an average of 17.7 opinions each year of which
14.2 were opinions of the Court, 0.9 were concurring opinions, and 2.6 were dissents.

Number-one opinion-writer (quantitatively) in the 183
years of Supreme Court history covered in this survey was
William O. Douglas (79). His 1,232 opinions included 524
opinions of the Court, 154 concurring opinions, and 486
opinions in dissent as of 1973. Second was Justice Oliver

---

13. Luther v. Borden, 48 U.S. (7 How.) 1 (1849).

Wendell Holmes (58) with 975 opinions, and in third place was Hugo L. Black (76) with a total of 923.

This should come as no surprise in view of the lengthy tenure which Douglas, Holmes, and Black enjoyed on the Supreme Court bench. Douglas had over 36 years of service and Black had thirty-four years. Holmes had just over twenty-nine. Yet longevity is not a sure guide to total productivity. Justice Bushrod Washington (11) wrote a total of only eighty-four opinions during his more than thirty years on the Court, and Justice James M. Wayne (23) wrote only one hundred and fifty-nine in thirty-two years.

Of course it must be noted that Justices Washington and Wayne served during the early years of the Court when far fewer opinions were being written. Yet John Marshall (13), a Washington contemporary, wrote 539 opinions in just four years more. And while Stephen J. Field (38), author of 659 opinions, was hardly a Wayne contemporary, these two justices were brothers on the bench for five years.

Sixteen of the one hundred justices each delivered more than five hundred opinions:

Rank	Justice	Number of Opinions
1.	Douglas (79)	1232*
2.	Holmes (68)	975
3.	Black (76)	923
4.	Waite (43)	908
5.	Fuller (50)	892
6.	Harlan I (44)	879
7.	Frankfurter (78)	697
8.	Miller (36)	691
9.	McKenna (57)	686
10.	Field (38)	659
11.	Harlan II (89)	626
12.	Brewer (51)	607
13.	McReynolds (66)	580
14.	Marshall (13)	539
15.	Brandeis (67)	532
16.	Brown (52)	511

Here are the total* numbers of opinions of the ten justices who served more than 30 years:

Justice	Years on Court	Number of Opinions
Douglas (79)	34*	1232
Field (38)	34	659
Marshall (13)	34	539
Black (76)	34	923
Harlan I (44)	34	879
Story (18)	33	288
Wayne (23)	32	159
McLean (21)	31	299
Washington (11)	30	84
Johnson (14)	30	162

*The survey was made when Justice Douglas had served 34 years on the Court. He served two additional years before retirement.

In the category of "average number of opinions per justice per term" (table 11), by far the most prolific of the 100 justices was Morrison R. Waite (43). In his 14 years on the bench, Chief Justice Waite wrote 908 opinions or 64.93 per term. Second was Chief Justice Melville W. Fuller (50) with an average of 42.48. Fifteen other justices averaged a total per term of more than thirty but less than forty opinions. This category includes Justices Douglas, Holmes, and Frankfurter but not Justices Black, Miller, or either of the Harlans.

Writing for the Court. Less than 20 percent of the 100 justices wrote more than half of the total number of opinions of the Court—19 justices having authored 10,915 of the 21,428 total. These 10,915 opinions were written by the 19 in 419 years on the bench, or 29 percent of the 1,458 total years of Supreme Court service.

Was there any relationship between this quantity and the factor of quality? Was there a higher percentage of "greats" and "near greats" among these men who spoke most often

for the Court and for their colleagues? Were these the justices most responsible for the course of Supreme Court history?

Here are the figures:

Quantita- tive Ranking	Justice	Years Served	Number of Opinions of the Court	Qualitative Ranking See Ch. Two
1.	Oliver W. Holmes (58)	29	873	Great
2.	Morrison R. Waite* (43)	14	872	Near Great
3.	Melville W. Fuller* (50)	21	750	Average
4.	John M. Harlan I (44)	34	737	Great
5.	Edward D. White* (55)	26	680	Near Great
6.	Joseph McKenna (57)	26	646	Average
7.	Samuel F. Miller (36)	28	608	Near Great
8.	Stephen J. Field (38)	34	544	Near Great
9.	David J. Brewer (51)	20	533	Average
10.	William O. Douglas (79)	36	524 (as of 1973)	Near Great
11.	John Marshall* (13)	34	508	Great
12.	James C. McReynolds (66)	26	488	Failure
13.	Hugo L. Black (76)	34	481	Great
14.	Harlan F. Stone* (73)	20	456	Great
15.	Louis D. Brandeis (67)	22	455	Great
16.	Henry B. Brown (52)	15	453	Average
17.	Horace Gray (47)	20	450	Average
18.	William R. Day (59)	19	430	Average
19.	Samuel Blatchford (48)	11	427	Average

*Chief Justice

Thus the 19 most prolific spokesmen for the Court included:

   6 of the 12 great justices
   5 of the 15 near-great justices
   7 of the 55 average justices
   1 of the 14 below-average justices and judicial failures

With half of the "greats" and only one of the "failures"
among the nineteen who wrote more than half of the opin-

ions of the Court, there is, evidently, some quantity–quality relationship. But it is not significant. As pointed out in Chapter Two, there is a high correlation between length of service and favorable ratings—no justice being classified as a "great" or "near great" unless he served long enough to be known. And there is the demonstrated high correlation between total number of opinions of the Court and length of service.

Mr. Justice [Blank] Dissenting. Although the statistics do not prove that a significant quality-quantity relationship exists, they do confirm the often-expressed view that the greatest—or most prolific—dissenters consistently have been among the most outstanding of the one hundred justices.

The leading writers of dissenting opinions were "greats" and "near greats": Douglas (79) with 486 written dissents as of 1973, Black (76) with 310, Frankfurter (78) with 251, and John M. Harlan II (89) with 242. Number five on the list is John M. Harlan I (44) with 119.

Justice Douglas's 486 dissenting opinions constitute more than twelve percent of the 3,915 handed down during the first 183 years of Supreme Court history. And the number written by the dozen leading dissenters constitutes more than 50 percent of the total. Justice Harlan II (89) was the author of the greatest number of dissents per term of Court, 15.13, followed by Douglas (79) with an average of 14.29. Frankfurter (78) was third with 10.91.

The statistics also reveal that the justice known in history as the "great dissenter," Oliver Wendell Holmes (63), is down in eleventh place on the list of those who have written the greatest number of dissenting opinions. His total was only 72, or 2.48 dissents per term.

This chapter must end with the same theme and the same questions with which it began—together with a plea for ideas on how these quantitative tabulations can be used.

APPENDIX

Table 1
Information on the Members of the Supreme Court

No.	Name	State	Party	Position Held Prior to Appointment
1	*John Jay	N.Y.	Federalist	Sec. of Foreign Affairs under Art. of Confed.
2	John Rutledge	S.C.	Federalist	State Judge
3	William Cushing	Mass.	Federalist	State Judge
4	James Wilson	Pa.	Federalist	Private Practice
5	John Blair	Va.	Federalist	State Judge
6	James Iredell	N.C.	Federalist	State Employee
7	Thomas Johnson	Md.	Federalist	State Judge
8	William Paterson	N.J.	Federalist	N.J. Governor
2	†John Rutledge	S.C.	Federalist	State Judge
9	Samuel Chase	Md.	Federalist	State Judge
10	*Oliver Ellsworth	Conn.	Federalist	U.S. Senate
11	Bushrod Washington	Va.	Federalist	Private Practice
12	Alfred Moore	N.C.	Federalist	State Judge
13	*John Marshall	Va.	Federalist	U.S. Sec. of State
14	William Johnson	S.C.	Dem.-Rep.	State Judge
15	Brockholst Livingston	N.Y.	Dem.-Rep.	State Judge
16	Thomas Todd	Ky.	Dem.-Rep.	State Judge
17	Gabriel Duvall	Md.	Dem.-Rep.	U.S. Comptroller of the Treasury
18	Joseph Story	Mass.	Dem.-Rep.	Private Practice
19	Smith Thompson	N.Y.	Dem.-Rep.	U.S. Sec. of Navy
20	Robert Trimble	Ky.	Dem.-Rep.	Federal Judge
21	John McLean	Ohio	Democrat	U.S. Postmaster-General
22	Henry Baldwin	Pa.	Democrat	Private Practice
23	James M. Wayne	Ga.	Democrat	U.S. House of Representatives
24	*Roger B. Taney	Md.	Democrat	Private Practice
25	Philip P. Barbour	Va.	Democrat	Federal Judge
26	John Catron	Tenn.	Democrat	Private Practice
27	John McKinley	Ala.	Democrat	U.S. House of Representatives
28	Peter V. Daniel	Va.	Democrat	Federal Judge
29	Samuel Nelson	N.Y.	Democrat	State Judge
30	Levi Woodbury	N.H.	Democrat	U.S. Senate
31	Robert C. Grier	Pa.	Democrat	State Judge
32	Benjamin R. Curtis	Mass.	Whig	Private Practice
33	John A. Campbell	Ala.	Democrat	Private Practice
34	Nathan Clifford	Maine	Democrat	Private Practice
35	Noah H. Swayne	Ohio	Republican	Private Practice
36	Samuel F. Miller	Iowa	Republican	Private Practice

*Chief Justice.

Appointing President	Age at Appoint- ment	Years of Service	Total Years of Service	Cause of Termination of Service	Death Date	Age
Washington	44	1789-1795	5	Resigned	1829	83
Washington	50	1789-1791	1	Resigned	1800	60
Washington	57	1789-1810	20	Death	1810	77
Washington	47	1789-1798	8	Death	1798	56
Washington	58	1789-1796	6	Resigned	1800	68
Washington	38	1790-1798	9	Death	1798	48
Washington	59	1791-1793	1	Resigned	1819	86
Washington	47	1793-1806	13	Death	1806	61
Washington	55	1795-1795	0	Rejected	1800	60
Washington	54	1796-1811	15	Death	1811	70
Washington	50	1796-1799	4	Resigned	1807	62
Adams	36	1798-1829	31	Death	1829	67
Adams	45	1799-1804	4	Resigned	1810	55
Adams	45	1801-1835	34	Death	1835	80
Jefferson	32	1804-1834	30	Death	1834	63
Jefferson	49	1806-1823	16	Death	1823	65
Jefferson	42	1807-1826	18	Death	1826	60
Madison	58	1812-1835	22	Resigned	1844	90
Madison	32	1811-1845	33	Death	1845	65
Monroe	55	1823-1843	20	Death	1843	75
Adams	49	1826-1828	2	Death	1828	51
Jackson	44	1829-1861	32	Death	1861	76
Jackson	50	1830-1844	14	Death	1844	64
Jackson	45	1835-1867	32	Death	1867	77
Jackson	59	1836-1864	28	Death	1864	87
Jackson	52	1836-1841	5	Death	1841	58
Jackson	51	1837-1865	28	Death	1865	79
Van Buren	57	1837-1852	15	Death	1852	72
Van Buren	57	1841-1860	19	Death	1860	76
Tyler	52	1845-1872	27	Retired	1873	81
Polk	55	1845-1851	5	Death	1851	61
Polk	52	1846-1870	23	Retired	1870	76
Fillmore	41	1851-1857	6	Resigned	1874	64
Pierce	41	1853-1861	8	Resigned	1889	77
Buchanan	54	1858-1881	23	Death	1881	78
Lincoln	57	1862-1881	18	Retired	1884	79
Lincoln	46	1862-1890	28	Death	1890	74

No.	Name	State	Party	Position Held Prior to Appointment
37	David Davis	Illinois	Republican	State Judge
38	Stephen J. Field	Calif.	Democrat	State Judge
39	*Salmon P. Chase	Ohio	Republican	U.S. Secretary of Treasury
40	William Strong	Pa.	Republican	Private Practice
41	Joseph P. Bradley	N.J.	Republican	Private Practice
42	Ward Hunt	N.Y.	Republican	State Judge
43	*Morrison R. Waite	Ohio	Republican	Private Practice
44	John M. Harlan	Ky.	Republican	Private Practice
45	William B. Woods	Ga.	Republican	Federal Judge
46	Stanley Matthews	Ohio	Republican	Private Practice
47	Horace Gray	Mass.	Republican	State Judge
48	Samuel Blatchford	N.Y.	Republican	Federal Judge
49	Lucius Q. C. Lamar	Miss.	Democrat	U.S. Secretary of Interior
50	*Melville W. Fuller	Illinois	Democrat	Private Practice
51	David J. Brewer	Kansas	Republican	Federal Judge
52	Henry B. Brown	Mich.	Republican	Federal Judge
53	George Shiras, Jr.	Pa.	Republican	Private Practice
54	Howell E. Jackson	Tenn.	Democrat	Federal Judge
55	Edward D. White	La.	Democrat	U.S. Senate
56	Rufus W. Peckham	N.Y.	Democrat	State Judge
57	Joseph McKenna	Calif.	Republican	U.S. Attorney General
58	Oliver W. Holmes	Mass.	Republican	State Judge
59	William R. Day	Ohio	Republican	Federal Judge
60	William H. Moody	Mass.	Republican	U.S. Attorney General
61	Horace H. Lurton	Tenn.	Democrat	Federal Judge
62	Charles E. Hughes	N.Y.	Republican	Governor of New York
55	*Edward D. White	La.	Democrat	Elevated to Chief Justice
63	Willis Van Devanter	Wyo.	Republican	Federal Judge
64	Joseph R. Lamar	Ga.	Democrat	Private Practice
65	Mahlon Pitney	N.J.	Republican	State Judge
66	James C. McReynolds	Tenn.	Democrat	U.S. Attorney General
67	Louis D. Brandeis	Mass.	Democrat	Private Practice
68	John H. Clarke	Ohio	Democrat	Federal Judge
69	*William H. Taft	Ohio	Republican	Professor of Law
70	George Sutherland	Utah	Republican	Private Practice
71	Pierce Butler	Minn.	Democrat	Private Practice
72	Edward T. Sanford	Tenn.	Republican	Federal Judge
73	Harlan F. Stone	N.Y.	Republican	U.S. Attorney General
62	*Charles E. Hughes	N.Y.	Republican	Judge of Internat. Court of Justice
74	Owen J. Roberts	Pa.	Republican	Private Practice
75	Benjamin N. Cardozo	N.Y.	Democrat	State Judge
76	Hugo L. Black	Ala.	Democrat	U.S. Senate
77	Stanley F. Reed	Ky.	Democrat	U.S. Solicitor General

*Chief Justice.

Appointing President	Age at Appoint- ment	Years of Service	Total Years of Service	Cause of Termination of Service	Death Date	Age
Lincoln	47	1862-1877	14	Resigned	1886	71
Lincoln	46	1863-1897	34	Retired	1899	82
Lincoln	56	1864-1873	8	Death	1873	64
Grant	61	1870-1880	10	Retired	1895	87
Grant	57	1870-1892	21	Death	1892	79
Grant	62	1873-1882	9	Disabled	1886	75
Grant	57	1874-1888	14	Death	1888	72
Hayes	44	1877-1911	34	Death	1911	78
Hayes	56	1881-1887	6	Death	1887	63
Garfield	56	1881-1889	7	Death	1889	64
Arthur	53	1882-1902	20	Death	1902	74
Arthur	62	1882-1893	11	Death	1893	73
Cleveland	62	1888-1893	5	Death	1893	68
Cleveland	55	1888-1910	21	Death	1910	76
Harrison	52	1890-1910	20	Death	1910	73
Harrison	54	1891-1906	15	Retired	1913	77
Harrison	60	1892-1903	10	Retired	1924	92
Harrison	60	1893-1895	2	Death	1895	63
Cleveland	48	1894-1910	16	Promoted	1921	75
Cleveland	57	1896-1909	13	Death	1909	71
McKinley	54	1898-1925	26	Retired	1926	83
Roosevelt	61	1902-1932	29	Retired	1935	93
Roosevelt	53	1903-1922	19	Retired	1923	74
Roosevelt	52	1906-1910	3	Disabled	1917	63
Taft	66	1910-1914	4	Death	1914	70
Taft	48	1910-1916	5	Resigned	1948	86
Taft	65	1910-1921	10	Death	1921	76
Taft	51	1911-1937	26	Retired	1941	81
Taft	53	1911-1916	5	Death	1916	58
Taft	54	1912-1922	10	Disabled	1924	66
Wilson	52	1914-1941	26	Retired	1946	84
Wilson	59	1916-1939	22	Retired	1941	84
Wilson	59	1916-1922	5	Resigned	1945	87
Harding	63	1921-1930	8	Retired	1930	72
Harding	60	1922-1938	15	Retired	1942	80
Harding	56	1922-1939	16	Death	1939	72
Harding	57	1923-1930	7	Death	1930	65
Coolidge	52	1925-1941	15	Promoted	1946	73
Hoover	67	1930-1941	11	Retired	1948	86
Hoover	55	1930-1945	15	Resigned	1955	80
Hoover	61	1932-1938	6	Death	1938	68
Roosevelt	51	1937-1971	34	Retired	1971	85
Roosevelt	53	1937-1957	19	Retired		

No.	Name	State	Party	Position Held Prior to Appointment
78	Felix Frankfurter	Mass.	Democrat	Professor of Law
79	William O. Douglas	Conn.	Democrat	U.S. Chairman, S.E.C.
80	Frank Murphy	Mich.	Democrat	U.S. Attorney General
81	James F. Byrnes	S.C.	Democrat	U.S. Senate
73	*Harlan F. Stone	N.Y.	Republican	Elevated to Chief Justice
82	Robert H. Jackson	N.Y.	Democrat	U.S. Attorney General
83	Wiley B. Rutledge	Iowa	Democrat	Federal Judge
84	Harold H. Burton	Ohio	Republican	U.S. Senate
85	*Fred M. Vinson	Ky.	Democrat	U.S. Secretary of Treasury
86	Tom C. Clark	Texas	Democrat	U.S. Attorney General
87	Sherman Minton	Ind.	Democrat	Federal Judge
88	*Earl Warren	Calif.	Republican	Governor of California
89	John M. Harlan	N.Y.	Republican	Federal Judge
90	William J. Brennan, Jr.	Ind.	Democrat	State Judge
91	Charles E. Whittaker	Mo.	Republican	Federal Judge
92	Potter Stewart	Ohio	Republican	Federal Judge
93	Byron R. White	Colo.	Democrat	U.S. Deputy Atty. General
94	Arthur J. Goldberg	Illinois	Democrat	U.S. Sec. of Labor
95	Abe Fortas	Wash,D.C.	Democrat	Private Practice
96	Thurgood Marshall	N.Y.	Democrat	U.S. Solicitor General
97	*Warren E. Burger	Minn.	Republican	Federal Judge
98	Harry A. Blackmun	Minn.	Republican	Federal Judge
99	Lewis F. Powell	Va.	Republican	Private Practice
100	William H. Rehnquist	Ariz.	Republican	Asst. Attorney General

*Chief Justice

Appointing President	Age at Appointment	Years of Service	Total Years of Service	Cause of Termination of Service	Death Date	Age
Roosevelt	56	1938-1962	23	Retired	1965	82
Roosevelt	40	1939-1975	36	Retired		
Roosevelt	49	1940-1949	9	Death	1949	59
Roosevelt	62	1941-1942	1	Resigned	1972	92
Roosevelt	68	1941-1946	5	Death	1946	73
Roosevelt	49	1941-1954	13	Death	1954	62
Roosevelt	48	1943-1949	6	Death	1949	55
Truman	57	1945-1958	13	Retired	1964	76
Truman	56	1946-1953	7	Death	1953	63
Truman	49	1949-1967	18	Retired		
Truman	58	1949-1956	7	Retired	1965	75
Eisenhower	62	1953-1969	16	Retired	1974	83
Eisenhower	55	1955-1971	16	Retired	1971	72
Eisenhower	50	1956-				
Eisenhower	56	1957-1962	5	Retired	1973	72
Eisenhower	43	1958-				
Kennedy	44	1962-				
Kennedy	54	1962-1965	3	Resigned		
Johnson	55	1965-1969	4	Resigned		
Johnson	59	1967-				
Nixon	61	1969-				
Nixon	61	1970-				
Nixon	64	1971-				
Nixon	47	1971-				

Table 2
Occupants of Supreme Court Seats One through Five

Chief Justice 1	Seat 2	Seat 3	Seat 4	Seat 5
John Jay (1) *Washington* *1789-1795*	John Rutledge (2) *Washington* *1789-1791*	William Cushing (3) *Washington* *1789-1810*	James Wilson (4) *Washington* *1789-1798*	John Blair (5) *Washington* *1789-1796*
John Rutledge (2) *Washington* *1795*	Thomas Johnson (7) *Washington* *1791-1793*	Joseph Story (18) *Madison* *1811-1845*	Bushrod Washington (11) *Adams* *1798-1829*	Samuel Chase (9) *Washington* *1796-1811*
Oliver Ellsworth (10) *Washington* *1796-1799*	William Paterson (8) *Washington* *1793-1806*	Levi Woodbury (30) *Polk* *1845-1851*	Henry Baldwin (22) *Jackson* *1830-1844*	Gabriel Duvall (17) *Madison* *1812-1835*
John Marshall (13) *Adams* *1801-1835*	Brockholst Livingston (15) *Jefferson* *1806-1823*	Benjamin R. Curtis (32) *Fillmore* *1851-1857*	Robert C. Grier (31) *Polk* *1846-1870*	Philip P. Barbour (25) *Jackson* *1836-1841*
Roger B. Taney (24) *Jackson* *1836-1864*	Smith Thompson (19) *Monroe* *1823-1843*	Nathan Clifford (34) *Buchanan* *1858-1881*	William Strong (40) *Grant* *1870-1880*	Peter V. Daniel (28) *Van Buren* *1841-1860*
Salmon P. Chase (9) *Lincoln* *1864-1873*	Samuel Nelson (29) *Tyler* *1845-1872*	Horace Gray (47) *Arthur* *1882-1902*	William B. Woods (45) *Hayes* *1881-1887*	Samuel F. Miller (36) *Lincoln* *1862-1890*
Morrison R. Waite (43) *Grant* *1874-1888*	Ward Hunt (42) *Grant* *1873-1882*	Oliver.W. Holmes (58) *Roosevelt* *1902-1932*	Lucius Q. C. Lamar (49) *Cleveland* *1888-1893*	Henry B. Brown (52) *Harrison* *1891-1906*

Chief Justice 1	Seat 2	Seat 3	Seat 4	Seat 5
Melville W. Fuller (50) *Cleveland* *1888-1910*	Samuel Blatchford (48) *Arthur* *1882-1893*	Benjamin N. Cardozo (75) *Hoover* *1932-1938*	Howell E. Jackson (54) *Harrison* *1893-1895*	William H. Moody (60) *Roosevelt* *1906-1910*
Edward D. White (55) *Taft* *1910-1921*	Edward D. White (55) *Cleveland* *1894-1910*	Felix Frankfurter (78) *Roosevelt* *1939-1962*	Rufus W. Peckham (56) *Cleveland* *1896-1909*	Joseph R. Lamar (64) *Taft* *1911-1916*
William H. Taft (69) *Harding* *1921-1930*	Willis Van Devanter (63) *Taft* *1911-1937*	Arthur J. Goldberg (94) *Kennedy* *1962-1965*	Horace H. Lurton (61) *Taft* *1910-1914*	Louis D. Brandeis (67) *Wilson* *1916-1939*
Charles E. Hughes (62) *Hoover* *1930-1941*	Hugo L. Black (76) *Roosevelt* *1937-1971*	Abe Fortas (95) *Johnson* *1965-1969*	James C. McReynolds (66) *Wilson* *1914-1941*	William O. Douglas (79) *Roosevelt* *1939-1975*
Harlan F. Stone (73) *Roosevelt* *1941-1946*	Lewis F. Powell (99) *Nixon* *1971-*	Harry A. Blackmun (98) *Nixon* *1970-*	James F. Byrnes (81) *Roosevelt* *1941-1942*	
Fred M. Vinson (85) *Truman* *1946-1953*			Wiley B. Rutledge (83) *Roosevelt* *1943-1949*	
Earl Warren (88) *Eisenhower* *1953-1969*			Sherman Minton (87) *Truman* *1949-1956*	
Warren E. Burger (97) *Nixon* *1969-*			William J. Brennan, Jr. (90) *Eisenhower* *1956-*	

Table 2
Occupants of Supreme Court Seats Six through Ten

Seat 6	Seat 7	Seat 8	Seat 9	Seat 10
James Iredell (6) *Washington* 1790-1799	Thomas Todd (16) *Jefferson* 1807-1826	John Catron (26) *Jackson* 1837-1865 died 1865 no new appointment	John McKinley (27) *Van Buren* 1837-1852	Stephen J. Field (38) *Lincoln* 1863-1897
Alfred Moore (12) *Adams* 1799-1804	Robert Trimble (20) *Adams* 1826-1828		John A. Campbell (33) *Pierce* 1853-1861	Joseph McKenna (57) *McKinley* 1898-1925
William Johnson (14) *Jefferson* 1804-1834	John McLean (21) *Jackson* 1829-1861		David Davis (37) *Lincoln* 1862-1877	Harlan F. Stone (73) *Coolidge* 1925-1941
James M. Wayne (23) *Jackson* 1835-1867	Noah H. Swayne (35) *Lincoln* 1862-1881		John M. Harlan (44) *Hayes* 1877-1911	Robert H. Jackson (82) *Roosevelt* 1941-1954
Joseph P. Bradley (41) *Grant* 1870-1892	Stanley Matthews (46) *Garfield* 1881-1889		Mahlon Pitney (65) *Taft* 1912-1922	John M. Harlan (89) *Eisenhower* 1955-1971
George Shiras, Jr. (53) *Harrison* 1892-1903	David J. Brewer (51) *Harrison* 1890-1910		Edwart T. Sanford (72) *Harding* 1923-1930	William H. Rehnquist (100) *Nixon* 1971-
William R. Day (59) *Roosevelt* 1903-1922	Charles E. Hughes (62) *Taft* 1910-1916		Owen J. Roberts (74) *Hoover* 1930-1945	

Seat 6	Seat 7	Seat 8	Seat 9	Seat 10
Pierce Butler (71) *Harding* *1922-1939*	John H. Clarke (68) *Wilson* *1916-1922*		Harold H. Burton (84) *Truman* *1945-1958*	
Frank Murphy (80) *Roosevelt* *1940-1949*	George Sutherland (70) *Harding* *1922-1938*		Potter Stewart (92) *Eisenhower* *1958-*	
Tom C. Clark (86) *Truman* *1949-1967*	Stanley F. Reed (77) *Roosevelt* *1938-1957*			
Thurgood Marshall (96) *Johnson* *1967-*	Charles Whittaker (91) *Eisenhower* *1957-1962*			
	Byron R. White (93) *Kennedy* *1962-*			

Table 3
An Alphabetical List of the First One Hundred Justices

Name of Justice	Appoint- ment Number	Political Party	State	Appointing President	Years Served	Seat No.
Baldwin, Henry	22	Democrat	Pa.	Jackson	14	4
Barbour, Philip P.	25	Democrat	Va.	Jackson	5	5
Black, Hugo L.	76	Democrat	Ala.	Roosevelt	34	2
Blackmun, Harry A.	98	Republican	Minn.	Nixon	. .	3
Blair, John	5	Federalist	Va.	Washington	6	5
Blatchford, Samuel	48	Republican	N.Y.	Arthur	11	2
Bradley, Joseph P.	41	Republican	N.J.	Grant	21	6
Brandeis, Louis D.	67	Democrat	Mass.	Wilson	22	5
Brennan, William J.	90	Democrat	N.J.	Eisenhower	. .	4
Brewer, David J.	51	Republican	Kansas	Harrison	20	7
Brown, Henry B.	52	Republican	Mich.	Harrison	15	5
*Burger, Warren E.	97	Republican	Minn.	Nixon	. .	1
Burton, Harold H.	84	Republican	Ohio	Truman	13	9
Butler, Pierce	71	Democrat	Minn.	Harding	16	6
Byrnes, James F.	81	Democrat	S.C.	Roosevelt	1	4
Campbell, John A.	33	Democrat	Ala.	Pierce	8	9
Cardozo, Benjamin N.	75	Democrat	N.Y.	Hoover	6	3
Catron, John	26	Democrat	Tenn.	Jackson	28	8
*Chase, Salmon P.	39	Republican	Ohio	Lincoln	8	1
Chase, Samuel	9	Federalist	Md.	Washington	15	5
Clark, Tom C.	86	Democrat	Texas	Truman	18	6
Clarke, John H.	68	Democrat	Ohio	Wilson	5	7
Clifford, Nathan	34	Democrat	Maine	Buchanan	23	3
Curtis, Benjamin R.	32	Whig	Mass.	Fillmore	6	3
Cushing, William	3	Federalist	Mass.	Washington	20	3
Daniel, Peter V.	28	Democrat	Va.	Van Buren	19	5
Davis, David	37	Republican	Ill.	Lincoln	14	9
Day, William R.	59	Republican	Ohio	Roosevelt	19	6
Douglas, William O.	79	Democrat	Conn.	Roosevelt	36	5
Duvall, Gabriel	17	Dem.-Rep.	Md.	Madison	22	5
*Ellsworth, Oliver	10	Federalist	Conn.	Washington	4	1
Field, Stephen J.	38	Democrat	Calif.	Van Buren	34	10
Fortas, Abe	95	Democrat	D.C.	Johnson	4	3
Frankfurter, Felix	78	Democrat	Mass.	Roosevelt	23	3
*Fuller, Melville W.	50	Democrat	Ill.	Cleveland	21	1
Goldberg, Arthur J.	94	Democrat	Ill.	Kennedy	3	3
Gray, Horace	47	Republican	Mass.	Arthur	20	3
Grier, Robert C.	31	Democrat	Pa.	Polk	23	4
Harlan, John M., I	44	Republican	Ky.	Hayes	34	9
Harlan, John M., II	89	Republican	N.Y.	Eisenhower	16	10
Holmes, Oliver W.	58	Republican	Mass.	Roosevelt	29	3
*Hughes, Charles E.	62	Republican	N.Y.	Taft & Hoover	16	7 & 1

*Chief Justice.

Name of Justice	Appointment Number	Political Party	State	Appointing President	Years Served	Seat No.
Hunt, Ward	42	Republican	N.Y.	Grant	9	2
Iredell, James	6	Federalist	N.C.	Washington	9	6
Jackson, Howell E.	54	Democrat	Tenn.	Harrison	2	4
Jackson, Robert H.	82	Democrat	N.Y.	Roosevelt	13	10
*Jay, John	1	Federalist	N.Y.	Washington	5	1
Johnson, Thomas	7	Federalist	Md.	Washington	1	2
Johnson, William	14	Dem.-Rep.	S.C.	Jefferson	30	6
Lamar, Joseph R.	64	Democrat	Ga.	Taft	5	5
Lamar, Lucius Q. C.	49	Democrat	Miss.	Cleveland	5	4
Livingston, Brockholst	15	Dem.-Rep.	N.Y.	Jefferson	16	2
Lurton, Horace H.	61	Democrat	Tenn.	Taft	4	4
McKenna, Joseph	57	Republican	Calif.	McKinley	26	10
McKinley, John	27	Democrat	Ala.	Van Buren	15	9
McLean, John	21	Whig	Ohio	Jackson	32	7
McReynolds, James C.	66	Democrat	Tenn.	Wilson	26	4
*Marshall, John	13	Federalist	Va.	Adams	34	1
Marshall, Thurgood	96	Democrat	N.Y.	Johnson	..	6
Matthews, Stanley	46	Republican	Ohio	Garfield	7	7
Miller, Samuel F.	36	Republican	Iowa	Lincoln	28	5
Minton, Sherman	87	Democrat	Ind.	Truman	7	2
Moody, William H.	60	Republican	Mass.	Roosevelt	3	5
Moore, Alfred	12	Federalist	N.C.	Adams	4	6
Murphy, Frank	80	Democrat	Mich.	Roosevelt	9	6
Nelson, Samuel	29	Democrat	N.Y.	Tyler	27	2
Paterson, William	8	Federalist	N.J.	Washington	13	2
Peckham, Rufus W.	56	Democrat	N.Y.	Cleveland	13	4
Pitney, Mahlon	65	Republican	N.J.	Taft	10	9
Powell, Lewis F., Jr.	99	Republican	Va.	Nixon	..	2
Reed, Stanley F.	77	Democrat	Ky.	Roosevelt	19	7
Rehnquist, William H.	100	Republican	Ariz.	Nixon	..	10
Roberts, Owen J.	74	Republican	Pa.	Hoover	15	9
*Rutledge, John	2	Federalist	S.C.	Washington	1	2 & 1
Rutledge, Wiley B.	83	Democrat	Iowa	Roosevelt	6	4
Sanford, Edward T.	72	Republican	Tenn.	Harding	7	9
Shiras, George, Jr.	53	Republican	Pa.	Harrison	10	6
Stewart, Potter	92	Republican	Ohio	Eisenhower	..	9
*Stone, Harlan F.	73	Republican	N.Y.	Coolidge & Roosevelt	20	10 & 1
Story, Joseph	18	Dem.-Rep.	Mass.	Madison	33	3
Strong, William	40	Republican	Pa.	Grant	10	4
Sutherland, George	70	Republican	Utah	Harding	15	7
Swayne, Noah H.	35	Republican	Ohio	Lincoln	18	7
*Taft, William H.	69	Republican	Ohio	Harding	8	1
*Taney, Roger B.	24	Democrat	Md.	Jackson	28	1
Thompson, Smith	19	Dem.-Rep.	N.Y.	Monroe	20	2

Name of Justice	Appointment Number	Political Party	State	Appointing President	Years Served	Seat No.
Todd, Thomas	16	Dem.-Rep.	Ky.	Jefferson	18	7
Trimble, Robert	20	Dem.-Rep.	Ky.	Adams	2	7
Van Devanter, Willis	63	Republican	Wyo.	Taft	26	2
*Vinson, Fred M.	85	Democrat	Ky.	Truman	18	1
*Waite, Morrison R.	43	Republican	Ohio	Grant	14	1
*Warren, Earl	88	Republican	Calif.	Eisenhower	16	1
Washington, Bushrod	11	Federalist	Va.	Adams	31	4
Wayne, James M.	23	Democrat	Ga.	Jackson	32	6
White, Byron R.	93	Democrat	Colo.	Kennedy	. .	7
*White, Edward D.	55	Democrat	La.	Taft & Cleveland	26	2 & 1
Whittaker, Charles E.	91	Republican	Mo.	Eisenhower	5	7
Wilson, James	4	Federalist	Pa.	Washington	8	4
Woodbury, Levi	30	Democrat	N.H.	Polk	5	3
Woods, William B.	45	Republican	Ga.	Hayes	6	4

*Chief Justice

Table 4
Judges of the Judges

Listed below, in alphabetical order, are the law school deans and professors of law, history, and political science who deal with constitutional law, and have participated in this study:

Henry J. Abraham
  University of Pennsylvania
Albert W. Alschuler
  University of Texas
Jerome A. Barron
  George Washington University
William M. Beaney
  University of Denver
Arthur Bestor
  University of Washington
Joseph W. Bishop, Jr.
  Yale University
Vincent A. Blasi
  University of Michigan
Edgar Bodenheimer
  University of California at Davis
Arthur E. Bonfield
  University of Iowa
Gerald Grob
  Rutgers University
Vern Countryman
  Harvard University
Lindsey Cowen
  University of Georgia
John E. Cribbet
  University of Illinois
Norman Dorsen
  New York University
Jesse Dukeminier, Jr.
  University of California at Los Angeles
David Fellman
  University of Wisconsin
Morris David Forkosch
  Brooklyn Law School
Ray Forrester
  Cornell University
Walter Gellhorn
  Columbia University
Morton Gitelman
  University of Arkansas
Stephen B. Goldberg
  University of Illinois

Dewey Grantham
  Vanderbilt University
Gerald Gunther
  Stanford University
Andrew Hacker
  Cornell University
Elwood Hain
  Wayne State University
Jerome Hall
  University of California at Hastings
Winfred A. Harbison
  Wayne State University
Geoffrey C. Hazard, Jr.
  University of Chicago
James Willard Hurst
  University of Wisconsin
Fred L. Israel
  City University of New York
Alfred Kelly
  Wayne State University
Charles D. Kelso
  University of Indiana at Indianapolis
Robert E. Knowlton
  Rutgers University (Newark)
Milton R. Konvitz
  Cornell University
Robert A. Leflar
  University of Arkansas
Leonard W. Levy
  Brandeis University
William B. Lockhard
  University of Minnesota
Alpheus T. Mason
  University of Virginia
Lester J. Mazor
  University of Utah
Robert B. McKay
  New York University
Wallace Mendelson
  University of Texas
Arthur S. Miller
  George Washington University

Table 4 — continued

Clarence Morris
  University of Pennsylvania
William H. Muir
  University of California at Berkeley
Paul Murphy
  University of Minnesota
John B. Neibel
  University of Houston
Dallin H. Oaks
  University of Chicago
Howard L. Oleck
  Cleveland State University
Owen Olpin
  University of Texas
Arnold M. Paul
  Michigan State University
Cornelius J. Peck
  University of Washington
Leo Pfeffer
  Long Island University
Ervin H. Pollack
  Ohio State University
Ralph S. Rice
  University of California at Los Angeles

John P. Roche
  Brandeis University
Richard S. L. Roddis
  University of Washington
George Schatzki
  University of Texas
Samuel I. Shuman
  Wayne State University
Allen E. Smith
  University of Texas
Howard J. Taubenfeld
  Southern Methodist University
John W. Wade
  Vanderbilt University
Russell J. Weintraub
  University of Texas
Alan Westin
  Columbia University
Walter O. Weyrauch
  University of Houston
Charles Alan Wright
  University of Texas

Table 5
Prior Judicial Experience

Justice	Year Judicial Oath Taken	Prior Judicial Experience in Years Federal	State	Total	Total Years Supreme Court Service
1 *John Jay	1789	0	2	2	6
2 *John Rutledge	1789, 1795*	0	6	6	2
3 William Cushing	1789	0	29	29	21
4 James Wilson	1789	0	0	0	9
5 John Blair	1789	0	11	11	7
6 James Iredell	1790	0	½	½	9
7 Thomas Johnson	1791	0	1½	1½	2
8 William Paterson	1793	0	0	0	13
9 Samuel Chase	1796	0	8	8	15
10 *Oliver Ellsworth	1793	0	5	5	4
11 Bushrod Washington	1798	0	0	0	31
12 Alfred Moore	1799	0	1	1	5
13 *John Marshall	1801	0	0	0	34
14 William Johnson	1804	0	6	6	30
15 Brockholst Livingston	1806	0	0	0	17
16 Thomas Todd	1807	0	6	6	20
17 Joseph Story	1811	0	0	0	34
18 Gabriel Duvall	1811	0	6	6	24
19 Smith Thompson	1823	0	16	16	20
20 Robert Trimble	1826	9	2	11	2
21 John McLean	1829	0	6	6	32
22 Henry Baldwin	1830	0	0	0	14
23 James M. Wayne	1835	0	5	5	32
24 *Roger B. Taney	1836	0	0	0	28
25 Philip B. Barbour	1836	6	2	8	5
26 John Catron	1837	0	10	10	28
27 John McKinley	1837	0	0	0	15
28 Peter V. Daniel	1841	4	0	4	19
29 Samuel Nelson	1845	0	22	22	27
30 Levi Woodbury	1845	0	6	6	6
31 Robert C. Grier	1846	0	13	13	24
32 Benjamin R. Curtis	1851	0	0	0	6
33 John A. Campbell	1853	0	0	0	8
34 Nathan Clifford	1858	0	0	0	23
35 Noah H. Swayne	1862	0	0	0	19
36 Samuel F. Miller	1862	0	0	0	28
37 David Davis	1862	0	14	14	15
38 Stephen J. Field	1863	0	6	6	34
39 *Salmon P. Chase	1864	0	0	0	9
40 William Strong	1870	0	11	11	10

*Chief Justice.

Justice	Year Judicial Oath Taken	Prior Judicial Experience in Years			Total Years Supreme Court Service
		Federal	State	Total	
41 Joseph P. Bradley	1870	0	0	0	22
42 Ward Hunt	1872	0	8	8	10
43 *Morrison R. Waite	1874	0	0	0	14
44 John M. Harlan, I	1877	0	1	1	34
45 William B. Woods	1880	12	0	12	7
46 Stanley Matthews	1881	0	4	4	8
47 Horace Gray	1881	0	18	18	21
48 Samuel Blatchford	1882	15	0	15	11
49 Lucius Q. C. Lamar	1888	0	0	0	5
50 *Melville W. Fuller	1888	0	0	0	22
51 David J. Brewer	1889	6	22	28	21
52 Henry B. Brown	1890	16	0	16	16
53 George Shiras, Jr.	1892	0	0	0	11
54 Howell E. Jackson	1893	7	0	7	2
55 *Edward D. White	1894, 1910*	0	1½	1½	27
56 Rufus W. Peckham	1895	0	9	9	14
57 Joseph McKenna	1898	5	0	5	27
58 Oliver W. Holmes	1902	0	20	20	30
59 William R. Day	1903	4	3	7	19
60 William H. Moody	1906	0	0	0	4
61 Horace H. Lurton	1909	16	10	26	5
62 *Charles E. Hughes	1910, 1930*	0	0	0	17
63 Willis Van Devanter	1910	7	1	8	27
64 Joseph R. Lamar	1910	0	2	2	6
65 Mahlon Pitney	1912	0	11	11	10
66 James C. McReynolds	1914	0	0	0	27
67 Louis D. Brandeis	1916	0	0	0	23
68 John H. Clarke	1916	2	0	2	6
69 *William H. Taft	1921	8	5	13	9
70 George Sutherland	1922	0	0	0	16
71 Pierce Butler	1922	0	0	0	17
72 Edward T. Sanford	1923	14	0	14	7
73 *Harlan F. Stone	1923, 1941*	0	0	0	23
74 Owen J. Roberts	1930	0	0	0	15
75 Benjamin N. Cardozo	1932	0	18	18	6
76 Hugo L. Black	1937	0	1½	1½	34
77 Stanley F. Reed	1937	0	0	0	19
78 Felix Frankfurter	1939	0	0	0	23
79 William O. Douglas	1939	0	0	0	35
80 Frank Murphy	1940	0	7	7	9
81 James F. Byrnes	1941	0	0	0	1
82 Robert H. Jackson	1941	0	0	0	13
83 Wiley B. Rutledge	1943	4	0	4	6

*Chief Justice.

Justice	Year Judicial Oath Taken	Prior Judicial Experience in Years			Total Years Supreme Court Service
		Federal	State	Total	
84 Harold H. Burton	1945	0	0	0	13
85 *Fred M. Vinson	1946	5	0	5	7
86 Tom C. Clark	1949	0	0	0	18
87 Sherman Minton	1949	8	0	8	7
88 *Earl Warren	1953	0	0	0	16
89 John M. Harlan, II	1955	1	0	1	16
90 William J. Brennan, Jr.	1956	0	7	7	
91 Charles E. Whittaker	1957	3	0	3	5
92 Potter Stewart	1958	4	0	4	
93 Byron R. White	1962	0	0	0	
94 Arthur J. Goldberg	1962	0	0	0	3
95 Abe Fortas	1965	0	0	0	4
96 Thurgood Marshall	1967	3½	0	3½	
97 *Warren E. Burger	1969	13	0	13	
98 Harry A. Blackmun	1970	11	0	11	
99 Lewis F. Powell, Jr.	1971	0	0	0	
100 William H. Rehnquist	1971	0	0	0	

*Chief Justice

Table 6
The 138 Nominees
Nominations[1] —Confirmations, Rejections, Acceptances

No.	Nominee	Appointed	Action[2]	Term	No. Serving
[1]	*John Jay	Sept. 24, 1789	C- Sept. 26, 1789	1789-1795	(1)
[2]	John Rutledge	Sept. 24, 1789	C- Sept. 26, 1789	1789-1791	(2)
[3]	William Cushing	Sept. 24, 1789	C- Sept. 26, 1789	1789-1810	(3)
[4]	Robert H. Harrison	Sept. 24, 1789	C- Sept. 26, 1789		
			D- Oct. 1, 1789		
[5]	James Wilson	Sept. 24, 1789	C- Sept. 26, 1789	1789-1798	(4)
[6]	John Blair	Sept. 24, 1789	C- Sept. 26, 1789	1789-1796	(5)
[7]	James Iredell	Feb. 9, 1790	C- Feb. 10, 1790	1790-1799	(6)
[8]	Thomas Johnson	Aug. 5, 1791	C- Nov. 7, 1791	1791-1793	(7)
[9]	William Paterson	Feb. 27, 1793	W- Feb. 28, 1793		
[10]	William Paterson	Mar. 4, 1793	C- Mar. 4, 1793	1793-1806	(8)
[11]	*John Rutledge[3]	Jul. 1, 1795	R- Dec. 15, 1795		
[12]	*William Cushing	Jan. 26, 1796	C- Jan. 27, 1796		
			D- Feb. 2, 1796		
[13]	Samuel Chase	Jan. 26, 1796	C- Jan. 27, 1796	1796-1811	(9)
[14]	*Oliver Ellsworth	Mar. 3, 1796	C- Mar. 4, 1796	1796-1799	(10)
[15]	Bushrod Washington	Sept. 29, 1798	C- Dec. 20, 1798	1798-1829	(11)
[16]	Alfred Moore	Oct. 20, 1799	C- Dec. 10, 1799	1799-1804	(12)
[- 17]	*John Jay	Dec. 18, 1800	C- Dec. 19, 1800		
			D- Jan. 2, 1801		
[18]	*John Marshall	Jan. 20, 1801	C- Jan. 27, 1801	1801-1835	(13)
[19]	William Johnson	Mar. 22, 1804	C- Mar. 24, 1804	1804-1834	(14)
[20]	Brockholst Livingston	Nov. 10, 1806	C- Dec. 17, 1806	1807-1823	(15)
[21]	Thomas Todd	Feb. 28, 1807	C- Mar. 3, 1807	1807-1826	(16)
[- 22]	Levi Lincoln	Jan. 2, 1811	C- Jan. 3, 1811		
			D- Jan. 20, 1811		
[- 23]	Alexander Wolcott	Feb. 4, 1811	R- Feb. 13, 1811		
[- 24]	John Q. Adams	Feb. 21, 1811	C- Feb. 22, 1811		
			D- Apr. 1811		
[25]	Joseph Story	Nov. 15, 1811	C- Nov. 18, 1811	1811-1845	(17)
[26]	Gabriel Duvall	Nov. 15, 1811	C- Nov. 18, 1811	1812-1835	(18)
[27]	Smith Thompson	Sept. 11, 1823	C- Dec. 19, 1823	1823-1843	(19)
[28]	Robert Trimble	Apr. 11, 1826	C- May 9, 1826	1826-1828	(20)
[29]	John J. Crittenden	Dec. 17, 1828	P- Feb. 12, 1829		
[30]	John McLean	Mar. 6, 1829	C- Mar. 7, 1829	1829-1861	(21)
[31]	Henry Baldwin	Jan. 4, 1830	C- Jan. 6, 1830	1830-1844	(22)
[32]	James M. Wayne	Jan. 7, 1835	C- Jan. 9, 1835	1835-1867	(23)
[33]	Roger B. Taney[4]	Jan. 15, 1835	P- Mar. 3, 1835		
[34]	*Roger B. Taney	Dec. 28, 1835	C- Mar. 15, 1836	1836-1864	(24)
[35]	Philip P. Barbour	Dec. 28, 1835	C- Mar. 15, 1836	1836-1841	(25)

*Chief Justice.

No.	Nominee	Appointed	Action	Term	No. Serving
[-36]	William Smith	Mar. 3, 1837	C- Mar. 8, 1837 D- Mar., 1837		
[37]	John Catron	Mar. 3, 1837	C- Mar. 8, 1837	1837-1865	(26)
[38]	John McKinley	Apr. 22, 1837	C- Sept. 25, 1837	1837-1852	(27)
[39]	Peter V. Daniel	Feb. 26, 1841	C- Mar. 2, 1841	1841-1860	(28)
[-40]	John C. Spencer	Jan. 8, 1844	R- Jan. 31, 1844		
[-41]	Reuben H. Walworth	Mar. 13, 1844	P- June. 15, 1844 W- June 17, 1844		
[-42]	Edward King	June 5, 1844	P- June 15, 1844		
[-43]	Edward King	Dec. 4, 1844	P- Jan. 23, 1845 W- Feb. 7, 1845		
[44]	Samuel Nelson	Feb. 4, 1845	C- Feb. 14, 1845	1845-1872	(29)
[-45]	John M. Read	Feb. 7, 1845	NA		
[-46]	George W. Woodward	Dec. 23, 1845	R- Jan. 22, 1846		
[47]	Levi Woodbury	Sept. 20, 1845	C- Jan. 3, 1846	1845-1851	(30)
[48]	Robert C. Grier	Aug. 3, 1846	C- Aug. 4, 1846	1846-1870	(31)
[49]	Benjamin R. Curtis	Sept. 22, 1851	C- Dec. 29, 1851	1851-1857	(32)
[-50]	Edward A. Bradford	Aug. 16, 1852	NA		
[-51]	George E. Badger	Jan. 10, 1853	P- Feb. 11, 1853		
[-52]	William C. Micou	Feb. 24, 1853	NA		
[53]	John A. Campbell	Mar. 21, 1853	C- Mar. 25, 1853	1853-1861	(33)
[54]	Nathan Clifford	Dec. 9, 1857	C- Jan. 12, 1858	1858-1881	(34)
[-55]	Jeremiah S. Black	Feb. 5, 1861	R- Feb. 21, 1861	(lame duck appointment)	
[56]	Noah H. Swayne	Jan. 21, 1862	C- Jan. 24, 1862	1862-1881	(35)
[57]	Samuel F. Miller	July 16, 1862	C- July 16, 1862	1862-1890	(36)
[58]	David Davis	Oct. 17, 1862	C- Dec. 8, 1862	1862-1877	(37)
[59]	Stephen J. Field	Mar. 6, 1863	C- Mar. 10, 1863	1863-1897	(38)
[60]	*Salmon P. Chase	Dec. 6, 1864	C- Dec. 6, 1864	1864-1873	(39)
[-61]	Henry Stanbery	Apr. 16, 1866	NA[5]		
[-62]	Ebenezer R. Hoar	Dec. 14, 1869	R- Feb. 3, 1870		
[-63]	Edwin M. Stanton	Dec. 20, 1869	C- Dec. 20, 1869	Died Dec. 24, 1869	
[64]	William Strong	Feb. 7, 1870	C- Feb. 18, 1870	1870-1880	(40)
[65]	Joseph P. Bradley	Feb. 7, 1870	C- Mar. 21, 1870	1870-1892	(41)
[66]	Ward Hunt	Dec. 3, 1872	C- Dec. 11, 1872	1873-1882	(42)
[-67]	*George H. Williams	Dec. 1, 1873	W- Jan. 8, 1874		
[-68]	*Caleb Cushing	Jan. 9, 1874	W- Jan. 13, 1874		
[69]	*Morrison R. Waite	Jan. 19, 1874	C- Jan. 21, 1874	1874-1888	(43)
[70]	John M. Harlan	Mar. 29, 1877	C- Nov. 29, 1877	1877-1911	(44)
[71]	William B. Woods	Dec. 15, 1880	C- Dec. 21, 1880	1881-1887	(45)
[-72]	Stanley Matthews	Jan. 26, 1881	NA		
[73]	Stanley Matthews	Mar. 14, 1881	C- May 12, 1881	1881-1889	(46)
[74]	Horace Gray	Dec. 19, 1881	C- Dec. 20, 1881	1882-1902	(47)

No.	Nominee	Appointed	Action	Term	No. Serving
[- 75]	Roscoe Conkling	Feb. 24, 1882	C- Mar. 2, 1882 D- Mar. 7, 1882		
[76]	Samuel Blatchford	Mar. 13, 1882	C- Mar. 27, 1882	1882-1893	(48)
[77]	Lucius Q. C. Lamar	Dec. 6, 1887	C- Jan. 16, 1888	1888-1893	(49)
[78]	*Melville W. Fuller	Apr. 30, 1888	C- July 20, 1888	1888-1910	(50)
[79]	David J. Brewer	Dec. 4, 1889	C- Dec. 18, 1889	1890-1910	(51)
[80]	Henry B. Brown	Dec. 23, 1890	C- Dec. 29, 1890	1891-1906	(52)
[81]	George Shiras, Jr.	July 19, 1892	C- July 26, 1892	1892-1903	(53)
[82]	Howell E. Jackson	Feb. 2, 1893	C- Feb. 18, 1893	1893-1895	(54)
[- 83]	William B. Hornblower	Sept. 19, 1893	R- Jan. 15, 1894		
[- 84]	Wheeler H. Peckham	Jan. 22, 1894	R- Feb. 16, 1894		
[85]	Edward D. White	Feb. 19, 1894	C- Feb. 19, 1894	1894-1910	(55)
[86]	Rufus W. Peckham	Dec. 3, 1895	C- Dec. 9, 1895	1896-1901	(56)
[87]	Joseph McKenna	Dec. 16, 1897	C- Jan. 21, 1898	1898-1925	(57)
[88]	Oliver W. Holmes	Aug. 11, 1902	C- Dec. 4, 1902	1902-1932	(58)
[89]	William R. Day	Feb. 19, 1903	C- Feb. 23, 1903	1903-1922	(59)
[90]	William H. Moody	Dec. 3, 1906	C- Dec. 12, 1906	1906-1910	(60)
[91]	Horace H. Lurton	Dec. 13, 1909	C- Dec. 20, 1909	1910-1914	(61)
[92]	*Edward D. White	Dec. 12, 1910	C- Dec. 12, 1910	1910-1921	(55)
[93]	Charles E. Hughes	Apr. 25, 1910	C- May 2, 1910	1910-1916	(62)
[94]	Willis Van Devanter	Dec. 12, 1910	C- Dec. 15, 1910	1911-1937	(63)
[95]	Joseph R. Lamar	Dec. 12, 1910	C- Dec. 15, 1910	1911-1916	(64)
[96]	Mahlon Pitney	Feb. 19, 1912	C- Mar. 13, 1912	1912-1922	(65)
[97]	James C. McReynolds	Aug. 19, 1914	C- Aug. 29, 1914	1914-1941	(66)
[98]	Louis D. Brandeis	Jan. 28, 1916	C- June 1, 1916	1916-1939	(67)
[99]	John H. Clarke	July 14, 1916	C- July 24, 1916	1916-1922	(68)
[100]	*William H. Taft	June 30, 1921	C- June 30, 1921	1921-1930	(69)
[101]	George Sutherland	Sept. 5, 1922	C- Sept. 5, 1922	1922-1938	(70)
[102]	Pierce Butler	Nov. 23, 1922[6]	C- Dec. 21, 1922	1922-1939	(71)
[103]	Edward T. Sanford	Jan. 24, 1923	C- Jan. 29, 1923	1923-1930	(72)
[104]	Harlan F. Stone	Jan. 25, 1925	C- Feb. 5, 1925	1925-1941	(73)
[105]	*Charles E. Hughes	Feb. 3, 1930	C- Feb. 13, 1930	1930-1941	(62)
[106]	Owen J. Roberts	May 9, 1930	C- May 20, 1930	1930-1941	(74)
[-107]	John J. Parker	Mar. 21, 1930	R- May 7, 1930		
[108]	Benjamin N. Cardozo	Feb. 15, 1932	C- Feb. 24, 1932	1932-1938	(75)
[109]	Hugo L. Black	Aug. 12, 1937	C- Aug. 17, 1937	1937-1971	(76)
[110]	Stanley F. Reed	Jan. 20, 1938	C- Jan. 25, 1938	1938-1957	(77)
[111]	Felix Frankfurter	Jan. 5, 1939	C- Jan. 17, 1939	1939-1962	(78)
[112]	William O. Douglas	Mar. 20, 1939	C- Apr. 5, 1939	1939-1975	(79)
[113]	Frank Murphy	Jan. 4, 1940	C- Jan. 16, 1940	1940-1949	(80)
[114]	*Harlan F. Stone	June 12, 1941	C- June 27, 1941	1941-1946	(73)
[115]	James F. Byrnes	June 3, 1941	C- June 13, 1941	1941-1942	(81)
[116]	Robert H. Jackson	June 12, 1941	C- July 7, 1941	1941-1954	(82)
[117]	Wiley B. Rutledge	Jan. 11, 1943	C- Feb. 8, 1943	1943-1949	(83)
[118]	Harold H. Burton	Sept. 18, 1945	C- Sept. 19, 1945	1945-1958	(84)

*Chief Justice.

No.	Nominee	Appointed	Action	Term	No. Serving
[119]	*Fred M. Vinson	June 6, 1946	C- June 20, 1946	1946-1953	(85)
[120]	Tom C. Clark	Aug. 2, 1949	C- Aug. 18, 1949	1949-1967	(86)
[121]	Sherman Minton	Sept. 15, 1949	C- Oct. 4, 1949	1949-1956	(87)
[122]	*Earl Warren	Oct. 2, 1953	C- Mar. 1, 1954	1953-1968	(88)
[123]	John M. Harlan, II	Oct. 9, 1954	C- Mar. 16, 1955	1955-1971	(89)
[124]	William J. Brennan, Jr.	Sept. 29, 1956	C- Mar. 19, 1957	1956-	(90)
[125]	Charles E. Whittaker	Mar. 1, 1957	C- Mar. 19, 1957	1957-1962	(91)
[126]	Potter Stewart[7]	Oct. 14, 1958	C- May 5, 1959	1959-	(92)
[127]	Byron R. White	Apr. 3, 1962	C- Apr. 11, 1962	1962-	(93)
[128]	Arthur J. Goldberg	Aug. 31, 1962	C- Sept. 25, 1962	1962-1965	(94)
[129]	Abe Fortas	July 28, 1965	C- Aug. 11, 1965	1965-1969	(95)
[130]	Thurgood Marshall	June 13, 1967	C- Aug. 30, 1967	1967-	(96)
[-131]	*Abe Fortas	June 26, 1968	W- Oct. 4, 1968[8]		
[-132]	Homer Thornberry	June 26, 1968	W- Oct. 4, 1968[9]		
[133]	*Warren E. Burger	May 23, 1969	C- June 3, 1969	1969-	(97)
[-134]	Clement F. Haynsworth	Sept. 25, 1969	R- Nov. 21, 1969		
[-135]	George Harrold Carswell	Jan. 19, 1970	R- Apr. 7, 1970		
[136]	Harry A. Blackmun	Apr. 14, 1970	C- May 12, 1970	1970-	(98)
[137]	Lewis F. Powell, Jr.	Oct. 21, 1971	C- Dec. 6, 1971	1971-	(99)
[138]	William H. Rehnquist	Oct. 21, 1971	C- Dec. 10, 1971	1971-	(100)

*   Indicates nomination as chief justice.
-   Indicates an appointment which did not result in a man serving on the Court, for whatever reason.

1   The dates of appointment, confirmation, or rejection, and the terms of the justices from John Jay in 1789 through William Howard Taft in 1921, were taken from Charles Warren's three volume work, *The Supreme Court in United States History,* © 1922, volume 3 (1856-1918), 479-483. All subsequent dates were taken from the Congressional Record, and show the date the nomination was received by the Senate.

2   The following letters have been used to indicate the action taken on the nomination: C - Confirmed; D - Declined appointment after confirmation by Senate; W - Withdrawn; R - Rejected; NA - No Action taken by Senate; P - Postponed by Senate.

3   Rutledge was commissioned, and sworn in Aug. 12, 1795, and presided over the August Term of the Court. Swindler, Politics of Advice and Consent, 56 A.B.A. J. 533, 536 n.2 (1970).

4   The Senate rejected the nomination as an attempt to control the Court through Taney's Cabinet affiliation. In the 1836 election, with six additional states voting, the Democrats won control of the Senate. Taney was renominated, this time for Chief Justice, and was confirmed, 29-15. Swindler, Politics of Advice and Consent, 56 A.B.A. J. 533, 536 n.3 (1970).

5   Congress passed a law reducing the size of the Court, keeping Stanbery out.

6   The 1922 Index to the Congressional Record, Volume 63, p. 14, cites to 63 Cong. Rec. 68, which indicates that the nomination was received by the Senate November 23, 1922. However, the 1922 Index, Volume 64, p. 57, cites to 64 Cong. Rec. 40, where it states that the Senate received the nomination December 5, 1922.

7   Took an interim appointment. Was later approved by Senate.

8   Nomination withdrawn from Senate Oct. 4, 1968 (114 Cong. Rec., 20084). Statement by President withdrawing nomination appears October 2, 1968 in 4 Weekly Compilation of Presidential Documents, 1438 (1968).

9   Thornberry's nomination depended on Fortas' confirmation as chief justice.

Table 7
The Eleven Multiple Nominees*

Multiple nominees who served on the Court

1. *Nominee confirmed by Senate following second nomination* 6

    (a)   As chief justice after prior service as associate justice................. 3
            Edward D. White (55) [85] [92 as chief justice]
            Harlan F. Stone (73) [104] [114 as chief justice]
            Charles E. Hughes (62) [93] [105 as chief justice]

    (b)   As chief justice following failure to receive confirmation
          after nomination as associate justice 1
            Roger B. Taney (24) [33] [34]

    (c)   As associate justice following failure to receive confirmation
          after prior nomination as associate justice 2
            William Paterson (8) [9] [10]
            Stanley Matthews (46) [72] [73]

2. *Nominee confirmed by Senate following second nomination, but*
   nominee declined appointment 2

    (a)   As chief justice 2
            William Cushing (3) [3] [12]
            John Jay (1) [1] [17]

    (b)   As associate justice 0

3. *Nominee's second nomination not confirmed by Senate* 3

    (a)   As chief justice after prior service as associate justice 2
            John Rutledge (2) [2] [11]
            Abe Fortas (95) [129] [131]

    (b)   Multiple nominee who did not serve on Court. Nominee's
          two nominations not confirmed by Senate 1
            Edward King [42] [43]

                                       Total   11

*No multiple nominee ever received a third nomination

Table 8
Supreme Court Opinions: Count Per Volume (United States Reports)
(Volumes 1-412)

Volume	Opinion of the Court	Con-curring	Con-curring without Opinion	Dissent-ing	Dissent-ing without Opinion	Other	Per Curiam	Total Opinions
1								
2			1	1		10		11
3	9	2	1	1		34		46
4	2					9		11
5	15					1		16
6	15	1				1		17
7	27	1	1	1		20		49
8	31	2	7	4	1	8		45
9	37		2	4				41
10	27	1		1	1	3		32
11	70	4	1	4	1	7		85
12	46			5	1	3		54
13	39	2		2	1	2		45
14	40	1		3	2	1		45
15	40			1		1		42
16	36			2	2	2		40
17	32		2		1	3		35
18	26			3		1		30
19	33			1		1		35
20	29			1	2			30
21	27			2		3		32
22	39	1		4				44
23	27							27
24	29					1		30
25	45	2		1	3			48
26	53	1		3				57
27	42	1		2				45
28	27	1		4	2	1		33
29	24			3	1			27
30	40	2		7	6	1		50
31	50	1		5	2	2		58
32	38			2				40
33	59			2				61
34	38	1		3		3		45
35	48			1				49
36	19	2		5	2	6		32
37	40	3		5	20	3		51
38	51	2		5	6			58
39	41	4	1	3	3	11		59
40	31				6	3		34

Volume	Opinion of the Court	Con-curring	Con-curring without Opinion	Dissent-ing	Dissent-ing without Opinion	Other	Per Curiam	Total Opinions
41	42	6		2	1	2		52
42	26			4				30
43	39	1	1	3		1		44
44	49			13	1	2		64
45	46	2		2	5	6		56
46	35	4	1	5	3	9		53
47	35	1	3	3	14	5		44
48	40		1	8	8	7		55
49	38			5	16			43
50	44			5	6	1		50
51	35			6	7	3		44
52	39			9	18			48
53	45	1		5	5	1		52
54	49	2	1	5	7			56
55	53		1	12	17	8		73
56	37	2	3	7	10	3		49
57	43	5		9	6	1		58
58	71	5	5	15	16	1		92
59	90	7	3	14	24	1		112
60	63	7		8	9			78
61	70	2	2	9	12			81
62	69	1		6	25			76
63	56		1	2	6	2		60
64	59			2	1			61
65	64			3	1			67
66	74	2	4	2	1			78
67	41			7	13		1	49
68	75	4	4	4	12			83
69	55	1	1	5	8	1	3	65
70	70	1	2	7	16	3	1	82
71	55	1	3	3	5	2		61
72	73	1		3	5			77
73	96			7	31	2		105
74	84	3	1	10	10			97
75	64		2	10	17	1	1	76
76	104			3	4	1		108
77	67	1		7	9			75
78	60		1	8	7	1		69
79	57	2	1	6	4	7		72
80	78		3	13	18	7		98
81	68			6	16			74
82	75	3		8	17	6		92
83	57	2	2	10	18	2		71
84	68	2	1	7	22	4		81

Volume	Opinion of the Court	Concurring	Concurring without Opinion	Dissenting	Dissenting without Opinion	Other	Per Curiam	Total Opinions
85	61	3		9	16	2		75
86	61	2	2	5	18	3		71
87	58	6	3	11	18	4		79
88	68		1	6	13		1	75
89	47		1	3	13			50
90	41			2	6	1		44
91	104			11	23			115
92	96	1		12	33			109
93	93	2		7	16	1		103
94	126	1		9	38			136
95	112	1	2	7	12	2		122
96	96	3		13	31	1		113
97	81	2		8	14			91
98	65	1		6	12			72
99	92	2	1	10	20	3		107
100	82	1	2	12	14	2		97
101	123			6	18			129
102	90	2		6	10	1		99
103	131			3	11	1		135
104	120		1	4	3			124
105	112			7	12	2		121
106	104			6	9	1		111
107	76	1	3	10	7	1		88
108	87	2		1	3	3		93
109	92	1		7	5			100
110	90			5	1	1		96
111	95	3	3	2	5	3		103
112	86			5	5			91
113	86	1	1	1	6			88
114	78	1		2	8			81
115	75			6	6			81
116	90	2	1	6	7			98
117	79			5	6			84
118	68	2		5	16			75
119	80	1		6	3			87
120	85			4	4			89
121	64							64
122	58			1	8			59
123	72	1		1		2		76
124	82	1		3	3			86
125	54	2		5	8			61
126	2			1	2			3
127	77			3	2	7		87
128	70			1	2		1	72

Volume	Opinion of the Court	Con-curring	Con-curring without Opinion	Dissent-ing	Dissent-ing without Opinion	Other	Per Curiam	Total Opinions
129	65	1		2				68
130	69			1	4			70
131	38			2	4		9	49
132	84			3	1			87
133	58		1	3	3	1		62
134	64	3		5	8			72
135	45			3	8			48
136	31			2	20		6	39
137	80		2		4		3	83
138	63				3			63
139	65	1		5	12	2	1	74
140	61	1	3	3	6		5	70
141	69		1	7	18	2		78
142	53	1		6	13	4		64
143	43	2	5	6	13	1		52
144	63			5	8	8	1	77
145	52			2	6	2		56
146	47			6	9	8		61
147	60			2	3	3		65
148	60		1	3	2	7		70
149	64		4	11	6	8		83
150	69	1		7	9	7		84
151	59		3	3	3	4		66
152	69		1	3	11	1		73
153	55		2	4	13	1	1	61
154	28		8	6	20			34
155	61		1	7	8	13		81
156	50			5	7	8		63
157	43	1		6	9	7		57
158	56			4	6			60
159	59		4	1	7	3		63
160	55			1	6	2		58
161	59		3	7	14	3		69
162	44	1	2	9	15	2		56
163	55		1	8	8	3		66
164	69		5	2	20	2	18	91
165	54		4	5	19	2	4	65
166	52		3	5	17	1	11	69
167	53		3		11	2	3	58
168	53	1	2	3	14	1	12	70
169	48			4	12		8	60
170	51	1	5	7	30	2	4	65
171	47	1	2	3	17		6	57
172	46			6	16	3	10	65

Volume	Opinion of the Court	Concurring	Concurring without Opinion	Dissenting	Dissenting without Opinion	Other	Per Curiam	Total Opinions
173	57	1	3	5	21	2	6	71
174	55		1	2	30	2	1	60
175	50		2	3	27		3	56
176	51	2	3	6	17		4	63
177	66	2	5	2	14	3	2	75
178	47		3	4	18	1	1	53
179	63	3	10	4	26		11	81
180	52		6	5	23	1	4	62
181	58		1	7	30	2	7	74
182	24	2	2	6	15			32
183	50	3	7	4	23		6	63
184	52		4	3	10		9	64
185	39		1	3	15	1	8	51
186	38		1	2	10	2	9	51
187	62		4	2	14	1	14	79
188	55	2	4	8	34		2	67
189	57		4	3	18	4	12	76
190	39	2	6	5	16	5	3	54
191	49		7	3	22	1	11	64
192	45		1	5	17			50
193	42	1	1	2	12	3	5	53
194	64	1	5	7	24		7	79
195	44	3	5	7	16	1	14	69
196	59	1	2	3	14	1	7	71
197	45	3	2	5	24		2	55
198	48	1	8	4	33		10	63
199	47	1	2	8	18	1	20	77
200	50	2	6	3	18	1	12	68
201	36	2	4	4	17	2	4	48
202	40		1	7	24		8	55
203	59		4	4	12		29	92
204	61		1		25	1	7	69
205	48	1	7	5	15	1	12	67
206	38	3	4	4	10		1	46
207	45	2	1	5	12		15	67
208	58		1	2	9		3	63
209	44	3	4	5	3	1	10	63
210	29		1	3	14		2	34
211	58	3	2	6	16			67
212	44			3	8		31	78
213	39			3	8			42
214	40			2	7	1	19	62
215	57	2		3	17		19	81
216	57	5	4	2	17		14	78

Volume	Opinion of the Court	Concurring	Concurring without Opinion	Dissenting	Dissenting without Opinion	Other	Per Curiam	Total Opinions
217	43		2	3	7		16	62
218	58		4	4	10	·	6	68
219	42	1	1	3	4		5	51
220	46		1	3	1		18	67
221	40		1	4	11			44
222	71		2	1	2	5	3	80
223	57		1	3		1	31	92
224	57			2	9	1		60
225	45			3	7	1	11	60
226	55			1	5	8	20	84
227	67		8		5	4	3	74
228	70	1	3	4	13	3		78
229	55			2	12	1	15	73
230	24		1	3	3	2		29
231	73		1		13	4	22	99
232	78	1	1		2	3	18	100
233	66	1	1	4	16	1		72
234	68	1	1	1	7	1	14	85
235	66	1	7	4	14	6	30	107
236	70			6	16	3		79
237	73			4	12	6		83
238	48		1	2	11		20	70
239	81			1	13	8	32	122
240	76	1	2	1	13	2		80
241	78		1	3	10		37	118
242	77		1	3	23	3	33	116
243	60	1	1	6	21	2	22	91
244	70		3	7	46	1	21	99
245	82		1	4	17	5	44	135
246	73	1		3	19	1	29	107
247	53		4	6	19	2	4	65
248	69		1	8	16	8	47	132
249	80		3	2	14	7	29	118
250	78		10	7	32	3	19	107
251	54	1	5	6	38	3	33	97
252	55		5	8	18	1	20	84
253	45	2	5	8	29	4	10	69
254	73	1	3	3	32	1	34	112
255	67	6	22	6	10		19	98
256	77		3	7	29	1	9	94
257	58		5	12	20	1	33	104
258	71		4	8	22		24	103
259	42	1	3	4	13		3	50
260	83			4	4	1	36	124

Volume	Opinion of the Court	Con-curring	Con-curring without Opinion	Dissent-ing	Dissent-ing without Opinion	Other	Per Curiam	Total Opinions
261	70			3	4	1	10	84
262	70	1	1	8	10		13	92
263	79	1	4	2	14		39	121
264	69	2	4	6	7		18	95
265	64			4	7	2	19	89
266	81			2	7	1	34	118
267	73		2	5	5			78
268	78			3	16		14	95
269	63		2	1	8	1	31	96
270	67		1	5	9		25	97
271	80		3	6	3		21	107
272	53	3	8	9	15	1		66
273	66		1	6	17		83	155
274	80	5	7	9	13		27	121
275	61		.	1	2	2	56	120
276	64	1	1	13	18	2	44	124
277	51	1	1	18	16		16	86
278	59	1	8	7	13		85	152
279	72	1	4	7	18		30	110
280	54	2	6	9	13		42	107
281	81		5	5	7		26	112
282	79	2	7	5	20		40	126
283	87		2	8	15		38	133
284	63			6	13		49	118
285	42		2	7	15		14	63
286	45	1		3	11		20	69
287	59	1		4			34	98
288	49		3	7	19		9	65
289	60		1	6	18		15	81
290	50		1	6	19		36	92
291	54	2	15	8	19		22	86
292	53	2	10	4	10		27	86
293	54	2	3	3	7		34	93
294	54	2	4	2	24		12	70
295	50	3	2	6	17		17	76
296	53		10	7	27		36	96
297	53	1	7	5	9		17	76
298	39	3	5	8	13		16	66
299	52		2	1	8		45	98
300	55	1	5	6	19		13	75
301	42	1	4	10	28		12	65
302	57	3	5	11	29	1	48	120
303	56	3	3	9	15		24	92
304	40	5	10	6	17	1	22	74

Volume	Opinion of the Court	Concurring	Concurring without Opinion	Dissenting	Dissenting without Opinion	Other	Per Curiam	Total Opinions
305	48	4	5	9	19		36	97
306	54	3	3	10	21		9	76
307	37	4	15	16	32	5	9	71
308	48	3	8	3	8		41	95
309	55	2	13	9	21	1	36	103
310	33		3	8	27		10	51
311	55	3	6	9	28	1	28	96
312	66	2	5	10	28		28	106
313	46		9	8	3		5	59
314	41	5	6	10	29		27	83
315	59	9	13	16	32	2	18	104
316	51	3	9	18	42	1	20	93
317	50	3	2	15	14	2	36	106
318	49	7	13	19	32	1	7	83
319	45	9	10	26	51	4	13	97
320	43	7	8	22	33	4	29	105
321	45	9	9	24	39	3	15	96
322	43	5	13	25	45	7	16	96
323	52	10	13	15	44	1	33	111
324	55	9	25	31	57	2	19	116
325	39	8	12	26	53	5	13	91
326	48	11	20	20	27	3	22	104
327	47	18	9	29	33	1	9	104
328	44	11	2	25	9	5	11	96
329	45	13	6	17	38	4	25	104
330	37	9	4	26	41	2	12	86
331	41	7	3	20	38		15	83
332	38	7	14	31	54	6	26	108
333	40	10	8	24	50	3	13	90
334	36	13	15	23	52	1	16	89
335	29	7	16	28	59	4	30	98
336	43	10	20	33	48	3	38	127
337	37	9	23	24	57	4	16	90
338	44	12	26	27	43	6	54	143
339	46	7	22	39	38	2	33	127
340	52	6	7	25	61	5	41	129
341	35	16	22	31	49	6	33	121
342	48	10	17	32	53	2	61	153
343	35	7	4	37	11	3	4	86
344	48	11	5	38	3	10	20	127
345	49	12	4	39	5	2	17	119
346	35	8	5	33	5	3	38	117
347	44	8	3	36	3	1	21	110
348	48	6	9	21	10	1	70	146

Volume	Opinion of the Court	Con- curring	Con- curring without Opinion	Dissent- ing	Dissent- ing without Opinion	Other	Per Curiam	Total Opinions
349	28	5	1	25	9	1	25	84
350	43	9	4	19	12	1	107	179
351	39	8	1	30	1	6	31	114
352	44	7	4	26	7	5	73	155
353	35	4	5	21	12	4	40	104
354	22	6	3	21	5	2	28	79
355	32		4	22	12	10	106	170
356	38	9	3	38	14	6	41	132
357	35	8	8	27	19	1	25	96
358	31	7	5	18	10	5	81	142
359	33	9	13	19	14	3	51	115
360	34	15	5	26	3	7	19	101
361	27	15	4	18	4	7	78	145
362	27	3	2	32	5	8	30	100
363	28	5	8	24	2	4	14	75
364	23	1	1	19	6	7	62	112
365	36	12	5	26	4	4	39	117
366	30	4	3	19	4	8	28	89
367	21	11	3	27	4	2	22	83
368	26	5	12	18	10	6	76	131
369	31	14	8	29	8	2	46	122
370	16	2	3	10	1	2	10	40
371	24	9	2	16	3	6	90	145
372	32	11	5	23	13	2	74	142
373	38	5	5	21	4	3	35	102
374	16	12	8	9	12	1	51	89
375	20	7	2	20	4	4	107	158
376	39	4	6	17	7	3	43	106
377	35	3	4	25	6	6	31	100
378	17	12		20		4	57	110
379	32	13	12	26	2	8	74	153
380	36	16	3	16	2	2	43	113
381	24	13	1	27	13	1	39	104
382	25	10		12		3	110	160
383	32	8	3	23		8	34	105
384	37	11	3	23		7	61	139
385	36	7		23	1	4	95	165
386	35	10	1	21		2	80	148
387	23	5	4	14		3	39	84
388	13	7	2	13	2	5	32	70
389	23	17	6	27	10	2	107	176
390	36	12	13	24	7	4	72	148
391	28	10		22		2	34	96
392	22	23	4	28	45	1	54	128

Volume	Opinion of the Court	Con-curring	Con-curring without Opinion	Dissent-ing	Dissent-ing without Opinion	Other	Per Curiam	Total Opinions
393	29	17	10	31	11	6	122	205
394	38	16	15	39	15	6	61	160
395	35	14	8	20	3	8	37	114
396	24	6	1	20	1	5	85	140
397	37	20		32	9	4	79	172
398	15	7	1	13	6	2	11	48
399	14	11		11		8	15	59
400	14	11	16	23	25	11	20	79
401	39	32	26	33	32	26	9	139
402	45	51	29	53	49	21	12	182
403	22	22	7	20	7	11	6	81
404	28	12	5	22	4	3	20	85
405	32	16	3	31	0	8	8	95
406	32	12	6	27	7	7	6	84
407	21	12	2	21		1	5	60
408	16	16	6	19		4	4	59
409	25	10	2	25	2	4	19	83
410	28	8	2	39	6	7	12	94
411	29	6	5	18	4	8	7	68
412	46	21	12	42	5	13	6	128
Totals	21,428	1,322	1,367	3,915	5,392	1,000	6,488	34,153
Averages	52.01	3.21	3.32	9.50	13.09	2.42	15.75	82.89

Table 9
Supreme Court Opinions: Count per Court Term

Court Term	Opinion of the Court	Con-curring	Con-curring without Opinion	Dissent-ing	Dissent-ing without Opinion	Other	Per Curiam	Total Opinions
Feb. 1790		1		1				2
Aug. 1792						5		5
Feb. 1793						5		5
Feb. 1794	1					8		9
Feb. 1795	1					5		6
Aug. 1795						4		4
Feb. 1796						2		2
Aug. 1796	3			1		1		5
Feb. 1797								
Aug. 1797	1	1				5		7
Feb. 1798	1					6		7
Aug. 1798								
Feb. 1799	2					3		5
Aug. 1799	2							2
Feb. 1800						5		5
Aug. 1800						4		4
Aug. 1801	1					1		2
Dec. 1801	3							3
Feb. 1803	11							11
Feb. 1804	15	1				1		17
Feb. 1805	10	1	1	1		3		15
Feb. 1806	17					17		34
Feb. 1807	10					2		12
Feb. 1808	21	2	7	4	1	6		33
Feb. 1809	37		2	4				41
Feb. 1810	27	1		1	1	3		32
Feb. 1812	31	1		1		3		36
Feb. 1813	39	3	1	3	1	4		49
Feb. 1814	46			5	1	3		54
Feb. 1815	39	2		2	1	2		45
Feb. 1816	40	1		3	2	1		45
Feb. 1817	40			1		1		42
Feb. 1818	36			2	2	2		40
Feb. 1819	32		2		1	3		35
Feb. 1820	26			3		1		30
Feb. 1821	33			1		1		35
Feb. 1822	29			1	2			30
Feb. 1823	27			2		3		32
Feb. 1824	39	1		4				44
Feb. 1825	27	1						28
Feb. 1826	29						1	30

Court Term	Opinion of the Court	Con-curring	Con-curring without Opinion	Dissent-ing	Dissent-ing without Opinion	Other	Per Curiam	Total Opinions
Jan. 1827	45	1		1	3			47
Jan. 1828	53	1		3				57
Jan. 1829	42	1		2				45
Jan. 1830	51	1		7	3	1		60
Jan. 1831	40	2		7	6	1		50
Jan. 1832	50	1		5	2	2		58
Jan. 1833	38			2				40
Jan. 1834	59			2				61
Jan. 1835	38	1		3		3		45
Jan. 1836	48			1				49
Jan. 1837	19	2		5	2	6		32
Jan. 1838	40	3		5	20	3		51
Jan. 1839	51	2		5	6			58
Jan. 1840	41	4	1	3	3	11		59
Jan. 1841	31				6	3		34
Jan. 1842	42	6		2	1	2		52
Jan. 1843	26			4				30
Jan. 1844	39	1	1	3		1		44
Jan. 1845	49			13	1	2		64
Jan. 1846	46	2		2	5	6		56
Jan. 1847	35	4	1	5	3	9		53
Jan. 1848	35	1	3	3	14	5		44
Jan. 1849	40		1	8	8	7		55
Jan. 1850	82			10	22	1		93
Dec. 1850	74			15	25	3		92
Dec. 1851	94	3	1	10	12	1		108
Dec. 1852	53		1	12	17	8		73
Dec. 1853	80	7	3	16	16	4		107
Dec. 1854	71	5	5	15	16	1		92
Dec. 1855	90	7	3	14	24	1		112
Dec. 1856	63	7	0	8	9			78
Dec. 1857	70	2	2	9	12			81
Dec. 1858	69	1		6	25			76
Dec. 1859	115		1	4	7	2		121
Dec. 1860	64			3	1			67
Dec. 1861	74	2	4	2	1			78
Dec. 1862	41			7	13		1	49
Dec. 1863	75	4	4	4	12			83
Dec. 1864	55	1	1	5	8	1	3	65
Dec. 1865	70	1	2	7	16	3	1	82
Dec. 1866	128	2	3	6	10	2		138
Dec. 1867	96			7	31	2		105
Dec. 1868	114	3	1	13	12			130
Dec. 1869	169		2	14	24	2	2	187

Court Term	Opinion of the Court	Con-curring	Con-curring without Opinion	Dissent-ing	Dissent-ing without Opinion	Other	Per Curiam	Total Opinions
Dec. 1870	151	3	2	15	15	8		177
Dec. 1871	148		3	21	34	7		176
Dec. 1872	157	7	3	23	46	12		199
Oct. 1873	193	9	4	21	60	7		230
Oct. 1874	186	2	3	17	35	3	1	209
Oct. 1875	200	1		23	56			224
Oct. 1876	219	3		16	54	1		239
Oct. 1877	248	4	2	21	54	3		276
Oct. 1878	198	5	1	23	35	4		230
Oct. 1879	205	1	2	18	32	2		226
Oct. 1880	221	2		9	21	2		234
Oct. 1881	232		1	11	15	2		245
Oct. 1882	267	3	3	17	19	5		292
Oct. 1883	277	4	3	14	11	4		299
Oct. 1884	271	2	1	11	24			284
Oct. 1885	280	4	1	18	30			302
Oct. 1886	298	1		12	15			311
Oct. 1887	287	4		13	15	9		313
Oct. 1888	242	1		6	10		10	259
Oct. 1889	282	3	1	16	40	1	6	308
Oct. 1890	297	2	5	14	42	3	9	325
Oct. 1891	252	3	6	20	41	16	1	292
Oct. 1892	231		5	22	20	24		277
Oct. 1893	280	1	14	23	56	13	1	318
Oct. 1894	225	1	5	23	37	31		280
Oct. 1895	257	1	6	25	43	10		293
Oct. 1896	228		15	12	67	7	36	283
Oct. 1897	184	3	9	16	65	3	25	231
Oct. 1898	173	1	4	14	75	7	22	217
Oct. 1899	214	4	13	15	76	4	10	247
Oct. 1900	197	5	19	22	94	3	22	249
Oct. 1901	179	3	13	12	58	3	32	229
Oct. 1902	213	4	18	18	82	10	31	276
Oct. 1903	208	3	15	20	87	4	23	258
Oct. 1904	194	7	16	17	77	2	34	254
Oct. 1905	168	5	14	22	76	4	43	242
Oct. 1906	205	4	15	12	61	2	49	272
Oct. 1907	176	5	7	15	38	1	30	227
Oct. 1908	181	3	2	14	39	1	50	249
Oct. 1909	175	7	9	9	46		55	246
Oct. 1910	168	1	4	13	21		23	205
Oct. 1911	230		3	9	18	8	45	292
Oct. 1912	271	1	12	10	38	18	38	338
Oct. 1913	285	3	4	5	38	9	54	356

Court Term	Opinion of the Court	Concurring	Concurring without Opinion	Dissenting	Dissenting without Opinion	Other	Per Curiam	Total Opinions
Oct. 1914	257	1	8	16	53	15	50	339
Oct. 1915	235	1	3	5	36	10	69	320
Oct. 1916	207	1	5	16	90	6	76	306
Oct. 1917	208	1	5	13	55	8	77	307
Oct. 1918	213		14	14	51	18	83	328
Oct. 1919	168	3	15	23	96	8	75	277
Oct. 1920	217	7	28	16	71	2	62	304
Oct. 1921	171	1	12	24	55	1	60	257
Oct. 1922	223	1	1	15	18	2	59	300
Oct. 1923	212	3	8	12	28	2	76	305
Oct. 1924	232		2	10	28	1	48	291
Oct. 1925	210		6	12	20	1	77	300
Oct. 1926	199	8	16	24	45	1	110	342
Oct. 1927	176	2	2	32	36	4	116	330
Oct. 1928	131	2	12	14	31		115	262
Oct. 1929	135	2	11	14	20		68	219
Oct. 1930	166	2	9	13	35		78	259
Oct. 1931	150	1	2	16	39		83	250
Oct. 1932	168	1	14	17	50		58	244
Oct. 1933	157	4	26	18	48		85	264
Oct. 1934	158	7	9	11	48		63	239
Oct. 1935	145	4	22	20	49		69	238
Oct. 1936	149	2	11	17	55		70	238
Oct. 1937	153	11	18	26	61	2	94	286
Oct. 1938	139	11	23	35	71	5	54	244
Oct. 1939	136	5	24	20	56	1	87	249
Oct. 1940	167	5	20	27	59	1	61	261
Oct. 1941	151	17	28	44	103	3	65	280
Special July term & Oct. term 1942	148	24	25	63	100	8	58	301
Oct. 1943	127	16	30	68	114	13	58	282
Oct. 1944	154	31	55	79	163	8	67	339
Oct. 1945	131	36	26	67	59	9	40	283
Oct. 1946	140	31	17	80	141	7	52	310
Oct. 1947	105	31	36	70	149	10	55	271
Oct. 1948	106	32	76	86	160	14	86	324
Oct. 1949	85	10	25	56	68	4	85	240
Oct. 1950	87	22	29	56	110	11	74	250
Oct. 1951	83	17	21	69	64	5	65	239
Oct. 1952	109	24	10	90	9	13	38	274
June 1953	2	2		3	3		2	9
Oct. 1953	65	13	7	53	4	3	56	190

Court Term	Opinion of the Court	Con-curring	Con-curring without Opinion	Dissent-ing	Dissent-ing without Opinion	Other	Per Curiam	Total Opinions
Oct. 1954	76	11	10	46	19	2	95	230
Oct. 1955	82	17	5	49	13	7	138	293
Oct. 1956	101	17	12	68	24	11	141	338
Oct. 1957	105	17	15	87	45	17	172	398
June 1958	2							2
Oct. 1958	96	31	13	63	27	15	151	356
Oct. 1959	82	25	16	74	11	19	122	322
Oct. 1960	110	28	12	91	18	21	151	401
Oct. 1961	73	21	23	57	19	10	132	293
Oct. 1962	110	37	20	69	32	12	250	478
Oct. 1963	111	26	12	82	17	17	238	474
Oct. 1964	92	42	16	69	17	11	156	370
Oct. 1965	94	29	6	58		18	205	404
Oct. 1966	107	29	7	71	3	14	246	467
Oct. 1967	109	62	23	101	62	9	267	548
Oct. 1968	102	47	33	90	29	20	220	479
Oct. 1969	90	44	2	76	16	19	190	419
Oct. 1970	120	114	78	127	114	70	47	478
Oct. 1971	129	68	20	120	12	24	42	383
Oct. 1972	128	45	17	128	5	31	44	376
Averages	114.59	7.07	7.16	20.94	28.23	5.35	34.70	182.63

Table 10
Opinions by Justice

Justice	Years Served	Opinion of the Court	Con-curring	Con-curring without Opinion	Dissent-ing	Dissent-ing without Opinion	Other	T
1 *John Jay (1789-1795)	5	1					2	
2 John Rutledge (1789-1791)	1						1	
3 William Cushing (1789-1810)	20	4	3				14	
4 James Wilson (1789-1798)	8	2			1		4	
5 John Blair (1789-1796)	6						3	
6 James Iredell (1790-1798)	9		1		1		8	
7 Thomas Johnson (1791-1793)	1						1	
8 William Paterson (1793-1806)	13	1			1		15	
2 *John Rutledge (1795)	0							
9 Samuel Chase (1796-1811)	15	1	1	2	1		8	
10 *Oliver Ellsworth (1796-1799)	4	9					2	
11 Bushrod Washington (1798-1829)	31	69		1	1	2	14	
12 Alfred Moore (1799-1804)	4						1	
13 *John Marshall (1801—1835)	34	508			6		25	
14 William Johnson (1804-1834)	30	109	11	3	30	3	12	
15 Brockholst Livingston (1806-1823)	16	38	3	2	7	3		
16 Thomas Todd (1807-1826)	18	12	1				1	
17 Gabriel Duvall (1812-1835)	22	16	1		1	2	1	
18 Joseph Story (1811-1845)	33	270	1	2	13	4	4	
19 Smith Thompson (1823-1843)	20	87	2		10	4	2	

*Chief Justice.

tice	Years Served	Opinion of the Court	Con- curring	Con- curring without Opinion	Dissent- ing	Dissent- ing without Opinion	Other	Total
Robert Trimble (1826-1828)	2	16				1		16
John McLean (1829-1861)	32	245	5	3	33	32	16	299
Henry Baldwin (1830-1844)	14	39	7		11	30	9	66
James M. Wayne (1835-1867)	32	144	6	5	5	35	4	159
*Roger B. Taney (1836-1864)	28	260	7	3	14	17	8	289
Philip P. Barbour (1836-1841)	5	17	1		2			20
John Catron (1837-1865)	28	157	12	2	26	23	15	210
John McKinley (1837-1852)	15	19	1		3	10	1	24
Peter V. Daniel (1841-1860)	19	87	9		47	43	4	147
Samuel Nelson (1845-1872)	27	290	6	6	22	27	3	321
Levi Woodbury (1845-1851)	5	42	2		9	5	4	57
Robert C. Grier (1846-1870)	23	194	2	7	12	55	4	212
Benjamin R. Curtis (1851-1857)	6	48	3	1	8	3	4	63
John A. Campbell (1853-1861)	8	92	5	4	18	11	1	116
Nathan Clifford (1858-1881)	23	395	8	1	60	73	7	470
Noah H. Swayne (1862-1881)	18	335	3	6	9	66	3	350
Samuel F. Miller (1862-1890)	28	608	6	4	67	90	10	691
David Davis (1862-1877)	14	192	2	5	10	61		204
Stephen J. Field (1863-1897)	34	544	19	8	84	147	12	659
*Salmon P. Chase (1864-1873)	8	134	2	1	8	30	28	172
William Strong (1870-1880)	10	238	2	3	19	50	4	263
Joseph P. Bradley (1870-1892)	21	389	17	2	60	68	6	472

Justice	Years Served	Opinion of the Court	Con-curring	Con-curring without Opinion	Dissent-ing	Dissent-ing without Opinion	Other	T
42 Ward Hunt (1873-1882)	9	141	4		5	17		
43 *Morrison R. Waite (1874-1888)	14	872	2	5	23	28	11	
44 John M. Harlan (1877-1911)	34	737	17	32	119	257	6	
45 William B. Woods (1881-1887)	6	164		2	1	7	1	
46 Stanley Matthews (1881-1889)	7	233	2		5	12		
47 Horace Gray (1882-1902)	20	450	4	14	11	64		
48 Samuel Blatchford (1882-1893)	11	427		1	2	6		
49 Lucius Q. C. Lamar (1888-1893)	5	101	1		2	9		
50 *Melville W. Fuller (1888-1893)	21	750	1	8	32	101	109	
51 David J. Brewer (1890-1910)	20	533	8	36	57	169	9	
52 Henry B. Brown (1891-1906)	15	453	10	21	44	89	4	
53 George Shiras, Jr. (1892-1903)	10	251		10	15	45	1	
54 Howell E. Jackson (1893-1895)	2	46			4	9	1	
55 Edward D. White (1894-1910)	16	375	9	40	44	126	1	
56 Rufus W. Peckham (1896-1909)	13	312	2	9	8	133	6	
57 Joseph McKenna (1898-1925)	26	646	4	38	30	197	6	
58 Oliver W. Holmes (1902-1932)	29	873	14	35	72	100	16	
59 William R. Day (1903-1922)	19	430	2	6	22	68	14	
60 William H. Moody (1906-1910)	3	62		2	4	11		
61 Horace H. Lurton (1910-1914)	4	96		1	2	15	2	
62 Charles E. Hughes (1910-1916)	5	144		5	6	26	4	
55 *Edward D. White (1910-1921)	10	305	2	8	5	44	41	

*Chief Justice.

stice	Years Served	Opinion of the Court	Con-curring	Con-curring without Opinion	Dissent-ing	Dissent-ing without Opinion	Other	Total
Willis Van Devanter (1911-1937)	26	360	1	9	4	105	3	368
Joseph R. Lamar (1911-1916)	5	112		2	2	18	2	116
Mahlon Pitney (1912-1922)	10	249	5	21	19	84	2	275
James C. McReynolds (1914-1941)	26	488	7	47	65	240	20	580
Louis D. Brandeis (1915-1939)	22	455	10	47	65	150	2	532
John H. Clarke (1916-1922)	5	128	2	13	22	78	1	153
*William H. Taft (1921-1930)	8	255	1		2	17	1	259
George Sutherland (1922-1938)	15	288	2	7	23	72	2	315
Pierce Butler (1922-1939)	16	325	6	12	35	91	1	367
Edward T. Sanford (1923-1930)	7	129	1	7	3	18	2	135
Harlan F. Stone (1925-1941)	15	360	27	33	58	68	2	447
*Charles E. Hughes (1930-1941)	11	251	2	9	11	42		264
Owen J. Roberts (1930-1945)	15	296	2	36	67	152	7	372
Benjamin N. Cardozo (1932-1938)	6	129	2	23	23	38		154
Hugo L. Black (1937-1971)	34	481	88	152	310	307	44	923
Stanley F. Reed (1938-1957)	19	228	21	34	79	125	9	337
Felix Frankfurter (1939-1962)	23	247	132	69	251	111	67	697
William O. Douglas (1939-1975)	36	524	154	96	486	309	68	1,232
Frank Murphy (1940-1949)	9	132	18	31	66	120	2	218
James F. Byrnes (1941-1942)	1	16		1		11		16
*Harlan F. Stone (1941-1946)	5	96	10	12	35	57	4	145
Robert H. Jackson (1941-1954)	13	150	47	45	107	123	12	316

Justice	Years Served	Opinion of the Court	Con- curring	Con- curring without Opinion	Dissent- ing	Dissent- ing without Opinion	Other	Tota
83 Wiley B. Rutledge (1943-1949)	6	65	34	43	59	90	6	1
84 Harold H. Burton (1945-1958)	13	96	15	39	50	97	5	1
85 *Fred M. Vinson (1946-1953)	7	76		9	12	55	3	
86 Tom C. Clark (1949-1967)	18	214	24	13	98	39	18	3
87 Sherman Minton (1949-1956)	7	66	7	9	35	19	1	1
88 *Earl Warren (1953-1969)	16	165	11	10	47	13	4	2
89 John M. Harlan (1955-1971)	16	166	143	67	242	58	75	6
90 William J. Brennan, Jr. (1956-)		210	61	13	101	21	30	4
91 Charles E. Whittaker (1957-1962)	5	42	7	6	33	11	9	
92 Potter Stewart (1958-)		188	72	30	102	19	22	3
93 Byron R. White (1962-)		141	58	17	87	35	26	3
94 Arthur J. Goldberg (1962-1965)	3	36	18	5	25	2	8	
95 Abe Fortas (1965-1969)	4	40	19	2	27	2	6	
96 Thurgood Marshall (1967-)		69	16	8	54	26	12	1
97 *Warren E. Burger (1969-)		53	29	21	35	19	14	1
98 Harry A. Blackmun (1970-)		38	24	19	30	14	11	1
99 Lewis F. Powell, Jr. (1971-)		26	13	3	11		2	
100 †William H. Rehnquist (1971-)		25	2	3	22	4	4	
TOTALS	1,458††	21,428	1,322	1,367	3,915	5,392	1,000	27,6

*Chief Justice.
†Not included in count.
††Includes years of justices now on court.

Table 11
Average Number of Opinions per Justice per Term

	Justice	Opinion	Con-curring	Con-curring without Opinion	Dissent-ing	Dissent-ing without Opinion	Other	Total
1	*John Jay	.20	—	—	—	—	.40	.60
2	John Rutledge	—	—	—	—	—	1.00	1.00
3	William Cushing	.20	.15	—	—	—	.70	1.05
4	James Wilson	.25	—	—	.13	—	.50	.88
5	John Blair	—	—	—	—	—	.50	.50
6	James Iredell	—	.11	—	.11	—	.89	1.11
7	Thomas Johnson	—	—	—	—	—	1.00	1.00
8	William Paterson	.08	—	—	.08	—	1.15	1.31
2	*John Rutledge	—	—	—	—	—	—	—
9	Samuel Chase	.07	.07	.13	.07	—	.53	.73
10	*Oliver Ellsworth	2.00	—	—	—	—	.50	2.50
11	Bushrod Washington	2.19	—	.03	.03	.06	.45	2.68
12	Alfred Moore	—	—	—	—	—	.25	.25
13	*John Marshall	14.91	—	—	.15	—	.76	15.82
14	William Johnson	3.60	.37	.10	1.00	.10	.40	5.37
15	Brockholst Livingston	2.31	.19	.13	.44	.19	—	2.94
16	Thomas Todd	.67	.06	.06	—	—	.06	.78
17	Gabriel Duvall	.68	.05	—	.05	.09	.05	.82
18	Joseph Story	8.15	.03	.06	.39	.12	.12	8.70
19	Smith Thompson	4.30	.10	—	.50	.20	.10	5.00
20	Robert Trimble	7.50	—	—	—	.50	—	7.50
21	John McLean	7.63	.16	.09	1.03	1.00	.50	9.31
22	Henry Baldwin	2.79	.50	—	.79	2.14	.64	4.71
23	James M. Wayne	4.50	.19	.16	.16	1.09	.13	4.97
24	*Roger B. Taney	9.29	.25	.11	.46	.61	.32	10.32
25	Philip P. Barbour	3.40	.20	—	.40	—	—	4.00
26	John Catron	5.61	.43	.07	.93	.82	.54	7.50
27	John McKinley	1.27	.07	—	.20	.67	.07	.85
28	Peter V. Daniel	4.58	.47	—	2.42	2.26	.21	7.68
29	Samuel Nelson	10.74	.22	.22	.78	1.00	.11	11.85
30	Levi Woodbury	8.40	.40	—	1.60	1.00	.80	11.20
31	Robert C. Grier	8.43	.09	.30	.48	2.39	.17	9.17
32	Benjamin R. Curtis	8.00	.50	.17	1.17	.50	.83	10.50
33	John A. Campbell	11.50	.63	.50	2.25	1.38	.13	14.50
34	Nathan Clifford	17.17	.35	.04	2.61	3.17	.30	20.43
35	Noah H. Swayne	18.61	.17	.33	.50	3.67	.17	19.44
36	Samuel F. Miller	21.71	.21	.14	2.39	3.21	.36	24.68
37	David Davis	13.71	.14	.36	.71	4.36	—	14.57
38	Stephen J. Field	16.00	.56	.24	2.47	4.32	.35	19.38
39	*Salmon P. Chase	16.75	.25	.13	1.00	3.75	3.50	21.50
40	William Strong	23.80	.20	.30	1.90	5.00	.40	26.30

*Chief Justice.

Justice	Opinion	Con-curring	Con-curring without Opinion	Dissent-ing	Dissent-ing without Opinion	Other	Total
41 Joseph P. Bradley	18.52	.81	.10	2.86	3.24	.29	22.4
42 Ward Hunt	15.67	.44	–	.56	1.89	–	16.6
43 *Morrison R. Waite	62.29	.14	.36	1.71	2.00	.79	64.9
44 John M. Harlan I	21.68	.50	.94	3.50	7.56	.18	25.8
45 William B. Woods	27.33	–	.33	.17	1.17	.17	27.6
46 Stanley Matthews	33.29	.29	–	.71	1.71	–	34.2
47 Horace Gray	22.50	.20	.70	.55	3.20	–	23.2
48 Samuel Blatchford	38.82	–	.09	.18	.55	–	39.0
49 Lucius Q. C. Lamar	20.20	.20	–	.40	1.80	–	20.8
50 *Melville W. Fuller	35.71	.05	.38	1.52	4.81	5.19	42.4
51 David J. Brewer	26.65	.40	1.80	2.80	8.45	.50	30.3
52 Henry B. Brown	30.20	.67	1.40	2.93	5.93	.27	34.0
53 George Shiras, Jr.	25.10	–	1.00	1.50	4.50	.10	26.7
54 Howell E. Jackson	23.00	–	–	2.00	4.50	.50	25.5
55 Edward D. White	23.44	.56	2.50	2.81	7.88	.06	26.8
56 Rufus W. Peckham	24.00	.15	.69	.62	10.23	.46	25.2
57 Joseph McKenna	24.85	.15	1.46	1.19	7.58	.23	26.4
58 Oliver W. Holmes	30.10	.48	1.21	2.48	3.45	.55	33.6
59 William R. Day	22.63	.11	.32	1.11	3.58	.79	24.6
60 William H. Moody	20.67	–	.67	1.33	3.67	–	22.0
61 Horace H. Lurton	24.00	–	.25	.50	3.75	.50	25.0
62 Charles E. Hughes	28.80	–	1.00	1.20	5.20	.80	30.8
55 *Edward D. White	30.50	.20	.80	.50	4.40	4.10	35.3
63 Willis Van Devanter	13.85	.04	.35	.15	4.04	.12	14.1
64 Joseph R. Lamar	22.40	–	.40	.40	3.60	.40	23.2
65 Mahlon Pitney	24.90	.50	2.10	1.80	8.40	.30	27.5
66 James C. McReynolds	18.77	.27	1.81	2.54	9.23	.77	22.3
67 Louis D. Brandeis	25.60	.40	2.60	4.40	15.60	.20	30.6
68 John H. Clarke	25.60	.40	2.60	4.40	15.60	.20	30.6
69 *William H. Taft	31.88	.13	–	.25	2.13	.13	32.3
70 George Sutherland	19.20	.13	.47	1.53	4.80	.13	21.0
71 Pierce Butler	20.31	.38	.75	2.19	5.69	.06	22.9
72 Edward T. Sanford	18.43	.14	1.00	.43	2.57	.29	19.2
73 Harlan F. Stone	24.00	1.80	2.20	3.87	4.53	.13	29.8
62 *Charles E. Hughes	22.82	.18	.82	1.00	3.82	–	24.0
74 Owen J. Roberts	19.73	.13	2.40	4.47	10.13	.47	24.8
75 Benjamin N. Cardozo	21.50	.33	3.83	3.83	6.33	–	25.6
76 Hugo L. Black	14.15	2.59	4.47	9.12	9.03	1.29	27.1
77 Stanley F. Reed	12.00	1.11	1.79	4.16	6.58	.47	17.7
78 Felix Frankfurter	10.74	5.74	3.00	10.91	4.83	2.91	30.3
79 William O. Douglas	15.41	4.53	2.82	14.29	9.09	2.00	36.2
80 Frank Murphy	14.67	2.00	3.44	7.33	13.33	.22	24.2
81 James F. Byrnes	16.00	–	1.00	–	11.00	–	16.0
73 *Harlan F. Stone	19.20	2.00	2.40	7.00	11.40	.80	29.0

Justice	Opinion	Con-curring	Con-curring without Opinion	Dissent-ing	Dissent-ing without Opinion	Other	Total
82 Robert H. Jackson	11.54	3.62	3.46	8.23	9.46	.92	24.31
83 Wiley B. Rutledge	10.83	5.67	7.17	9.83	15.00	1.00	27.33
84 Harold H. Burton	7.38	1.15	3.00	3.85	7.46	.38	12.77
85 *Fred M. Vinson	10.86	—	1.29	1.71	7.86	.43	13.00
86 Tom C. Clark	11.89	1.33	.72	5.44	2.17	1.00	19.67
87 Sherman Minton	9.43	1.00	1.29	5.00	2.71	.14	15.57
88 *Earl Warren	10.31	.69	.63	2.94	.81	1.25	14.10
89 John M. Harlan, II	10.38	8.94	4.19	15.13	3.63	4.69	39.13
90 William J. Brennan, Jr.	12.35	3.59	. .76	5.94	1.24	1.76	23.65
91 Charles E. Whittaker	8.40	1.40	1.20	6.60	2.20	1.80	18.20
92 Potter Stewart	12.53	4.80	2.00	6.80	1.27	1.47	25.60
93 Byron R. White	12.82	5.27	1.55	7.91	3.18	2.36	28.36
94 Arthur J. Goldberg	12.00	6.00	1.67	8.33	.67	1.00	27.33
95 Abe Fortas	10.00	4.75	.50	6.75	.50	1.50	23.00
96 Thurgood Marshall	11.50	2.67	1.33	9.00	4.33	2.00	25.17
97 *Warren Earl Burger	13.25	7.25	5.25	8.75	4.75	3.50	32.75
98 Harry A. Blackmun	12.67	8.00	6.33	10.00	4.67	3.67	34.33
99 Lewis F. Powell, Jr.	13.00	6.50	1.50	5.50	0	1.00	26.00
100 William H. Rehnquist	12.50	1.00	1.50	.11	2.00	2.00	26.50
Average	**15.16**	**1.09**	**1.05**	**2.83**	**3.83**	**.71**	**19.44**

*Chief Justice.

SELECTED BIBLIOGRAPHY

Introduction

This bibliography represents the continuing effort by the editors over the years to group together titles of interest to the Supreme Court buff. It is not the definitive bibliographical work in this area. Indeed, with the avalanche of titles on the Supreme Court appearing in recent years, it would be nearly impossible to give a complete listing.[14] However, it certainly provides a good starting point for the reader interested in the Supreme Court.

Some explanation of the subject grouping for this bibliography is in order. Most of the titles fall naturally under the broad heading "Supreme Court—Books." No further breakdown was attempted here as most titles could easily be included under several topical headings. "Supreme Court—Bibliography" is the appropriate place for efforts at listing all Supreme Court oriented books similar to but older than this one. "Supreme Court—Biography" may appear to be a misnomer in some instances. The works included under this heading are not all strictly biographical but all deal with the life, the work, or the writings of specific individuals.

---

14. For a thorough examination of the literature related to the Supreme Court published in the last twelve years, see Mersky and Parrish, "The Supreme Court in Current Literature." *Supreme Court Historical Society Yearbook 1977*, 101.

The titles under "Articles" represent a selective grouping of journal and law review pieces of interest to the Supreme Court scholar as well as the reader just getting started in this area. Finally, "Other Publications Dealing with Analysis of Supreme Court Decisions or Pending Cases" is a catch-all category for annual, semiannual, and irregularly published pieces which do not fit under "Supreme Court—Books" or "Supreme Court—Articles."

Apologies are extended by the authors in advance for any omissions. We, of course, welcome suggestions for future updating.

Supreme Court—Bibliography

Abraham, Henry J. *The Judicial Process: An Introductory Analysis of the Courts of the United States, England, and France.* 3d ed., rev. and enl., New York: Oxford University Press, 1975, 428–438.

Haines, C. G. *"Histories of the Supreme Court of the United States Written from the Federalist Point of View."* Reprinted from the *Southwestern Political and Social Science Quarterly,* v. 4, no. 1, June, 1923. Austin, Tex., 1923.

Mersky, R. M. *Louis Dembitz Brandeis, 1856–1941; a Bibliography.* Published for the Yale Law Library by the Yale Law School, 1958.

————, comp. *A Selected Bibliography on the History of the United States Supreme Court.* Austin, Tex., 1969.

Mitchell, Broadus. *A Bibliography of the Constitution of the United States.* New York: Oxford University Press, 1964.

Senior, M. R., comp. *The Supreme Court: Its Power of Judicial Review with Respect to Congressional Legislation: Selected References.* Washington: Division of Library Science, George Washington University, 1937.

Servies, James, comp. *A Bibliography of John Marshall.* Washington, 1956. Published by U.S. Commission for Celebration of 200th Birthday of John Marshall.

Tompkins, D. L. *Supreme Court of the United States: A Bibliography.* Berkeley, Calif.: University of California, Bureau of Public Administration, 1959.

U.S. Library of Congress. Division of Bibliography. *List of Works Relating to the Supreme Court of the United States.* Washington: U.S. Govt. Print. Off., 1909.

Supreme Court—Biography

Asch, S. H. *The Supreme Court and Its Great Justices.* New York: Arco, 1971.

Ball, Howard. *The Vision and the Dream of Justice Hugo L. Black.* University, Ala.: University of Alabama Press, 1975.

Bander, Edward, ed. *Justice Holmes, Ex Cathedra*. Charlottesville, Va.: Michie, 1966.

Beveridge, Albert J. *The Life of John Marshall*. Boston: Houghton Mifflin, 1919.

Biddle, Francis. *Mr. Justice Holmes*. New York: Scribner, 1942.

Black, Hugo. *My Father, A Remembrance*. New York: Random
House, 1975.

Bowen, C. D. *Yankee from Olympus: Justice Holmes and His
Family*. Boston: Little, Brown, 1945.

Brown, W. G. *The Life of Oliver Ellsworth*. New York: DaCapo
Press, 1970.

Campbell, T. W. *Four Score Forgotten Men: Sketches of the
Justices of the U.S. Supreme Court*. Little Rock, Ark.:
Pioneer Pub. Co., 1950.

Connor, Henry. *John Archibald Campbell, Associate Justice of
the United States Supreme Court 1853-1861*. Boston:
Houghton Mifflin, 1920.

Countryman, Vern. *The Judicial Record of Justice William O.
Douglas*. Cambridge, Mass.: Harvard University Press, 1974.

Cuneo, J. R. *John Marshall: Judicial Statesman*. New York:
McGraw-Hill, 1975.

Danelski, David J., ed. *The Autobiographical Notes of Charles
Evans Hughes*. Cambridge, Mass.: Harvard University
Press, 1973.

Douglas, William O. *Go East, Young Man*. New York: Random
House, 1974.

Dunham, Allison, ed. *Mr. Justice*. Chicago: University of Chicago Press, 1956.

Ewing, C. A. M. *The Judges of the Supreme Court, 1789-1937;
A Study of Their Qualifications*. Minneapolis: University of Minnesota Press, 1938.

Fairman, C. *Mr. Justice Miller and the Supreme Court, 1862-
1890*. New York: Russell & Russell, 1966.

Flanders, Henry. *The Lives and Times of the Chief Justices of
the Supreme Court of the United States*. Philadelphia:
T. & T. W. Johnson, 1881.

Flynn, J. J. *Famous Justices of the Supreme Court*. New York:
Dodd, Mead, 1968.

Frank, John P. *Mr. Justice Black, the Man and His Opinions*.
New York: Knopf, 1949.

————— . *The Warren Court*. New York: MacMillan, 1964.

Frankfurter, Felix, ed. *Mr. Justice Brandeis.* New York: DaCapo Press, 1972.

————. *Mr. Justice Holmes and the Supreme Court.* 2d ed. Cambridge, Mass.: Belknap Press of Harvard University Press, 1961.

Friedman, Leon, ed. *The Justices of the United States Supreme Court, 1789–1969: Their Lives and Major Opinions.* New York: Bowker, 1969.

Gehart, E. C. *Supreme Court Justice Jackson: Lawyer's Judge.* New York: Q Corp., 1961.

Glad, Betty. *Charles Evans Hughes and the Illusions of Innocence: A Study in American Diplomacy.* Urbana: University of Illinois Press, 1966.

Goldberg, Dorothy. *A Private View of a Public Life.* New York: Charterhouse, 1975.

Harper, F. V. *Justice Rutledge and the Bright Constellation.* New York: Bobbs-Merrill, 1965.

Howard, J. W. *Mr. Justice Murphy: A Political Biography.* Princeton, N.J.: Princeton University Press, 1968.

Howe, Mark De Wolfe. *Justice Oliver Wendell Holmes.* v. 1. *The Shaping Years, 1841–1870.* v. 2. *The Proving Years, 1870–1882.* Cambridge, Mass.: Belknap Press of Harvard University Press, 1957–1963.

————. *Touched with Fire, Civil War Letters and Diary of Oliver Wendell Holmes, Jr., 1861–1864.* New York: DaCapo Press, 1969.

Huston, Luther. *Pathway to Judgment: A Study of Earl Warren.* Philadelphia: Chilton Books, 1966.

Jones, W. M., ed. *Chief Justice John Marshall, a Reappraisal.* New York: DaCapo Press, 1971.

King, Willard. *Melville Weston Fuller, Chief Justice of the United States, 1888–1910.* Chicago: University of Chicago Press, 1967.

Konefsky, S. J. *John Marshall and Alexander Hamilton, Architects of the American Constitution.* New York: Macmillan, 1964.

Kurland, Philip. *Mr. Justice Frankfurter and the Constitution.* Chicago: University of Chicago Press, 1971.

————, ed. *Felix Frankfurter on the Supreme Court.* Cambridge, Mass.: Belknap Press of Harvard University Press, 1970.

Lash, Joseph P. *From the Diaries of Felix Frankfurter.* New York: Norton, 1975.

Latham, Frank. *The Great Dissenter: Supreme Court Justice John Marshall Harlan, 1833-1911.* New York: Cowles Book Co., 1970.

Lief, Alfred. *Brandeis, the Personal History of an American Ideal.* New York: Stackpole Sons, 1936.

McBride, Howard E., and Douglas, William O. *Impeach Justice Douglas: v. 1. Subversion.* Hicksville, New York: Exposition, 1971.

McClellan, James, and Story, Joseph. *Joseph Story and the American Constitution: A Study in Political Legal Thought.* Norman: University of Oklahoma, 1971.

McDevitt, M. *Joseph McKenna.* New York: DaCapo Press, 1974. (Originally published in 1946.)

Marshall, John. *Papers of John Marshall.* Norman: University of Oklahoma Press, 1969. 2 volumes.

Mason, A. T. *William Howard Taft, Chief Justice.* New York: Simon and Schuster, 1965.

————. *Brandeis, A Free Man's Life.* New York: Viking Press, 1956.

Mendelson, Wallace, ed. *Felix Frankfurter, A Tribute.* New York: William Morrow, 1964.

————; Frankfurter, Felix; and Black, Hugo. *Justices Black and Frankfurter: Conflict in the Court.* 2d ed. Chicago: University of Chicago Press, 1964.

Monaghan, Frank. *John Jay, Defender of Liberty.* New York: Bobbs-Merrill, 1935.

Morris, R. B. *John Jay, the Nation and the Court.* Boston: Boston University Press, 1968.

Norris, Harold. *Mr. Justice Murphy and the Bill of Rights.* Dobbs Ferry, N.Y.: Oceana Publications, 1965.

O'Brien, F. *Justice Reed and the First Amendment: The Religion Clauses.* Washington: Georgetown University Press, 1958.

Palmer, B. W. *Marshall and Taney: Statesmen of the Law.* New York: Russell & Russell, 1939.

Pearson, Drew. *The Nine Old Men.* Garden City, N.Y.: Doubleday, Doran & Co., 1937.

Pollard, Joseph P. *Mr. Justice Cardozo: A Liberal Mind in Action.* New York: Yorktown Press, 1935.

Proceedings of the Bar and Officers of the Supreme Court of the United States. *Proceedings before the Supreme Court of the United States . . . In memory of (Justices of the Supreme Court)*, Washington, D.C.

Schwartz, Mortimer, ed. *Joseph Story, a Collection of Writings by and about an Eminent American Jurist.* Dobbs Ferry, N.Y.: Oceana Publications, 1959.

Semmes, T. J. *Address on the Personal Characteristics of the Chief Justices, Delivered by Thomas J. Semmes, Esq., in New York, on Feburary 4th, 1890, at the Centennial Celebration of the Opening of the Supreme Court of the United States.* New Orleans: L. Graham & Son, 1890.

Shriver, Harry. *What Gusto: Stories and Anecdotes About Justice Oliver Wendell Holmes.* Potomac, Md.: Fox Hills Press, 1970.

Strickland, Stephen, ed. *Hugo Black and the Supreme Court, a Symposium.* Indianapolis: Bobbs-Merrill, 1967.

Swisher, Carl Brent. *Roger B. Taney.* New York: Macmillan, 1961.

———— . *Stephen J. Field: Craftsman of Law.* New York: Irvington, 1930.

Thomas, H. S. *Felix Frankfurter, Scholar on the Bench.* Baltimore: Johns Hopkins Press, 1960.

Umbreit, K. B. *Our Eleven Chief Justices: a History of the Supreme Court in Terms of Their Personalities.* Port Washington, N.Y.: Kennikat Press, 1969, c1938.

United States. Congress. Senate Committee on the Judiciary. *George Harrold Carswell Hearings.* 91st Congress. 2d Session. New York: DaCapo Press, 1973.

Urofsky, M. I. *A Mind of One Piece: Brandeis, and American Reform.* New York: Scribner, 1971.

Van Santvoord, George. *Sketches of the Lives, Times and Judicial Services of the Chief Justices of the Supreme Court of the United States: Jay, Rutledge, Ellsworth, Marshall, Taney, Chase, and Waite.* 2d ed. Albany, N.Y.: W. C. Little & Co., 1882.

Williams, Charlotte. *Hugo Black, a Study in Judicial Process.* Baltimore: Johns Hopkins Press, 1950.

Wolfman, Bernard. *Dissent Without Opinion: The Behavior of Justice William O. Douglas in Federal Tax Cases.* Philadelphia: University of Pennsylvania Press, 1975.

Supreme Court—Books

Abraham, H. J. *Freedom and the Court: Civil Rights and Liberties in the United States.* 2d ed. New York: Oxford University Press, 1972.

————. *The Judicial Process: An Introductory Analysis of the Courts of the United States, England, and France.* 3d ed., rev. and enl., New York: Oxford University Press, 1975.

————. *The Judiciary: the Supreme Court in the Governmental Process.* 3d ed. Boston: Allyn and Bacon, 1973.

————. *Justices and Presidents: A Political History of Appointments to the Supreme Court.* New York: Oxford University Press, 1974.

Acheson, P. C. *The Supreme Court, America's Judicial Heritage.* New York: Dodd, Mead, 1961.

Alfange, Dean. *The Supreme Court and the National Will.* Garden City, N.Y.: Doubleday, Doran & Co., 1937.

Alsop, Joseph. *The 168 days.* Garden City, N.Y.: Doubleday, Doran & Co., 1938.

American Bar Association. *Report of some members of the committee of the American Bar Association on the subject of delays incident to the determination of suits in the United States Supreme Court.* New Haven, Conn.: Tuttle, Morehouse & Taylor, Printers, 1882.

————. Special Committee on the Supreme Court Proposal. *Proposed Remaking of the Federal Judiciary: Analysis of Logan-Hatch-Ashurst Amendment Regarding the Federal Courts.* Chicago, 1937.

————. Standing Committee on the Federal Judiciary. *Report Recommending Action by the American Bar Association with Respect to Appointments to the Supreme Court of the United States.* Chicago, 1970.

Andrews, W. G., comp. *Coordinate Magistrates: Constitutional Law by Congress and President.* New York: Van Nostrand Reinhold, 1969.

Angell, Ernest. *Supreme Court Primer.* New York: Reynal & Hitchcock, 1937.

April, Nathan. *A Guide to Federal Appellate Procedure: Handbook for Counsel About to Engage in a Federal Appeal.* New York: Prentice-Hall, 1936.

Association of the Bar of the City of New York. Committee on
    Federal Legislation. *Report . . . on Senate bill 1392,
    House Bill 4417.* Approved at a special meeting of the
    Association at 8:30 P.M., February 24, 1937. New York,
    1937.
Auerbach, C. A. *The Legal Process.* San Francisco: Chandler
    Pub. Co., 1961.
Baer, Herbert R. *Admiralty Law of the Supreme Court.* Char-
    lottesville, Va.: Michie, 1969 with 1975 Cum. Supp.
Baker, L. *Back to Back, the Duel Between F.D.R. and the Supreme
    Court.* New York: Macmillan, 1967.
————. *John Marshall: A Life in Law.* New York: Macmillan,
    1974.
Balch, T. W. *A World Court in the Light of the United States
    Supreme Court.* Philadelphia: Allen, Lane and Scott,
    1918.
Ball, Howard. *The Warren Court's Conceptions of Democracy:
    An Evaluation of the Supreme Court's Apportionment
    Opinions.* Rutherford, N.J.: Fairleigh Dickinson Uni-
    versity Press, 1971.
Barbar, James. *The Honorable Eighty-Eight.* New York: Van-
    tage Press, 1957.
Barnes, W. R., ed. *The Supreme Court Issue and the Constitution:
    Comments Pro and Con by Distinguished Men.* New
    York: Barnes and Noble, 1937.
Barth, Alan. *The Heritage of Liberty.* St. Louis: McGraw-
    Hill, 1965.
————. *Prophets With Honor: Great Dissents and Great Dissen-
    ters.* New York: Knopf, 1974.
Bass, S. A. *United States Supreme Court Decisions During the
    Last Decade: Has the Court Exceeded Its Powers?* Chi-
    cago: American Bar Foundation, 1964.
Bates, E. S. *The Story of the Supreme Court.* Indianapolis:
    Bobbs-Merrill, 1936.
Baxter, M. G. *Daniel Webster and the Supreme Court.* Amherst:
    University of Massachusetts Press, 1966.
Beard, C. A. *The Supreme Court and the Constitution.* New
    York: Prentice-Hall 1962.
Becker, Theodore L. *The Impact of Supreme Court Decisions.*
    2d ed. New York: Oxford University Press, 1973.

Bedi, A. S. *Freedom of Expression and Security: a Comparative Study of the Function of the Supreme Courts of the United States of America and India*. Bombay: Asia Pub. House, 1966.

Beer, H. W. *Federal Trade Law and Practice Before the Federal Trade Commission, United States District Courts, United States Circuit Courts of Appeals, and United States Supreme Court in Federal Trade Commission Cases*. Chicago: Callaghan, 1942.

Bellot, H. H. L. *Texts Illustrating the Constitution of the Supreme Court of the United States and the Permanent Court of International Justice*. London: Sweet and Maxwell, 1921.

Benson, Paul R. *Supreme Court and the Commerce Clause, 1937–1970*. Port Washington, N.Y.: Dunellen, 1971.

Berger, Raoul. *Congress v. the Supreme Court*. Cambridge, Mass.: Harvard University Press, 1969.

Berle, A. A. *The Three Faces of Power*. New York: Harcourt, Brace & World, 1967.

Bickel, Alexander M. *The Caseload of the Supreme Court, and What, If Anything, To Do About It*. Washington: American Enterprise Institute for Public Policy Research, 1973.

————. *Politics and the Warren Court*. New York: Harper & Row, 1965.

————. *The Supreme Court and the Idea of Progress*. New York: Harper & Row, 1970.

Bickford, H. C. *Court Procedure in Federal Tax Cases*. New York: Prentice-Hall, 1928.

Biddle, Francis. *Justice Holmes, Natural Law and the Supreme Court*. New York: Macmillan, 1961.

Billikoph, D. M. *The Exercise of Judicial Power, 1789–1864*. New York: Vantage Press, 1973.

Black, C. L. *The People and the Court: Judicial Review in a Democracy*. New York: Macmillan, 1960.

Black, Hugo. *A Constitutional Faith*. New York: Knopf, 1968.

Bland, Randall W. *Private Pressure on Public Law: Legal Career of Justice Thurgood Marshall*. Port Washingon, New York: Kennikat, 1973.

Blaustein, A. P. *Desegregation and the Law: The Meaning and Effect of the School Segregation Cases*. 2d ed. New York: Vantage Books, 1962.

Bloch, C. J. *States' Rights: The Law of the Land.* Atlanta: Harrison, 1958.

Bolmeier, E. C. *Landmark Supreme Court Decisions on Public School Issues.* Charlottesville, Va.: Michie Co., 1973.

Boudin, L.B. *Government by Judiciary.* New York: W. Godwin, 1932.

Bozell, L. B. *The Warren Revolution: Reflections on the Consensus Society.* New Rochelle, N.Y.: Arlington House, 1966.

Brandeis, L. D. *The Unpublished Opinions of Mr. Justice Brandeis: the Supreme Court at Work,* ed. by Alexander M. Bickel. Cambridge, Mass.: Belknap Press of Harvard University Press, 1957.

The Brandeis Guide to the Modern World. Boston: Little, Brown, 1941.

Breckenridge, A. C. *Congress Against the Court.* Lincoln: University of Nebraska Press, 1970.

Brest, P. *Process of Constitutional Decisionmaking: Cases and Materials.* Boston: Little, Brown, 1975.

Brett, Peter. *Supreme Court and Free Speech: The Evils of Legalism.* [No pub.,] 1967.

Brewer, D. J. *Two periods in the History of the Supreme Court.* A paper read before the Arkansas and Texas Bar Associations July 11, 1906. [No pub.,] 1906.

Butler, C. H. *A Century at the Bar of the Supreme Court of the United States.* New York: G. P. Putnam, 1942.

CBS Reports (Television program), *Storm Over the Supreme Court.* A CBS News Broadcast as presented over the CBS television network, Wednesday, February 20, 1963, 7:30-8:30 p.m., E.S.T. Reporter Eric Sevareid Producer: Gene DePoris. Executive producer: Fred W. Friendly. New York, 1963.

Cahn, E. N., ed. *Supreme Court and Supreme Law.* Bloomington: Indiana University Press, 1954.

Cardozo, B. N. *The Nature of the Judicial Process.* New Haven: Yale University Press, 1960.

Carmichael, P. A. *The South and Segregation.* Washington: Public Affairs Press, 1965.

Carr, R. K. *Democracy and the Supreme Court.* Norman: University of Oklahoma Press, 1965.

————. *The Supreme Court and Judicial Review.* New York: Farrar and Rinehart, 1942.

Carson, H. L. *The History of the Supreme Court of the United States; With Biographies of all the Chief and Associate Justices.* Philadelphia: P. W. Ziegler Co., 1902–04.

————. *The Supreme Court of the United States: Its History and its Centennial Celebration, February 4th, 1890.* Philadelphia: J. Y. Huber Co., 1891.

Carter, John Denton. *The Warren Court and the Constitution: A Critical View of Judicial Activism.* Gretna, La.: Pelican Pub. Co., 1973.

Carter, Robert. *Equality.* New York: Random House, 1965.

Casper, J. D. *Lawyers Before the Warren Court: Civil Liberties and Civil Rights, 1957–66.* Urbana: University of Illinois Press, 1972.

Chaplin, H. W. *Principles of the Federal Law as Presented in Decisions of the Supreme Court, Citing Something Over 3,500 Cases; 2 Dallas-241 U.S. (Congressional legislation to February 1, 1917)* Washington: J. Byrne, 1917.

Chicago, University of, Law School. *The Supreme Court and the Constitution.* Chicago: University of Chicago Press, 1965.

Clark, C. E. *The Judicial Process: A Series of Cases Illustrating the Place of the United States Supreme Court in Our Legal System.* New Haven: Yale University Press, 1933.

Claude, Richard. *The Supreme Court and the Electoral Process.* Baltimore: Johns Hopkins Press, 1970.

Clayton, J. E. *The Making of Justice: The Supreme Court in Action.* New York: Dutton, 1964.

Cohen, S. *A Law Enforcement Guide to United States Supreme Court Decisions.* Springfield, Ill.: C. C. Thomas, 1972.

Congressional Quarterly, Inc. *The Supreme Court, Justice and the Law.* Washington, 1973.

Continuing Challenge: The Past and the Future of Brown v. Board of Education. Evanston, Ill. Integrated Education Association, 1975.

Cope, A. H., ed. *Franklin D. Roosevelt and the Supreme Court.* rev. ed. Lexington, Mass.: Heath, 1969.

Cord, R. L. *Protest, Dissent and the Supreme Court.* Cambridge, Mass.: Winthrop Publications, 1971.

Cortner, Richard C. *The Supreme Court and Civil Liberties Policy.* Palo Alto, Calif.: Mayfield, 1975.

Corwin, E. S. *A Constitution of Powers in a Secular State: Three*

Lectures on the William H. White Foundation at the University of Virginia, April 1950, and An Additional Chapter. Charlottesville, Va.: Michie, 1951.

————. *Court over Constitution: A Study of Judicial Review as an Instrument of Popular Government.* Princeton, N.J.: Princeton University Press, 1938.

————. *The Doctrine of Judicial Review: Its Legal and Historical Basis, and Other Essays.* Princeton, N.J.: Princeton University Press, 1914.

————. *John Marshall and the Constitution: A Chronicle of the Supreme Court.* New Haven: Yale University Press, 1919.

————. *Our Constitutional Revolution and How To Round It Out.* Philadelphia: Brandeis Lawyers Society, 1951.

————. *The Twilight of the Supreme Court: A History of Our Constitutional Theory.* New Haven: Yale University Press, 1934.

Cotton, Joseph. *The Constitutional Decisions of John Marshall.* New York: DaCapo Press, 1969.

Countryman, Edwin. *The Supreme Court of the United States With a Review of Certain Decisions Relating to its Appellate Power Under the Constitution.* Albany: Bender, 1913.

Cox, Archibald. *The Role of the Supreme Court in American Government.* New York: Oxford University Press, 1976.

————. *The Warren Court: Constitutional Decision as an Instrument of Reform.* Cambridge, Mass.: Harvard University Press, 1968.

Cox, Joseph. *United States Supreme Court: Its Organization and Judges to 1835.* Cincinnati, [No pub.], 1890.

The Criminal Law Revolution and Its Aftermath, 1960–1972, ed. by Criminal Law Reporter. Washington: Bureau of National Affairs, 1973.

Crosskey, W. W. *Politics and the Constitution in the History of the United States.* Chicago: University of Chicago Press, 1953.

Curtis, B. R. *Jurisdiction, Practice, and Peculiar Jurisprudence of the Courts of the United States.* 2d ed., rev. and enl. Boston: Little, Brown, 1896.

Curtis, C. P. *Law as Large as Life: A Natural Law for Today and the Supreme Court as its Prophet.* New York: Simon and Schuster, 1959.

————. *Lions Under the Throne. A Study of the Supreme Court of the United States, Addressed Particularly to Those Laymen Who Know More Constitutional Law Than They Think They Do, and To Those Lawyers Who Know Less.* Boston: Houghton Mifflin, 1947.

Curtis, G. T. *Commentaries on the Jurisdiction, Practice and Peculiar Jurisprudence of the Courts of the United States.* Philadelphia: T. & J. W. Johnson, 1854.

Cushman, Robert F., and Robert E. *Leading Constitutional Decisions.* 14th ed. New York: Appleton-Century-Crofts, 1971.

Cushman, R. E. *The Supreme Court and the Constitution.* Washington: Public Affairs Committee, 1937.

Daly, J. J. *The Use of History in the Decisions of the Supreme Court: 1900–1930.* Washington: Catholic University of America Press, 1954.

D'Amato, Anthony A., and O'Neil, Robert. *Judiciary and Vietnam.* New York: St. Martin's, 1972.

Danelski, D. J. *A Supreme Court Justice is Appointed.* New York: Random House, 1964.

————. *The Chief Justice and the Supreme Court.* Chicago: Dept. of Photoduplication, University of Chicago Lirary, 1961.

Davis, Abraham L., ed. *U.S. Supreme Court and the Uses of Social Science Data.* New York: MSS Information, 1975.

Davis, H. A. *The Judicial Veto.* Boston: Houghton Mifflin, 1914.

Davis, J. C. B., ed. *Centennial Celebration of the Organization of the Federal Judiciary, Held at New York, February 4, 1890,* [No pub.].

Davis, Warren. *Law of the Land.* New York: Carlton Press, 1962.

Devol, Kenneth S., ed. *Mass Media and the Supreme Court.* 2d ed. New York: Hastings House, 1976.

Dodd, E. M. *The Supreme Court and Organized Labor (and) the Supreme Court and Fair Labor Standards.* New York: Published for the Association of American Law Schools by the Practising Law Institute, 1946.

Douglas, W. O. *A Living Bill of Rights.* New York: Doubleday, 1961.

Drinan, Robert. *Religion, the Courts and Public Policy.* New York: McGraw-Hill, 1963.

Duane, Morris. *The New Deal in Court (With a Digest of Decisions)*. Philadelphia: G. T. Bisel, 1935.

Dunham, Allison. *Mr. Justice*. rev. and enl. Chicago: University of Chicago Press, 1964.

Dunne, G. T. *Justice Joseph Story and the Rise of the Supreme Court*. New York: Simon and Schuster, 1971.

————. *Monetary Decisions of the Supreme Court*. New Brunswick, N.J.: Rutgers University Press, 1960.

Eastland, J. O. *Is the Supreme Court Pro-Communist? Here are Facts as Disclosed by U.S. Senator James O. Eastland*. Richmond: Patrick Henry Group, 1962.

Elder, C. B. *A Handbook of the Interstate Commerce Act: The Parts of the Statute, Cases and Excerpts Principally from the Decisions of the Supreme Court of the United States, and Other Material, Analytically Arranged, With an Introductory History of the Act*. Evanston, Ill.: Northwestern University, 1931.

Elliott, Ward E. Y. *The Rise of Guardian Democracy: The Supreme Court's Role in Voting Rights Disputes, 1845–1969*. Cambridge, Mass.: Harvard University Press, 1974.

Elliott, William Y. *The Need For Constitutional Reform: A Program for National Security*. New York: Whittlesey House, McGraw-Hill, 1835.

Eriksson, E. M. *The Supreme Court and the New Deal: A Study of Recent Constitutional Interpretation*. Los Angeles: Lymanhouse, 1941.

Ernst, Morris L. *The Great Reversals: Tales of the Supreme Court*. New York: Weybright and Talley, 1973.

————. *The Law of the Land*. New York: Weybright and Talley, 1969.

Ervin, S. J. *Role of the Supreme Court: Policymaker or Adjudicator?* Washington: American Enterprise Institute for Public Policy Research, 1970.

Ettrude, D. J., comp. *Power of Congress to Nullify Supreme Court Decisions*. New York: H. W. Wilson, 1924.

Everson, D. H., ed. *The Supreme Court as Policymaker: Three Studies on the Impact of Judicial Decisions*. Carbondale, Ill.: Southern Illinois University Public Affairs Research Bureau, 1968.

Ewing, C. A. M. *The Judges of the Supreme Court: 1789–1937.* Minneapolis: University of Minnesota Press, 1938.

Fairman, C. *Mr. Justice Miller and the Supreme Court, 1862–1890.* New York: Russell & Russell, 1939.

Feinstein, Isidor. *The Court Disposes.* New York: Covici, Friede, 1937.

Fellman, D. *Supreme Court and Education.* New York: Teachers College, Columbia University, 1960.

Finkelstein, Maurice. *The Dilemma of the Supreme Court: Is the N.R.A. Constitutional?* New York: John Day, 1933.

Foley, J. P. *Natural Law, Natural Right and the Warren Court.* Rome: Pontificia Sutiorum Universitasa. S. Thoma Aq., 1965.

Forte, D. F. *The Supreme Court in American Politics: Judicial Activism v. Judicial Restraint.* Lexington, Mass.: Heath, 1972.

Foundation of the Federal Bar Association, Washington, D.C. *Equal Justice Under Law: the Supreme Court in American Life.* Washington, 1965.

Fraenkel, Osmond, ed. *The Course of Bigness, Miscellaneous Papers of Louis D. Brandeis.* Port Washington, N.Y.: Kennikat Press, 1965, c1934.

————. *The Rights We Have.* 2d ed. New York: Crowell, 1974.

————. *The Supreme Court and Civil Liberties: How the Court Has Protected the Bill of Rights.* 2d ed. Dobbs Ferry, N.Y.: Published for the American Civil Liberties Union by Oceana Publications, 1963.

Frank, John P. *Marble Palace: The Supreme Court in American Life.* New York: Knopf, 1958.

Frank, Theodore D. *A Footnote to a Dialogue: Some Reflections on Congressional Power and the Supreme Court's Appellate Jurisdiction.* Cambridge, Mass.: Harvard Law School, 1969.

Frankfurter, Felix. *The Business of the Supreme Court: A Study in the Federal Judicial System.* New York: Macmillan, 1928.

————. *The Commerce Clause Under Marshall, Taney and*

Waite. Chapel Hill: University of North Carolina Press, 1937.

———— . *Felix Frankfurter: A Register of His Papers in the Library of Congress*. Library of Congress, Manuscript Division, 1971.

———— . *Felix Frankfurter on the Supreme Court: Extrajudicial Essays on the Court and the Constitution*. Cambridge, Mass.: Belknap Press of Harvard University Press, 1970.

———— . *Law and Politics*. Gloucester, Mass.: Peter Smith, 1971.

———— . *Some Observations on Supreme Court Litigation and Legal Education*. Chicago: Law School, University of Chicago, 1954.

Freedman, Max. *Perspectives on the Court*. Evanston, Ill.: Northwestern University Press, 1967.

———— . *Roosevelt and Frankfurter, Their Correspondence 1928–1945*. Boston: Little, Brown, 1967.

Freund, P. A. *On Law and Justice*. Cambridge, Mass.: Belknap Press of Harvard University Press, 1968.

———— . *On Understanding the Supreme Court*. Boston: Little, Brown, 1949.

———— . *The Supreme Court in Contemporary Life*. Dallas: Southern Methodist University School of Law, 1965.

———— . *The Supreme Court of the United States*. New York: Meridian Books, 1961.

Fribourg, M. G. *The Supreme Court in American History*. Philadelphia: Macrae Smith Co., 1965.

Friedman, Leon. *Obscenity: The Complete Oral Arguments Before the Supreme Court in the Major Obscenity Areas*. New York: Chelsea House Publishers, 1970.

Fuller, H. B. *The Act to Regulate Commerce, Construed by the Supreme Court*. Washington: Byrne, 1915.

Funston, Richard. *Judicial Crisis: The Supreme Court in a Changing America*. New York: Wiley, 1974.

Galloway, John. *The Supreme Court and the Rights of the Accused*. New York: Facts on File, Inc., 1973.

Garland, A. H. *Experience in the Supreme Court of the United States, With Some Reflections and Suggestions as to the Tribunal*. Washington: Byrne, 1898.

Garraty, J. H., ed. *Quarrels that Have Shaped the Constitution*. New York: Harper & Row, 1964.

Garvey, G. *Constitutional Bricolage.* Princeton, N.J.: Princeton University Press, 1971.

Gaskin, S. *The Grass Case.* Summertown, Tenn.: Bool Pub. Co. Fdn., 1974.

Gavit, B. C. *The Commerce Clause of the United States Constitution.* Bloomington, Ind.: Principia Press, 1932.

Ginger, Ann F., ed. *Human Rights Casefinder, 1953–1969.* Berkeley, Calif.: Meiklejohn Civil Liberties Library, 1972.

————. *Law, the Supreme Court, and People's Rights.* Woodbury, New York: Educational Series, 1974.

Glick, Henry P. *Supreme Court in State Politics: An Investigation of the Judicial Role.* New York: Basic, 1971.

Goldberg, A. J. *Equal Justice.* New York: Farrar, Straus, & Giroux, 1972.

Goldman, Alvin L., *Supreme Court and Labor-Management Relations Law.* Lexington, Mass.: Lexington Books, 1976.

Goldman, Solomon, ed. *The Words of Justice Brandeis.* New York: Henry Schuman, 1953.

Goodman, E. *The Rights of the People.* New York: Farrar, Straus & Giroux, 1971.

Gorden, William I. *Nine Men Plus: Supreme Court Opinions on Free Speech and Free Press: An Academic Game-Simulation.* Dubuque, Iowa: W. C. Brown Co., 1971.

Gordon, R. M. *Nine Men Against America: The Supreme Court and Its Attack on American Liberties.* New York: Devin-Adair, 1958.

Graglia, Lino A. *Disaster by Decree: The Supreme Court Decisions on Race and the Schools.* Ithaca, N.Y.: Cornell University Press, 1976.

Great Cases of the Supreme Court. Boston: Houghton Mifflin, 1971.

Gressman, E. *Supreme Court Practice.* Washington: Bureau of National Affairs, 1963.

Grey, D. L. *The Supreme Court and the News Media.* Evanston, Ill.: Northwestern University Press, 1968.

Griffin, G. E. *The Great Prison Break: The Supreme Court Leads the Way.* Boston: Western Islands, 1968.

————. *A Memorandum on Supreme Court Decisions.* Belmont, Mass.: [No pub.], 1968.

Grossman, J. B., ed. *Constitutional Law and Judicial Policy Making.* New York: Wiley, 1972.

Gunther, Gerald, ed. *John Marshall's Defense of* McCullough *v.* Maryland. Stanford, Calif.: Stanford University Press, 1969.

Habenstreit, Barbara. *Changing America and the Supreme Court.* New York: J. Messner, 1970.

Hackten, W. A. *The Supreme Court on Freedom of the Press: Decisions and Dissents.* Ames, Iowa: Iowa State University Press, 1968.

Haines, Charles G. *The Role of the Supreme Court in American Government and Politics.* Berkeley: University of California Press, 1944–57.

Hall, T. B. *The Infringement of Patents for Inventions, Not Designs, With Sole Reference to the Opinions of the Supreme Court of the United States.* Cincinnati: R. Clarke & Co., 1893.

———. *Outline of the Infringement of Patents for Inventions, Not Designs, Based Solely on the Opinions of the Supreme Court of the United States.* New York: Banks, 1895.

Hamilton, J. A. *The Supreme Court, Guardian or Ruler?* New York: Scholastic Book Services, 1968.

Hand, Learned. *The Bill of Rights.* Cambridge, Mass.: Harvard University Press, 1960.

Harlan, J. M. *Manning the Dikes: Some Comments on the Statutory Certiorari Jurisdiction and Jurisdictional Statement Practice of the Supreme Court of the United States.* New York: Association of the Bar of the City of New York, 1958.

Harrell, Mary Ann, and Jones, Stuart E. *Equal Justice Under Law: The Supreme Court in American Life.* Washington, D.C.: The Foundation of the Federal Bar Association, 1975.

Harris, Richard. *Decision.* New York: Dutton, 1971.

Harris, Robert J. *The Judicial Power of the United States.* University, La.: Louisiana State University Press, 1940.

Henry, J. M. *Nine Above the Law: Our Supreme Court.* Pittsburgh, Pa.: R. T. Lewis, 1936.

Hirschfield, R. S. *The Constitution and the Court: The Development of the Basic Law Through Judicial Interpretation.* New York: Random House, 1963.

Hollingsworth, Harold M. *Essays on the New Deal.* Arlington, Tex.: University of Texas Press, 1969.

Honnold, A. B. *Supreme Court Law.* St. Paul: West, 1933.

Howe, M. D., ed. *Holmes-Pollack letters, the Correspondence of Mr. Justice Holmes and Sir Frederick Pollack, 1874–1932.* Cambridge, Mass.: Harvard University Press, 1941.

Hudgins, H. C. *The Warren Court and the Public Schools: An Analysis of Landmark Supreme Court Decisions.* Danville, Ill.: Interstate Printers and Publishers, 1970.

Hughes, C. E. *The Supreme Court of the United States: Its Foundation, Methods and Achievements: An Interpretation.* New York: Columbia University Press, 1928.

Hugo Black and the Supreme Court: A Symposium. Strickland, S. P., ed. Indianapolis: Bobbs-Merrill, 1967.

Hyneman, C. S. *The Supreme Court on Trial.* New York: Atherton, 1963.

Illinois. University. Edmund J. James Lectures on Government. Urbana: University of Illinois, 1938; 2d series, 1941; 3d series, 1944; 4th series, 1947; 5th series, 1951; 6th series, 1954.

Jackson, P. E. *Dissent in the Supreme Court: A Chronology.* Norman: University of Oklahoma Press, 1969.

Jackson, Percival E. *The Wisdom of the Supreme Court.* Westport, Conn.: Greenwood Press, 1962.

Jackson, R. H. *Advocacy before the United States Supreme Court.* Morrison Foundation Lecture, San Francisco, 1951.

———. *The Struggle for Judicial Supremacy: A Study of a Crisis in American Power Politics.* New York: Knopf, 1941.

———. *The Supreme Court in the American System of Govment.* Cambridge, Mass.: Harvard University Press, 1955.

Jacob, Herbert. *Justice in America.* Boston: Little, Brown, 1965.

Jacobs, C. *Justice Frankfurter and Civil Liberties.* New York: DaCapo Press, 1974.

James, L. F. *The Supreme Court in American Life.* New York: Scott, 1964.

Johnson, G. W. *The Supreme Court.* New York: Morrow, 1961.

Johnson, R. M. *The Dynamics of Compliance; Supreme Court Decision Making from a New Perspective.* Evanston, Ill.: Northwestern University Press, 1967.

Johnston, Henry. *The Correspondence and Public Papers of John Jay, 1763–1826.* New York: DaCapo Press 1971.

Justice and Equity in the International Sphere. London: Constable, 1936.

Kauper, P. G. *The Supreme Court: Hybrid Organ of State.* Dallas: School of Law, Southern Methodist University, 1967.

Kirkpatrick, Dick. *U.S. Supreme Court Upsets Tradition.* Washington: U.S. Govt. Print. Off., 1967.

Kluger, Richard. *Simple Justice: The History of Brown v. Board of Education and Black America's Struggle for Equality.* New York: Knopf, 1976.

Kohlmeier, L. M. *God Save This Honorable Court.* New York: Scribner, 1972.

Konefsky, Samuel. *The Legacy of Holmes and Brandeis.* New York: Macmillan, 1956.

————. *Chief Justice Stone and the Supreme Court.* Boston: Houghton Mifflin, 1971.

Kramer, P. R. *Jury Trials Before the Supreme Court of the United States.* Washington, [no pub.], 1961.

Krislov, S. *The Supreme Court and Political Freedom.* New York: Free Press, 1968.

————. *The Supreme Court in the Political Process.* New York: Macmillan, 1965.

Kurland, Philip B. *Church and State: The Supreme Court and the First Amendment.* Chicago: University of Chicago Press, 1976.

————. *Free Speech and Association: The Supreme Court and the First Amendment.* Chicago: University of Chicago Press, 1975.

————, and Casper, Gerhard. *Landmark Briefs and Arguments of the Supreme Court of the United States' Constitutional Law.* 80 vols. Arlington, Va.: University Publications of America, Inc., 1975.

————., ed. *Politics, the Constitution and the Warren Court.* Chicago: University of Chicago Press, 1970.

————. *The Supreme Court and the Constitution.* Chicago: University of Chicago Press, 1965.

————. *The Supreme Court and the Judicial Function.* Chicago: University of Chicago Press, 1976.

Kutler, S. I. *Judicial Power and Reconstruction Politics.* Chicago: University of Chicago Press, 1968.

————. *The Supreme Court and the Constitution.* Boston: Houghton Mifflin, 1969.

Kutler, Stanley I. *Privilege and Creative Destruction: The Charles River Bridge Case.* Philadelphia: J. B. Lippincott, 1971.

Landynski, J. W. *Search and Seizure and the Supreme Court.* Baltimore: Johns Hopkins Press, 1966.

Latham, F. B. *The Dred Scott Decision, March 6, 1857: Slavery and the Supreme Court's "Self-inflicted Wound."* New York: F. Watts, 1968.

————. *FDR and the Supreme Court Fight, 1937.* London: F. Watts, 1972.

Lawrence, David. *Nine Honest Men.* New York: Appleton-Century, 1936.

————. *Supreme Court or Political Puppets? Shall the Supreme Court be Free or Controlled by a Supreme Executive?* New York: Appleton-Century, 1937.

Lawson, J. F. *The General Welfare Clause: A Study of the Power of Congress Under the Constitution of the United States.* Washington: pub. by author, 1934.

Lee, C. B. T. *One Man, One Vote: WMCA and the Struggle for Equal Representation.* New York: Scribner, 1967.

Leonard, C. A. *A Search for a Judicial Philosophy: Mr. Justice Roberts and the Constitutional Revolution of 1937.* Port Washington, N.Y.: Kennikat Press, 1971.

Levy, B. H. *Our Constitution: Tool or Testament?* New York: Knopf, 1941.

Levy, Leonard. *Against the Law: The Nixon Court and Criminal Justice.* New York: Harper & Row, 1974.

Levy, L. W. *Judicial Review and the Supreme Court: Selected Essays.* New York: Harper & Row, 1967.

————. *Legacy of Suppression.* Cambridge, Mass.: Harvard University Press, 1960.

————. *The Supreme Court under Earl Warren.* New York: Quadrangle Books, 1972.

Lewinson, J. L. *Limiting Judicial Review.* Los Angeles: Parker, Stone & Baird, 1937.

Lewis, Anthony. *Clarence Earl Gideon and the Supreme Court.* New York: Random House, 1967.

————. *Gideon's Trumpet.* New York: Random House, 1964.

————. *The Supreme Court and How It Works: The Story of the Gideon Case.* New York: Random House, 1967.

————. *The Supreme Court: Process and Change.* Iowa City: College of Law, State University of Iowa, 1963.

Lippe, Emil. *Cases on the Jury System in the United States.* New York: Western, 1971.

Lippmann, Walter. *The Supreme Court, Independent or Controlled?* New York: Harper, 1937.

Liston, R. A. *Tides of Justice: The Supreme Court and the Constitution in Our Time.* New York: Dell, 1966.

Lusky, Louis. *By What Right? A Commentary on the Supreme Court's Power to Revise the Constitution.* Charlottesville, Va.: Michie, 1975.

Lyons, Thomas. *Supreme Court and Individual Rights in Contemporary Society.* Menlo Park, Calif.: Addison-Wesley, 1975.

Lytle, C. M. *The Warren Court and Its Critics.* Tucson: University of Arizona Press, 1968.

MacKenzie, John P. *The Appearance of Justice.* New York: Scribner, 1974.

MacLeish, Archibald. *Law and Politics, Occasional Papers of Felix Frankfurter 1913-38.* New York: Harcourt, Brace, 1939.

McCloskey, R. G. *The American Supreme Court.* Chicago: University of Chicago Press, 1960.

————. *The Modern Supreme Court.* Cambridge, Mass.: Harvard University Press, 1972.

McCune, Wesley. *The Nine Young Men.* New York: Harper, 1947.

McLaughlin, Kenneth F. *Color Me Justice: An Analysis and Collection of the Leading Supreme Court Cases of our Time.* Washington: Equity, 1969.

Macey, Robert L. *Our American Leviathan Unbound: The Judicial Perversion of American Freedom.* Brooklyn: Gaus, 1974.

Manzullo, Donald A. *Neither Sacred Nor Profane: The Supreme Court and the Church.* Hicksville, N.Y.: Exposition, 1973.

Marke, Julius. *The Holmes Reader.* 2d ed. New York: Oceana Publications, 1964.

Marnell, W. H. *The First Amendment.* New York: Doubleday, 1964.

Maslow, R. M. *"Coddling Criminals" Under the Warren Court.* Washington: Coiner Publications, 1969.

Mason, A. T. *Harlan Fiske Stone: Pillar of the Law.* New York: Viking Press, 1956.

————. *The Supreme Court from Taft to Warren.* rev. and enl. Baton Rouge: Louisiana State University Press, 1968.

————. *Supreme Court in a Free Society*. New York: Norton, 1960.

————. *The Supreme Court: Palladium of Freedom*. Ann Arbor: University of Michigan Press, 1962.

————. *The Supreme Court: Vehicle of Revealed Truth or Power Group, 1930–1937*. Boston: Boston University Press, 1953.

Mays, D. J. *A Question of Intent: The States, Their Schools and the 14th Amendment*. Statement before a Subcommittee of the United States Senate, May 14, 1959. Richmond: Virginia Commission on Constitutional Government, 1959.

Meador, D. J. *Mr. Justice Black and His Books*. Charlottesville: University Press of Virginia, 1974.

Meltsner, M. *Cruel and Unusual*. New York: Random House, 1973.

Mendelson, W. *Capitalism, Democracy and the Supreme Court*. New York: Appleton-Century-Crofts, 1960.

————. *The Constitution and the Supreme Court*. 2d ed. New York: Dodd, Mead, 1965.

————. *The Supreme Court: Law and Discretion*. Indianapolis: Bobbs-Merrill, 1967.

Mersky, Roy M., and Jacobstein, J. Myron, eds. *The Supreme Court of the United States: Hearings and Reports on Successful and Unsuccessful Nominations of Supreme Court Justices by the Senate Judiciary Committee, 1916–1975*. Buffalo, N.Y.: Hein, 1977.

Midwest Debate Bureau. *Supreme Court and Congress*. Normal, Ill., 1960.

Miller, A. S. *The Supreme Court and American Capitalism*. New York: Free Press, 1967.

————. *The Supreme Court and the Living Constitution*. Washington: Lerner Law Book Co., 1968.

Miller, C. A. *The Supreme Court and the Uses of History*. Cambridge, Mass.: Belknap Press of Harvard University Press, 1969.

Miller, Loren. *The Petitioners: The Story of the Supreme Court of the United States and the Negro*. New York: Pantheon Books, 1966.

Mr. Justice Jackson: Four Lectures in His Honor. New York: Columbia University Press, 1969.

Mitau, G. T. *Decade of Decision: The Supreme Court and the Constitutional Revolution, 1954–64.* New York: Scribner, 1967.

Monsman, Gerald. *A New Look at Constitutional Construction.* no pub., 1972.

Moore, Blaine F. *The Supreme Court and Unconstitutional Legislation.* New York: Columbia University, 1913.

Morgan, R. E. *The Supreme Court and Religion.* New York: Free Press, 1972.

Morris, R. B. *John Jay, the Nation and the Court.* Boston: Boston University Press, 1967.

Moschzisker, Robert von. *Judicial Review of Legislation: A Consideration of the Warrants for and Merits of Our American System of Judicially Reviewing Legislation to Ascertain Its Constitutional Validity.* Washington: National Association for Constitutional Government, 1923.

Muller, W. H. *Early History of the Federal Supreme Court.* Boston: Chipman Law Pub. Co., 1922.

Murphy, Walter F. *Congress and the Court.* Chicago: University of Chicago Press, 1962.

―――. *Elements of Judicial Strategy.* Chicago: University of Chicago Press, 1964.

―――. *Public Evaluations of Constitutional Courts: Alternative Explanations.* Beverly Hills, Calif.: Sage Publ., 1974, c1971.

Murray, W.H. *The Presidency, the Supreme Court and Seven Senators.* Boston: Meador Pub. Co., 1939.

Myers, Gustavus. *History of the Supreme Court of the United States.* New York: B. Franklin, 1968. (Originally published in 1925.)

National Consumers' League. *The Supreme Court and Minimum Wage Legislation: Comment by the Legal Profession on the District of Columbia Case.* New York: New Republic, 1925.

Nearing, Scott. *The Debs Decision.* New York: Rand School of Social Science, 1919.

Newmyer, R. K. *The Supreme Court Under Marshall and Taney.* New York: Crowell, 1968.

Nichols, E. R. *Congress or the Supreme Court: Which Shall Rule America? Containing the Principal Arguments both For and Against the Proposition: Resolved that Congress should have the power to over-ride, by a two-thirds majority vote, decisions of the Supreme Court declaring laws passed by Congress unconstitutional.* New York: Noble and Noble, 1935.

North, A. A. *The Supreme Court: Judicial Process and Judicial Politics.* New York: Appleton-Century-Crofts, 1966.

O'Brien, F. *Justice Reed and the First Amendment: The Religion Clauses.* Washington: Georgetown University Press, 1958.

O'Brien, J. Stephen, and Vacca, Richard S. *The Supreme Court and the Religion-Education Controversy: A Tightrope to Entanglement.* Durham, N.C.: Moore, 1974.

Oliver Wendell Holmes Devise History of the Supreme Court of the United States. General Editor: Paul Freund. New York: Macmillan, 1971—.

Volume I: Goebel, Julius, Jr. *Antecedents and Beginnings to 1801.* (1971).

Volume II: Haskins, George L. *Foundations of Power— John Marshall, 1801–1815.* (to be published).

Volume III: Gunther, Gerald. *The Struggle for Nationalism: The Marshall Court, 1815–1825.* (to be published).

Volume IV: Gunther, Gerald. *The Challenge of Jacksonian Democracy: the Marshall Court, 1826–1835.* (to be published).

Volume V: Swisher, Carl B. *The Taney Period, 1835–64.* (1974).

Volume VI: Fairman, Charles. *Reconstruction and Reunion, 1864–88.* Part I. (1971).

Volume VII: Fairman, Charles. *Reconstruction and Reunion, 1864–88.* Part II. (to be published).

Volume VIII: Neal, Phillip C., and Fiss, Owen M. *National Expansion and Economic Growth, 1888–1910.* (to be published).

Volume IX: Bickel, Alexander M. *The Judiciary and Responsible Government, 1910–21.* (to be published).

Volume X: Bickel, Alexander M. *The Judiciary and Responsible Government, 1921–30.* (to be published).

Volume XI: Freund, Paul A. *Depression, New Deal, and the Court in Crisis, 1930-41.* (to be published).

Palmer, B. W. *Marshall and Taney: Statesmen of the Law*. New York: Russell & Russell, 1939.

Palmer, W. J. *The Court v. the People*. Chicago: Hallberg, 1969.

Paul, A. M., comp. *Black Americans and the Supreme Court Since Emancipation: Betrayal or Protection?* New York: Holt, Rinehart and Winston, 1972.

Pearson, Drew. *The Nine Old Men*. Garden City, N.Y.: Doubleday, Doran, 1936.

———. *Nine Old Men at the Crossroads*. Garden City, N.Y.: Doubleday, Doran, 1937. (Sequel to *The Nine Old Men*.)

Petersen, Arnold. *The Supreme Court*. New York: New York Labor News, 1971.

Peterson, Helen S. *Supreme Court in America's Story*. Champaign, Ill.: Garrard, 1976.

Pfeffer, Leo. *The Liberties of an American: The Supreme Court Speaks*. 2d ed. Boston: Beacon Press, 1963.

———. *This Honorable Court*. Boston: Beacon Press, 1965.

Phillips, Philip. *The Statutory Jurisdiction and Practice of the Supreme Court of the United States, Together With Forms of Process and Rules Established for the Supreme Court, the Court of Claims, the Courts of Equity, the Courts of Admiralty, and the Courts in Bankruptcy*. rev. ed. Washington: W. H. & O. H. Morrison, 1878.

The Politics of Judicial Review, 1937–1957: A Symposium. Dallas: Southern Methodist University Press, 1957.

Pollack, E. H., ed. *The Brandeis Reader*. New York: Oceana Publications, 1956.

Pollak, L. H. *The Constitution and the Supreme Court: A Documentary History*. Cleveland: World Pub. Co., 1966.

Pollitt, B. H. *Justice and the Justices*. Daytona Beach, Fla.: College Pub. Co., 1954.

Post, C. G. *The Supreme Court and Political Questions*. Baltimore: Johns Hopkins Press, 1936.

Powell, T. R. *The Supreme Court and State Police Power, 1922–1930*. Charlottesville, Va.: Michie, 1932.

———. *The Supreme Court's Construction of the Federal Constitution in 1920–1921*. Ann Arbor: Michigan Law Review Association, 1922.

Practising Law Institute. *Schools and the Supreme Court*. New York: Practising Law Institute, 1972.

Pratt, John E. *Robbery, Rape, Burglary, Riot, Murder, Arson, Bombings: The Earl Warren Supreme Court.* Columbus, Ohio: Bourke, 1970.

Prettyman, B. *Death and the Supreme Court.* New York: Harcourt, Brace & World, 1961.

Pritchett, C. H. *Civil Liberties and the Vinson Court.* Chicago: University of Chicago Press, 1954.

———. *Congress versus the Supreme Court, 1957–1960.* Minneapolis: University of Minnesota Press, 1961.

———. *The Political Offender and the Warren Court.* Boston: Boston University Press, 1958.

———. *The Roosevelt Court: A Study in Judicial Politics and Values, 1937–1947.* New York: Macmillan, 1948.

———. *The Third Branch of Government.* New York: Harcourt, Brace & World, 1963.

Pusey, M. J. *The Supreme Court Crisis.* New York: Macmillan, 1937.

Ramaswamy, M. *The Creative Role of the Supreme Court of the United States.* Stanford, Calif.: Stanford University Press, 1956.

Ratcliffe, R. H. *Great Cases of the Supreme Court.* Boston, New York: Houghton Mifflin, 1975.

Reeder, R. P. *The First Homes of the Supreme Court of the United States.* Lancaster, Pa.: Lancaster Press, 1936.

Report of the Study Group on the Caseload of the Supreme Court. Washington: Federal Justice Center, 1972.

Rhodes, I. S., ed. *The Papers of John Marshall, a Descriptive Calendar.* Norman: University of Oklahoma Press, 1969.

Rice, C. E. *The Supreme Court and Public Prayer.* New York: Fordham University Press, 1964.

Roberts, O. J. *The Court and the Constitution.* Cambridge, Mass.: Harvard University Press, 1951.

Robertson, Reynolds. *Jurisdiction of the Supreme Court of the United States.* St. Paul: West, 1936.

———. *Practice and Procedure in the Supreme Court of the United States.* rev. ed. New York: Prentice-Hall, 1929.

Roche, J. P. *Courts and Rights.* New York: Random House, 1961.

———. *The Judiciary.* New York: Harcourt, 1964.

Rodell, Fred. *Fifty-Five Men.* New York: Telegraph, 1936.

———. *Nine Men: A Political History of the Supreme Court from 1790 to 1955.* New York: Random House, 1955.

Roettinger, R. L. *The Supreme Court and State Police Power: A Study in Federalism.* Washington: Public Affairs Press, 1957.

Rogge, O. J. *The First and the Fifth.* New York: Thomas Nelson, 1960.

Rohde, David W., and Spaeth, Harold J. *Supreme Court Decision Making.* San Francisco: W. H. Freeman, 1975.

Rosen, P. L. *The Supreme Court and Social Science.* Urbana: University of Illinois Press, 1972.

Rosenblum, Victor G., and Castberg, A. Didrick. *Cases on Constitutional Law: Political Roles of the Supreme Court.* Homewood, Ill.: Dorsey, 1973.

Rossiter, C. L. *The Supreme Court and the Commander-in-Chief.* Ithaca, N.Y.: Cornell University Press, 1976.

Rostow, E. V. *The Sovereign Prerogative: The Supreme Court and the Quest for Law.* New Haven: Yale University Press, 1962.

Rutledge, Wiley. *A Declaration of Legal Faith.* New York: DaCapo Press, 1970.

Solomon, L. I. *The Supreme Court.* New York: H.W. Wilson, 1961.

Schlesinger, A. M. *The Supreme Court: 1947.* New York: Time, 1947.

Schmidhauser, J. R., ed. *Constitutional Law in the Political Process.* Chicago: Rand McNally, 1963.

———. *The Supreme Court and Congress: Conflict and Interaction, 1945–1968.* New York: Free Press, 1972.

———. *The Supreme Court as Final Arbiter in Federal-State Relations, 1789–1957.* Chapel Hill: University of North Carolina Press, 1958.

———. *Supreme Court: Its Politics, Personalities and Procedures.* New York: Holt, Rinehart and Winston, 1960.

Schubert, G. A. *Constitutional Politics: The Political Behavior of Supreme Court Justices and the Constitutional Policies That They Make.* New York: Holt, Rinehart and Winston, 1960.

———. *The Constitutional Polity.* Boston: Boston University Press, 1970.

———. *The Future of the Nixon Court.* Honolulu: [No pub.], 1972.

———. *The Judicial Mind: The Attitudes and Ideologies of Supreme Court Justices, 1946–1963.* Evanston, Ill.: Northwestern University Press, 1965.

_____ . *Judicial Mind Revisited: Psychometric Analysis of the Supreme Court Ideology.* New York: Oxford University Press, 1974.

_____ . *Quantitative Analysis of Judicial Behavior.* Glencoe, Ill.: Free Press, 1960.

Schwartz, Bernard. *A Basic History of the United States Supreme Court.* Princeton, N. J.: Van Nostrand, 1968.

_____ . *The Supreme Court, Constitutional Revolution in Retrospect.* New York: Ronald Press, 1957.

Scigliano, R. G. *The Supreme Court and the Presidency.* New York: Free Press, 1971.

Scott, A. M. *The Supreme Court v. the Constitution.* New York: Exposition Press, 1963.

Scott, J. B. *The Judicial Settlement of International Disputes: Addresses at the Geneva Institute of International Relations, August 16th and 17th, 1926.* London: Oxford University Press, 1927.

_____ . *Sovereign States and Suits Before Arbitral Tribunals and Courts of Justice.* New York: New York University Press, 1925.

Selakovitch, D. *Supreme Court: Does It Protect or Limit Our Liberties?* Boston: Allyn, 1976.

Shamon, E. F. *Does the U. S. Supreme Court Govern the United States?* Boston: Old South Book Co., 1969.

Shapiro, D. L., ed. *The Evaluation of a Judicial Philosophy: Selected Opinions and Papers of Justice John Harlan.* Cambridge, Mass.: Harvard University Press, 1969.

Shapiro, Martin. *Freedom of Speech: The Supreme Court and Judicial Review.* Englewood Cliffs, N.J.: Prentice-Hall, 1966.

_____ . *Law and Politics in the Supreme Court.* New York: Free Press of Glencoe, 1964.

_____ . *The Supreme Court and Administrative Agencies.* New York: Free Press, 1968.

_____ . *The Supreme Court and Constitutional Rights: Readings in Constitutional Law.* Atlanta: Scott, Foresman, 1967.

_____ . *The Supreme Court and Public Policy.* Atlanta: Scott, Foresman, 1969.

Sheldon, Charles. *The Supreme Court: Politicians in Robes.* Beverly Hills, Calif.: Glencoe Press, 1970.

Shirley, J. M. *The Dartmouth College Case and the Supreme Court of the United States.* New York: DaCapo Press, 1971. (Originally published in 1879.)

Shogan, Robert. *A Question of Judgment: The Fortas Case and the Struggle for the Supreme Court.* Indianapolis: Bobbs-Merrill, 1972.

Silver, D. M. *Lincoln's Supreme Court.* Urbana: University of Illinois Press, 1956.

————. *The Supreme Court During the Civil War.* Urbana: University of Illinois Press, 1940.

Simon, James F. *In His Own Image: The Supreme Court in Richard Nixon's America.* New York: D. McKay, 1973.

Smith, H. A. *The American Supreme Court as an International Tribunal.* New York: Oxford University Press, 1920.

Snow, A. H. *The Development of the American Doctrine of Jurisdiction of Courts Over States.* Baltimore: American Society for Judicial Settlement of International Disputes, 1911.

Sokol, Ronald P. *Law-abiding Policeman: A Guide to Recent Supreme Court Decisions.* Charlottesville, Va.: Michie, 1966.

Spaeth, H. J. *An Introduction to Supreme Court Decision Making.* rev. and enl. San Francisco: Chandler Pub. Co., 1972.

————. *The Warren Court: Cases and Commentary.* San Francisco: Chandler Pub. Co., 1966.

Spahr, Margaret. *The Supreme Court on the Incidence and Effects of Taxation: An Analysis of Economic Theory Embedded in the Constitutional Law Derived from the Explicit Tax Clauses.* Northhampton, Mass.: Dept. of History, Smith College, 1925.

Spicer, G. W. *Supreme Court and Fundamental Freedoms.* 2d ed. New York: Appleton-Century-Crofts, 1967.

Sprague, J. D. *Voting Patterns of the U.S. Supreme Court: Cases in Federalism, 1889-1959.* Indianapolis: Bobbs-Merrill, 1968.

Spurlock, Clark. *Education and the Supreme Court.* Urbana: University of Illinois Press, 1955.

Starr, I. *The Supreme Court and Contemporary Issues.* Chicago: Encyclopedia Britannica Educational Corp., 1969.

Steamer, R. J. *The Supreme Court: Constitutional Revision and the New Strict Constructionism.* Minneapolis: Burgess Pub. Co., 1973.

———— . *The Supreme Court in Crisis: A History of Conflict.* Amherst: University of Massachusetts Press, 1971.

Steiner, H. A. *Significant Supreme Court Decisions, 1934-1936.* Los Angeles: Students's Co-operative Store, University of California at Los Angeles, 1936.

Stephens, Otis H. *The Supreme Court and Confessions of Guilt.* Knoxville: University of Tennessee Press, 1973.

Stern, R. L. *Supreme Court Practice: Jurisdiction, Procedure, Arguing and Briefing Techniques, Forms, Statutes, Rules for Practice in the Supreme Court of the United States.* 5th ed. Washington: Bureau of National Affairs, 1974.

Stites, Francis N. *Private Interest and Public Gain: The Dartmouth College Case, 1819.* Amherst: University of Massachusetts, 1972.

Story, W. W., ed. *Miscellaneous Writings of Joseph Story.* New York: DaCapo Press, 1972.

Strum, Philippa. *The Supreme Court and "Political Questions": A Study in Judicial Evasion.* University, Alabama: University of Alabama Press, 1974.

Sutherland, A. E. *Apology for Uncomfortable Change, 1865–1965.* New York: Macmillan, 1965.

———— ., ed. *Government Under Law—A Conference Held at Harvard Law School on the Occasion of the Bicentennial of Justice Marshall.* New York: DaCapo Press, 1968.

Swindler, W. F. *Court and Constitution in the Twentieth Century.* Indianapolis: Bobbs-Merrill.
Volume I: *The Old Legality, 1889–1932.* (1969).
Volume II: *The New Legality, 1932–1968.* (1970).
Volume III: *A Modern Interpretation.* (1974).

Swisher, Carl B. *Historic Decisions of the Supreme Court.* 2d ed. New York: Van Nostrand Reinhold, 1969.

———— . *The Supreme Court in Modern Role.* rev. ed. New York: New York University Press, 1965.

Taft, W. H. *The Anti-Trust Act and the Supreme Court.* Mamaroneck, N.Y.: Kraus Reprint Corp., 1969.

———— . *United States Supreme Court: The Prototype of a World Court.* Baltimore: American Society for Judicial Settlement of International Disputes, 1915.

Taylor, Albion G. *Labor and the Supreme Court.* 2d ed. Ann Arbor, Mich: Braun-Brumfield, 1961.

Taylor, Hannis. *Jurisdiction and Procedure of the Supreme Court of the United States.* Rochester, N.Y.: Lawyers' Cooperative Pub. Co., 1905.

Thomas, William R. *The Burger Court and Civil Liberties.* Brunswick, Ohio: King's Court Communications, 1976.

Todd, A. L. *Justice on Trial: The Case of Louis Brandeis.* New York: McGraw-Hill, 1964.

Treacy, K. W. *The Collisions of the Supreme Court of the United States and the States: the Marshall Court, 1801–1833.* Ann Arbor, Mich.: University Microfilms, 1958.

Tresolini, R. J. *Justice and the Supreme Court.* Philadelphia: Lippincott, 1963.

Tully, A. *Supreme Court.* New York: Simon and Schuster, 1963.

Tussman, J., ed. *The Supreme Court on Racial Discrimination.* New York: Oxford University Press, 1963.

Twiss, B. R. *Lawyers and the Constitution: How Laissez-Faire Came to the Supreme Court.* Princeton, N.J.: Princeton University Press, 1942.

U. S. Congress. House. Committee on the Judiciary. *Composition and Jurisdiction of the Supreme Court. Hearing before Subcommittee No. 4 of the Committee on the Judiciary, House of Representatives, Eighty-third Congress, Second session, on S. J. Res. 44 and H. J. Res. 194, joint resolutions proposing an amendment to the Constitution of the United States relating to the composition and jurisdiction of the Supreme Court; H. J. Res. 27, joint resolution proposing an amendment to the Constitution of the United States to fix the number of Justices of the Supreme Court; H. J. Res. 91, joint resolution proposing an amendment to the Constitution relating to the terms of office of judges of the Supreme Court of the United States and inferior courts. June 23, 1954.* Washington: U.S. Govt. Print. Off., 1954.

U.S. Congress. House. Committee on the Judiciary. *To Change the Quorum of the Supreme Court of the United States. Hearings before Subcommittee No. 4 of the Committee on the Judiciary, House of Representatives, Seventy-eighth Congress, First session of H. R. 2808, a bill to amend section 215 of the Judicial Code, relating to the quorum of the Justices of the Supreme Court of the United States.*

June 11 and 24, 1943. Serial no. 14. Washington: U.S. Govt. Print. Off., 1944.

U.S. Congress. Senate. Committee on the Judiciary. *Adverse Report of the Committee on the Judiciary on a Bill to Reorganize the Judicial Branch of the Government.* Stamford, Conn.: Overbrook Press, 1937.

U.S. Congress. Senate. Committee on the Judiciary. *Composition and Jurisdiction of the Supreme Court. Hearing before a Subcommittee of the Committee on the Judiciary, United States Senate, Eighty-third Congress, Second session, on S. J. Res. 44, joint resolution proposing an amendment to the Constitution of the United States relating to the composition and jurisdiction of the Supreme Court. January 29, 1954.* Washington: U.S. Govt. Print. Off., 1954.

U.S. Congress. Senate. Committee on the Judiciary. *Reorganization of the Federal Judiciary. Hearings before the Committee on the Judiciary, United States Senate, Seventy-fifth Congress, First session, on S. 1392, a bill to reorganize the judicial branch of the government.* Washington: U.S. Govt. Print. Off., 1937.

U.S. Congress. Senate. Committee on the Judiciary. *Reorganization of the Federal Judiciary . . . Adverse Report (to accompany S. 1392)* Washington: U.S. Govt. Print. Off., 1937.

U.S. Congress. Senate. Committee on the Judiciary. Subcommittee on Separation of Powers. *The Supreme Court. Hearings, Ninetieth Congress, Second session.* Washington: U.S. Govt. Print. Off., 1968.

U.S. Supreme Court. *Historic Decisions of the Supreme Court.* 2d ed. New York: Van Nostrand Reinhold, 1969.

U.S. Supreme Court. *Proceedings at the Ceremonies in Commemoration of the One Hundred and Fiftieth Anniversary of the First Meeting of the Supreme Court of the United States, February 1, 1940.* Washington: U.S. Govt. Print. Off., 1940.

Urofsky, Melvin, ed. *Letters of Louis D. Brandeis.* v. I: 1870–1907. v. II: 1907–1912. Albany: State University of New York Press, 1971.

Vance, D. F. *The Supreme Court and the Definition of Religion.* Bloomington, Ind.: Dept. of Government, Indiana University, 1970.

Vance, W. R. *The Supreme Court of the United States as an International Tribunal.* Baltimore: American Society for Judicial Settlement of International Disputes, 1915.

Van Cise, J. G. *The Supreme Court and the Antitrust Laws 1966–1967.* New York: Practising Law Institute, 1967.

Virginia. Commission on Constitutional Government. *The Supreme Court of the United States: A Review of the 1964 Term.* Richmond, 1965.

Vose, Clement E. *Constitutional Change: Amendment Politics and Supreme Court Litigation Since 1900.* Lexington, Mass.: Lexington, 1972.

Walch, John W. *Debate Handbook on Power of the Supreme Court.* Portland, Me., 1959.

Walker, Mary M. *The Evolution of the United States Supreme Court.* Morristown, N.J.: General Learning Press, 1974.

Warren, Charles. *Congress, the Constitution, and the Supreme Court.* rev. and enl. Boston: Little, Brown, 1935.

————. *The Making of the Constitution.* Boston: Little, Brown, 1928.

————. *The Supreme Court and Sovereign States.* Princeton, N.J.: Princeton University Press, 1924.

————. *The Supreme Court and the World Court, 1832 and 1932. Record of ratifications and signatures to: the protocol of signature of the World Court, the optional clause recognizing the Court's jurisdiction, the protocol of revision of the statute, the protocol of accession of the United States.* Worcester, Mass.: Carnegie Endowment for International Peace, Division of Intercourse and Education, 1933.

————. *The Supreme Court in United States History.* rev. ed. Boston: Little, Brown, 1935.

The Warren Court: A Critical Analysis. New York: Chelsea House, 1969.

Wasby, Stephen L. *Continuity and Change: From the Warren Court to the Burger Court.* Monica, Calif.: Goodyear, 1976.

————. *The Impact of the United States Supreme Court.* Homewood, Ill.: Dorsey Press, 1970.

Weaver, J. D. *Warren: the Man, the Court, the Era.* Boston: Little, Brown, 1967.

Webster, Sidney. *Two Treaties of Paris and the Supreme Court.* New York: Harper, 1901.

Wechsler, Herbert. *Principles, Politics and Fundamental Law.* Cambridge, Mass.: Harvard University Press, 1961.

Weeks, K. M. *Adam Clayton Powell and the Supreme Court.* New York: Dunellen Pub. Co., 1971.

Weinberger, A. D. *Freedom and Protection.* San Francisco: Chandler Pub. Co., 1962.

Westin, A. F. *An Autobiography of the Supreme Court: Off-the-Bench Commentary by the Justices.* New York: Macmillan, 1963.

————, ed. *The Supreme Court: Views from Inside.* New York: Norton, 1961.

White, G. Edward. *The American Judicial Tradition.* New York: Oxford University Press, 1976.

Wilkinson, J. Harvie, III. *Serving Justice: A Supreme Court Clerk's View.* New York: Charterhouse, 1974.

Williams, Jerre S. *The Supreme Court Speaks.* Austin: University of Texas Press, 1956.

Willoughby, W. W. *The Supreme Court of the United States: Its History and Influence in Our Constitutional System.* Baltimore: Johns Hopkins Press, 1890.

Wilcox, T. *States' Rights vs. the Supreme Court.* Boston: Forum Pub. Co., 1960.

Witkowiak, S. B. *Limitations Imposed Upon the Rights and Powers of Respective States Over Education by the United States Supreme Court.* Washington: Catholic University of America Press, 1942.

Wood, V. L. *Due Process of Law, 1932–1949: the Supreme Court's Use of a Constitutional Tool.* Baton Rouge: Louisiana State University Press, 1951.

Wright, B. F. *The Content Clause of the Constitution.* Cambridge, Mass.: Harvard University Press, 1938.

————. *The Growth of American Constitutional Law.* Boston: Published for Reynal & Hitchcock by Houghton Mifflin, 1942.

Wyzanski, C. E. *Whereas—A Judge's Premises, Essays in Judgment, Ethics and the Law.* Boston: Little, Brown, 1965.

Ziegler, B. M. *The Supreme Court and American Economic Life.* Evanston, Ill.: Row Peterson, 1962.

Articles and Short Monographs

Alsop, S. "The Myth and William Rehnquist." 78 no. 23 *News-week* 124 (1971).

Atkinson, D. N. "From New Deal Liberal to Supreme Court Conservative: The Metamorphosis of Justice Sherman Minton." 1975 *Washington University Law Quarterly* 361.

————. "Justice Sherman Minton and Behavior Patterns Inside the Supreme Court." 69 *Northwestern University Law Review* 716 (1974).

————. "Minor Supreme Court Justices: Their Characteristics and Importance." 3 *Florida State University Law Review* 348 (1975).

————. "Opinion Writing on the Supreme Court, 1949–1956: The Views of Justice Sherman Minton." 49 *Temple Law Quarterly* 105 (1975).

Baker, L. "With All Deliberate Speed." 24 no. 2 *American Heritage* 42 (1973).

Baldwin, F. N. "United States Supreme Court: A Creative Check of Institutional Misdirection?" 45 *Indiana Law Journal* 550 (1970).

Bartholomew, P. C. "Supreme Court of the United States, 1967–1968." 21 *Western Political Quarterly* 560 (1968).

————. "The Supreme Court of the United States, 1970–1971." 24 *Western Political Quarterly* 687 (1971).

Beck, James Montgomery. "The Old and the New Supreme Court: An Address . . . Before the Law Academy of Philadelphia, January 18, 1923." Philadelphia: *The Law Academy of Philadelphia*, 1923.

Beytagh, F. X. "Mr. Justice Stevens and the Burger Court's Uncertain Trumpet." 51 *Notre Dame Lawyer* 946 (1976).

Bickel, A. M. "The Making of Supreme Court Justices." 53 no. 11 *The New Leader* 14 (1970).

Bland, R. W. "Justice Thurgood Marshall: An Analysis of His First Years on the Court, 1967–1971." 4 *North Carolina Central Law Journal* 183 (1973).

Blaustein, A. P., and Mersky, R. M. "Rating Supreme Court Justices." 58 *American Bar Association Journal* 1183 (1972).

Blumstein, J. F. "Supreme Court's Jurisdiction—Reform Proposals, Discretionary Review, and Writ Dismissals." 26 *Vanderbilt Law Review* 895 (1973).

Bork, R. H. "Supreme Court Needs a New Philosophy." 78 *Fortune* 138 (December 1968).

Brennan, D. M. "Mr. Justice Brennan after Five Years: Speeches and Articles." 11 *Catholic University Law Review* 1 (1962).

Brennan, W. J. "The Bill of Rights and the States." 36 *New York University Law Review* 761 (1961).

————— . "State Supreme Court Judge versus United States Supreme Court Justice: A Change in Function and Perspective." 19 *University of Florida Law Review* 225 (1966).

Browning, J. R. "The Supreme Court Collection at the National Archives." 4 *American Journal of Legal History* 241 (1960).

Burger, W. E.; Warren, E. "Retired Chief Justice Warren Attacks, Chief Justice Burger Defends Freund Study Group's Composition and Proposal." 59 *American Bar Association Journal* 721 (1973).

Burns, R. D., and Yerby, R. D. "John Jay: Political Jurist." 13 *Journal of Public Law* 222 (1964).

Campbell, B. A. "John Marshall, the Virginia Political Economy, and the Dartmouth College Decision." 19 *American Journal of Legal History* 40 (1975).

Cannon, M. W. "Administrative Change and the Supreme Court." 57 *Judicature* 334 (1974).

Casey, G. "Supreme Court and Myth: An Empirical Investigation." 8 *Law and Social Review* 385 (1974).

Casper, G., and Posner, R. A. "Study of the Supreme Court's Caseload." 3 *Journal of Legal Studies* 339 (1974).

Catton, B. "Black Pawn on a Field of Peril: *Dred Scott* v. *Sanford*." 15 no. 1 *American Heritage* 66 (1963).

"Chief Justice Earl Warren: A Tribute" (Rosett, Hoenig, Moore, Jr., Pollak, Ehrenhaft, Bice, Moody, Jr., Hoerner) 2 *Hastings Constitutional Law Quarterly* 1 (1975).

Choper, J. H. "Supreme Court and the Political Branches: Democratic Theory and Practice." 122 *University of Pennsylvania Law Review* 810 (1974).

Clark, T. C. "The Court and Its Functions." 34 *Albany Law Review* 497 (1970).

———— . "The Supreme Court Conference." 37 *Texas Law Review* 273 (1959).

Clarke, John Hessin. "Observations and Reflections on Practice in the Supreme Court of the United States," An address delivered at the annual dinner of New York University Law Alumni, February 4, 1922.

Cohen, J. A. "Mr. Justice Frankfurter." 50 *California Law Review* 591 (1962).

Cooper, Charles P. "The Power of the Supreme Court of the United States to Declare Acts of Congress Void. Did the Framers of the Constitution and the American People Intend to Confer Such Power?" Discussions of the judicial power, by the delegates to the constitutional conventions. Jacksonville, Fla.: Cooper Press, 1935.

Cooper, Drury Walls. "Some Comments on the President's Bill to Increase the Membership of the Supreme Court." New York, 1937.

Cooper, J. A. "Mr. Justice Hugo La Fayette Black, of Alabama, 1886–1971." 33 *Alabama Lawyer* 17 (1972); 37 *Alabama Lawyer* 433 (1976).

Coudert, Frederic Rene. "The New Deal and the United States Supreme Court." A lecture delivered before the University of Oxford. Oxford: Clarendon Press, 1936.

Countryman, V. "Contribution of the Douglas Dissents." 10 *Georgia Law Review* 331 (1976).

Current, R. N. " 'It is . . . a small college . . . yet, there are those who love it': *Dartmouth College* v. *Woodward*." 14 no. 5 *American Heritage* 10 (1963).

Dangerfield, G. "The Steamboats' Charter of Freedom. *Gibbons* v. *Ogden*." 14 no. 6 *American Heritage* 38 (1963).

Daniels, W. J. "Supreme Court and Its Publics." 37 *Albany Law Review* 632 (1973).

Davis, J. F., and Reynolds, W. L. "Juridical Cripples: Plurality Opinions in the Supreme Court." 1974 *Duke Law Journal* 59.

Dedication. "In Honor of Mr. Justice Douglas." "Mr. Justice Douglas." C.E. Ares; "Even-Handed Justice." V. Countryman; "Mr. Justice Douglas." S. Duke. 11 *Harvard Civil Rights Civil Liberties Law Review* 227 (1976).

Dedication. "William O. Douglas: An Appreciation." A. Fortas;
    "Mr. Justice Douglas." R. A. Sprecher; "Justice Douglas
    and the Equal Protection Clause." K. L. Karst; "Justice
    William O. Douglas: The Constitution in a Free Society."
    W. N. Beaney; "An Appreciative Note on Mr. Justice
    Douglas' View of the Court's Role in Environmental Cases."
    P. Baude. 51 *Indiana Law Journal* 1 (1975).
Denenberg, R. V. "U.S. Supreme Court—An Introductory Note."
    29 *Cambridge Law Journal* 134 (1971).
Dionisopoulos, P. A. "Uniqueness of the Warren and Burger
    Courts in American Constitutional History." 22 *Buffalo
    Law Review* 737 (1973).
Dodd, Walter Fairleigh. "The United States Supreme Court as the
    Final Interpreter of the Federal Constitution." Chicago,
    1912.
Duke, S. "Tribute to Mr. Justice Douglas." 9 *Akron Law Re-
    view* 399 (1976).
Dunford, Edward Bradstreet. "The Supreme Court and the
    Eighteenth Amendment, Address Delivered . . . Before
    the Congress of the World League Against Alcoholism,
    on Saturday, August 20, 1927 at Winona Lake." Wester-
    ville, Ohio: American Issue Pub. Co., 1927.
Dunne, G. T. "Justice Hugo Black and Robert Jackson: The
    Great Feud." 19 *St. Louis University Law Journal* 465
    (1975).
Edgerton, H. W. "The Incidence of Judicial Control over Con-
    gress." 22 *Cornell Law Quarterly* 299 (1937).
Farrand, Max. "The First Hayburn Case, 1792." 13 *American
    Historical Review* 281 (1906).
Felix Frankfurter—In Memoriam. 37 *New York State Bar Jour-
    nal* 203 (1965).
Fennell, W. G. "The 'Reconstructed Court' and Religious Free-
    dom, the Gobitis Case in Retrospect." 19 *New York
    University Law Quarterly Review* 31 (1941).
Finlay, Luke W. "The Kings and the Courts." New York, 1937.
"Five-Four Decisions of the United States Supreme Court: Resur-
    rection of the Extraordinary Majority." 7 *Suffolk Uni-
    versity Law Review* 807 (1973).
Fleishmann, M., and Jensen, R. H. "American Bar Association and
    the Supreme Court—Old Wine in a New Bottle?" 20
    Buffalo Law Review 61 (1970).

Flesch, Richard Charles. "Review of Supreme Court's Tax Decisions, 1946–47 Term." Washington: Federal Bar Association, 1947.

Fletcher, John Lockwood. "The Segregation Case and the Supreme Court." Boston, 1958.

Fordham, J. B. "Earl Warren, a Man for All Men." 1 no. 2 *Human Rights* 1 (1971).

————. "The Present Supreme Court: Social Legislation and the Judicial Process." 37 *West Virginia Law Quarterly* 167 (1931).

Fortas, A. "Chief Justice Warren: The Enigma of Leadership." 84 *Yale Law Journal* 405 (1970).

Frank, J. P. "Conflict of Interest and U.S. Supreme Court Justices." 18 *American Journal of Comparative Law* 744 (1970).

————. "Legal Ethics of Louis D. Brandeis." 17 *Stanford Law Review* 683 (1965).

Frankfurter, F. "Supreme Court in the Mirror of Justices." 44 *American Bar Association Journal* 723 (1958).

Franklin, M. "Contribution to an Explication of the Activity of the Warren Majority of the Supreme Court." 24 *Buffalo Law Review* 487 (1975).

Freund, P. A. "National Court of Appeals." 25 *Hastings Law Journal* 130 (1974).

————. "Supreme Court under Attack." 25 *University of Pittsburgh Law Review* 1 (1963).

————. "The Supreme Court Crisis." 31 *New York State Bar Bulletin* 66 (1959).

Friedenthal, J. H. "Rulemaking Power of the Supreme Court: A Contemporary Crisis." 27 *Stanford Law Review* 673 (1975).

Garraty, J. A. "The Case of the Missing Commissions: *Marbury v. Madison.*" 14 no. 4 *American Heritage* 5 (1963).

Gavagan, Joseph Andrew. "Powers of the United States Supreme Court: Power to Declare Void Acts of Congress Repugnant to the Constitution—A Reply to Recent Criticisms of the Court Expressed Both In and Out of Congress. *Congressional Record*, March 11, 1936.

Gilkey, R. C. "Felix Frankfurter's Role as a Progressive in Politics and Liberal Disciple of Brandeis on the Labor Question." 33 *University of Missouri-Kansas City Law Review* 264 (1965).

————— . "Mr. Justice Frankfurter and Freedom of Religion in Terms of Separation of Church and State." 27 *University of Kansas City Law* Review 3 (1958).

Goldberg, A. J. "Constitutional Faith." 26 *Alabama Law Review* 295 (1974).

————— . "Mr. Justice Douglas: One Man's Opinions." 3 *Hastings Constitutional Law Quarterly* 1 (1976).

"Governor on the Bench: Charles Evans Hughes as Associate Justice." 89 *Harvard Law Review* 961 (1976).

Graham, H. J. "The Supreme Court of History." 10 *Vanderbilt Law Review* 395 (1957).

Gressman, E. "Constitution v. the Freund Report." 41 *Washington Law Review* 951 (1973).

Griffin, R. P. "The Fortas Controversy: The Senate's Role of Advise and Consent to Judicial Nominations. The Broad Role." 2 *Prospectus* 283 (1969).

Griswold, E. N. "Appellate Advocacy with Particular Reference to the United States Supreme Court." 44 *New York State Bar Journal* 375 (1972). 26 *Record of the Association of the Bar of the City of New York* 342 (1971).

————— . "Practice Before the Supreme Court of the United States." 29 *Federal Bar Journal* 147 (1970).

————— . "Rationing Justice—the Supreme Court's Caseload and What the Court Does Not Do." 60 *Cornell Law Review* 335 (1975).

Grossman, J. B., and Wasby, S. "Haynesworth and Parker: History Does Live Again." 23 *South Carolina Law Review* 345 (1971).

————— . "Senate and Supreme Court Nominations: Some Reflections." 1972 *Duke Law Journal* 557.

Gunther, G. "In Search of Judicial Quality on a Changing Court: The Case of Justice Powell." 24 *Stanford Law Review* 1001 (1972).

————— . "The Subtle Vices of the 'Passive Virtues'—A Comment on Principle and Expediency in Judicial Review." 64 *Columbia Law Review* 1 (1964).

Halper, T. "Senate Rejection of Supreme Court Nominees." 22 *Drake Law Review* 102 (1972).

Hart, H. M. "The Supreme Court, 1958 Term Forward: The Time Chart of the Justices." 73 *Harvard Law Review* 84 (1959).

Hendricks, Thomas Andrews. "The Supreme Court of the United States, and the Influences that have Contributed to Make it the Greatest Judicial Tribunal in the World." An oration delivered before the graduating classes and alumni of the Yale Law School at its sixty-first anniversary, June 23, 1885. New Haven, Law Dept. of Yale College, 1885.

Hills, R. M. "A Law Clerk at the Supreme Court of the United States." 33 *Los Angeles Bar Bulletin* 333 (1958).

Hoar, George Frisbie. "The Charge Against President Grant and Attorney General Hoar of Packing the Supreme Court of the United States, to Secure the Reversal of the Legal Tender Decision, by the Appointment of Judges Bradley and Strong, Refuted." Letter to the *Boston Herald.* Worcester, Mass.: Press of C. Hamilton, 1896.

Hogan, H. J. "Supreme Court and the Crisis in Liberalism." 33 *Journal of Politics* 257 (1971).

Holtzoff, Alexander. "Trends of Supreme Court Decisions." An address before the Cleveland Bar Association, Cleveland, Ohio, October 5, 1937.

Howard, A. E. D. "Mr. Justice Powell and the Emerging Nixon Majority." 70 *Michigan Law Review* 445 (1972).

Hruska. R. L. "National Court of Appeals: An Analysis of Viewpoints." 9 *Creighton Law Review* 286 (1975).

Hudon, E. G. "The Supreme Court of the United States." 19 *Federal Bar Journal* 185 (1959).

"In Honor of Mr. Justice William O. Douglas." (Warren, Burger, Sovern, Davis,) "Mr. Justice Douglas' Contribution to the Law. The First Amendment." T. I. Emerson; "Equal Protection of the Laws." N. Dorsen; "Constitutional Criminal Law." C. Ares; "Business Regulation." V. Countryman; Evolution to Absolutism: Justice Douglas and the First Amendment." L. A. Powe, Jr. 74 *Columbia Law Review* 341 (1974).

"Interpenetration of Narrow Construction and Policy: Mr. Justice Steven's Circuit Opinions." 13 *San Diego Law Review* 899 (1976).

Isenbergh, M. "Frankfurter as a Policymaker." 85 *Yale Law Journal* 280 (1975).

Jacobsohn, G. J. "Felix Frankfurter and the Ambiguities of Judicial Statesmanship." 49 *New York University · Law Review* 1 (1974).

Jaeger, W. H. E. "John Marshall: The Man, the Judge and the Law of Nations." 8 *American University Law Review* 28 (1959).

Johnsen, J. E., comp. "Limitation of Power of Supreme Court to Declare Acts of Congress Unconstitutional." 10 no. 6 *Reference Shelf* 1 (1935).

————— . "Reorganization of the Supreme Court." 11 no. 4 *Reference Shelf* 1 (1937).

Johnson, H. A. "John Jay: Lawyer in a Time of Transition, 1764–1774." 124 *University of Pennsylvania Law Review* 1260 (1976).

Johnson, Marian. "Preliminary Inventory of the Records of the Supreme Court of the United States." Washington: National Archives and Record Service, 1973.

"Judicial Philosophy of William H. Rehnquist." 45 *Mississippi Law Journal* 224 (1974).

Judicial Secrecy: A Symposium. "Secrecy and the Supreme Court: On the Need for Piercing the Red Velour Curtain." A. S. Miller, D. S. Sastri: "Irreverent Questions about Piercing the Red Velour Curtain." E. Gressman; "Comments on 'Secrecy and the Supreme Court,'" J. B. Grossman; "Comment on Secrecy and the Supreme Court." J. W. Howard, Jr.; "Comment on the Miller-Sastri Article." W. Probert; "One Touch of Adonis: On Ripping the Lid off Pandora's Box." G. Schubert's Comments on "Secrecy and the Supreme Court." R. Young; "Judicial Secrecy and Institutional Legitimacy: Max Weber Revisited." J. R. Schmidhauser, L. L. Berg, J. J. Green. 22 *Buffalo Law Review* 797 (1973).

"Justice Douglas and the Supreme Court." 122 *America* 464 (1970).

"Justice George Sutherland." S. D. Thurman; "A Study in Judicial Motivation: Mr. Justice Sutherland and Economic Regulation." R. A. Maidment. 1973 *Utah Law Review* 153.

Kauper, P. G. "Church and State: Cooperative Separatism." 60 *Michigan Law Review* 1 (1961).

King, W. L. "Mr. Justice Frankfurter Retires." 48 *American Bar Association Journal* 1143 (1962).

Knowlton, R. E. "Supreme Court, *Mapp* v. *Ohio* and Due Process of Law." 49 *Iowa Law Review* 14 (1963).

Kuchel, T. H.; Williams, E. B.; and Beytagh, F. X. "In Memoriam: Earl Warren." 6 *California Law Review* 3 (1976).

Kurland, P. B. "Appointment and Disappointment of Supreme Court Justices." 1972 *Law and the Social Order* 183.

――――. "Jurisdiction of the United States Supreme Court: Time for a Change?" 59 *Cornell Law Review* 616 (1974).

――――. "New Supreme Court." 7 *John Marshall Journal of Practice and Procedure* 1 (1973).

――――. "Of Church and State and the Supreme Court." 29 *University of Chicago Law Review* 2 (1961).

Lamb, C. M. "Judicial Policy-Making and Information Flow to the Supreme Court." 29 *Vanderbilt Law Review* 45 (1976).

Law Association of Philadelphia. "The Argument on Behalf of Certain Proposed Legislation to be Laid Before the Judiciary Committees of the Senate and the House of Representatives of the United States, at the Forty-Eighth Congress." Prepared by the Committee of the Law Association of Philadelphia, appointed December 5, 1882, to consider the subject of the delays to suitors in the Supreme Court of the United States and the various plans for the relief of that Court which have been suggested. Philadelphia: Collins Printer, 1884.

Leuchtenburg, W. E. "Klansman Joins the Court: The Appointment of Hugo L. Black." 41 *University of Chicago Law Review* 1 (1973).

Lewis, A. "The 3rd Branch, Lately Active, May Have Too Much Work To Do." *New York Times.* Sunday, Jan. 13, 1974.

Lillich, R. B. "Chase Impeachment." 4 *American Journal of Legal History* 49 (1960).

MacGrath, C. P. "A Foot in the Door: *Munn* v. *Illinois.*" 15 no. 2 *American Heritage* 44 (1964).

McKay, R. B. "Selection of U.S. Supreme Court Justices." 9 *Kansas Law Review* 109 (1960).

――――. "The Supreme Court and Its Lawyer Critics." 28 *Fordham Law Review* 615 (1959–1960).

McLain, J. D., Jr. "Supreme Court Controversies of Presidents Roosevelt and Nixon: A Consideration of the Political Nature of the Presidential Power of Judicial Appointment." 8 *Georgia State Bar Journal* 145 (1971).

McLauchlan, W. P. "Research Note: Ideology and Conflict in Supreme Court Opinion Assignment, 1946–1962." 25 *Western Political Quarterly* 16 (1972).

"Marshall Court: A Symposium." 21 *Stanford Law Review* 449 (1969).

Mason, A. T. "Burger Court in Historical Perspective." 47 *New York State Bar Journal* 87 (1975).

——— . "Chief Justice of the United States: *Primus Inter Pares.*" 17 *Journal of Public Law* 20 (1968).

——— . "President by Chance, Chief Justice by Choice." 55 *American Bar Association Journal* 35 (1969).

Maury, William Arden. "The Supreme Court of the United States: A Discussion of Its Wants and the Remedy for Them, With the Draught of a Statute Embodying a Plan of Relief." Washington: W. H. Morrison, 1881.

Meador, D. J. "Justice Black and His Law Clerks." 15 *Alabama Law Review* 57 (1962).

"Memorial to James Francis Byrnes. Introductory Remarks of Memorial Proceedings." E. N. Griswold; "Resolutions of the Bar of the Supreme Court. Response." E. N. Burger; "Remarks on the life of James F. Byrnes." D. S. Russell; "James F. Byrnes and the Supreme Court." R.M. Figg, Jr. 25 *South Carolina Law Review* 515 (1973).

Mendelsohn, R. H. "Senate Confirmation of Supreme Court Appointments: The Nomination and Rejection of John J. Parker." 14 *Howard Law Journal* 105 (1968).

Meredith, J. H. "Supreme Court of the United States and the Proposed National Court of Appeals." 29 *Journal of the Missouri Bar* 441 (1973).

Moore, R. H., Jr. "Justices View Supreme Court Workload: A Subjective Appraisal." 17 *Air Force Law Review* 31 (1975).

"Mootness Doctrine in the Supreme Court." 88 *Harvard Law Review* 373 (1974).

Morris, R. B. "The Jay Papers III: The Trials of Chief Justice Jay." 20 no. 4 *American Heritage* 80 (1969).

"Mr. Justice Clark: A Tribute by Earl Warren;" "A Personal note by D. F. Turner;" "Justice Tom Clark and Judicial Administration" by J. P. Frank. 46 *Texas Law Review* 1 (1967).

"Mr. Justice Goldberg." 48 *American Bar Association Journal* 1146 (1962).

Nagel, S. S. "Characteristics of Supreme Court Greatness." 56 *American Bar Association Journal* 957 (1970).

O'Brien, F. W. "Bicentennial Reflections on Herbert Hoover and the Supreme Court." 61 *Iowa Law Review* 397 (1975).

O'Mahoney, J. C. "The Judiciary Bill Should Not Pass." Radio address by Joseph C. O'Mahoney of Wyoming on May 5, 1937. 81 pt. 9 *Congressional Record* 1077 (1937).

"One Hundred and First Justice: An Analysis of the Opinions of Justice John Paul Stevens, Sitting as Judge on the Seventh Circuit Court of Appeals." 29 *Vanderbilt Law Review* 125 (1976).

O'Reilly, J. D., Jr. "Hugo L. Black—Legal Craftsman." 56 *Massachusetts Law Quarterly* 323 (1971).

Osborne, J. "One Supreme Court." 44 *Life* 92 (June 16, 1958).

Owens, J. B. "Hruska Commission's Proposed National Court of Appeals." 23 *U.C.L.A. Law Review* 580 (1976).

Patterson, Caleb Perry. "The Supreme Court and the Constitution." Dallas, Tex.: Southern Methodist University, 1936.

Paulsen, M. G. "Some Insights into the Burger Court." 27 *Oklahoma Law Review* 677 (1974).

Peebles, T. H. "Mr. Justice Frankfurter and the Nixon Court: Some Reflections on Contemporary Judicial Conservatism." 24 *American University Law Review* 1 (1974).

Peterson, Arnold. "The Supreme Court." New York: New York Labor News Company, 1937.

Phelps, Edward John. "The United States Supreme Court and the Sovereignty of the People." An address at the centennial celebration of the Federal judiciary, New York, February 4, 1890.

Pierce, C. A. "Vacancy on the Supreme Court: The Politics of Judicial Appointment, 1893-94." 39 *Tennessee Law Review* 555 (1972).

Pillen, Herbert George. "Majority Rule in the Supreme Court." Washington: Georgetown University, 1924.

Pollack, L. H. "Securing Liberty through Litigation—The Proper Role of the United States Supreme Court." 36 *Modern Law Review* 113 (1973).

Powe, L. A., Jr. "Senate and the Court: Questioning a Nominee." 54 *Texas Law Review* 891 (1976).

Powell, L. F., Jr. "Myths and Misconceptions about the Supreme Court." 48 *New York State Bar Journal* 6 (1976).

Powell, T. R. "The Supreme Court and the Adamson law." 65
    no. 7 *University of Pennsylvania Law Review and Ameri-
    can Law Register* 607 (1917).
Pusey, M. J. "F.D.R. vs. the Supreme Court." 9 no. 3 *American
    Heritage* 24 (1958).
Randolph, Carman Fitz. "The Insular Cases." New York:
    Columbia University Press, 1901.
Rauh, J. L., Jr. "Felix Frankfurter: Civil Libertarian." 11 *Har-
    vard Civil Rights Law Review* 496 (1976).
"Recollections of Mr. Justice Warren." 9 *Trial Lawyer's Quar-
    terly* 5 (1973).
Redlich, N. "Supreme Court—1833 Term. The Constitution—
    A Rule for the Government of Courts, as well as of the
    Legislature." 40 *New York University Law Review* 1 (1965).
Rehnquist, W. H. "Supreme Court: Past and Present." 59
    American Bar Association Journal 361 (1973).
Reich, C. A. "Mr. Justice Black and the Living Constitution."
    76 *Harvard Law Review* 673 (1963).
Remington, F. J. "The Role of the Supreme Court." 60 *Current
    History* 353 (1971).
Rhodes, I. S. "Legal Records as a Source of History." 59 *Ameri-
    can Bar Association Journal* 635 (1973).
Rodell, F. "The Great Chief Justice." 7 no. 1 *American Heritage*
    10 (1955).
Roe, D. B., and Osgood, R. K. "United States Supreme Court." 60
    Current History 353 (1971).
Ryerson, Hal. "The Place of the Supreme Court in Our Con-
    stitutional   Form   of   Government."   Washington:
    Georgetown University, 1937.
Schultz, W. B., and Howard, P. K. "Myth of Swing Voting: An
    Analysis of Voting Patterns on the Supreme Court." 50
    New York University Law Review 798 (1975).
Seddig, R. G. "John Marshall and the Origins of Supreme Court
    Leadership." 36 *University of Pittsburgh Law Review*
    785 (1975).
Shapiro, D. L. "Mr. Justice Rehnquist: A Preliminary View."
    90 *Harvard Law Review* 293 (1977).
Smith, E. A. "The Interstate Commerce Commission, the De-
    partment of Justice and the Supreme Court." 36 *Ameri-
    can Economic Review* 479 (1946).

Sommer, F. H. "Bill for 'Reforming' the Supreme Court." 23
     American Bar Association Journal 347 (1937).
Spaeth, H. J. "The Judicial Restraint of Mr. Justice Frank-
     furter—Myth or Reality?" 8 *Midwest Journal of Po-
     litical Science* 22 (1964).
Starr, Isidore. "The Federal Judiciary." New York: Oxford
     University Press, 1957.
Steele, T. M. " 'October term, 1936' . . . A study of Recent
     Supreme Court Decisions in the Light of Attacks upon
     the Court." 12 *Connecticut Bar Journal* 14 (1938).
Stevenson, J. "Rosa Parks Wouldn't Budge." 23 no. 2 *American
     Heritage* 56 (1972).
Studies in Judicial Biography. "Chief Justice Taft at the Helm."
     A. T. Mason; "Experience or Reason: The Tort Theories
     of Holmes and Doe." J. P. Reid; "In Search of Holmes
     From Within." S. Touster; "Justice Murphy: The
     Freshman Year." W. Howard; "Chief Justice Waite and
     the 'Twin Relic;' *Reynolds* v. *United States.*" C. P.
     Magrath; "Theodore Roosevelt and the Appointment of
     Mr. Justice Moody." P. T. Heffron; "Salmon P. Chase:
     Chief Justice." D. F. Hughes; "Justice Brewer and
     Substantive Due Process: A Conservative Court Revisited."
     R. E. Gamer; "Justice Joseph Story: A Study of the Legal
     Philosophy of a Jeffersonian Judge." M. D. Dowd;
     "W. O. Douglas—His Work." J. W. Hopkins; "Justice
     W. O. Douglas and the Concept of a 'Fair Trial.' " H. S.
     Thomas. 18 *Vanderbilt Law Review* 367 (1965).
"Summary Disposition of Supreme Court Appeals: The Signifi-
     cance of Limited Discretion and a Theory of Limited
     Precedent." 52 *Boston University Law Review* 373
     (1972).
Swift, Morrison Isaac. "The American House of Lords: Supreme
     Court Usurpation." Boston: *Supreme Court Reform
     League*, 1911.
Swindler, W. F. "Court, the Constitution and Chief Justice
     Burger." 27 *Vanderbilt Law Review* 443 (1974).
————— . "Supreme Court, the President and Congress." 19
     International and Comparative Law Quarterly 671 (1970).
————— . "Warren Court: Compilation of a Constitutional
     Revolution." 23 *Vanderbilt Law Review* 205 (1970).

Symposium: The Burger Court: "New Directions in Judicial Policy-
    Making Foreword." R. Runston; "The Changing Para-
    meters of Substantive Equal Protection: From the Warren
    to the Burger Era." A. B. Winter; "One man, one vote,
    and 'political fairness'—or How the Burger Court Found
    Happiness by Rediscovering *Reynolds* v. *Sims*." G. E.
    Baker; "Variations in Congressional Responses to the
    Warren and Burger Courts." J. J. Green, J. R. Schmid-
    hauser, and L. L. Berg; "Discussant's Remarks: Is the
    Burger Court a Nixon Court?" J. W. Howard, Jr.;
    "Discussant's Remarks." J. S. Ish; "Rejoinder." G. W.
    Baker. 23 *Emory Law Journal* 643 (1974).

Symposium: "Should the Appellate Jurisdiction of the United
    States Supreme Court be Changed? An Evaluation of
    the Freund Report Proposals. The Freund Report: A
    Statistical Analysis and Critique. The Proposed Na-
    tional Court of Appeals: A Critical Analysis. Indigent
    Criminals and the Supreme Court. Impact of the Supreme
    Court's Summary Disposition Practice on its Appeals Juris-
    diction. Interlocutory Appeals under the Antitrust Ex-
    pediting Act. 27 *Rutgers Law Review* 878 (1974).

Symposium: "The Warren Court." 67 *Michigan Law Review* 219
    (1968).

Tipton, S. V. "Warren Court versus the Burger Court." 48 *Florida
    Bar Journal* 560 (1974).

Totenberg, N. "Behind the Marble, Beneath the Robes." *New
    York Times Magazine*, March 16, 1975, p. 15.

————. "The Supreme Court: The Last Plantation." *New
    Times*, July 26, 1974, p. 26.

Ulmer, S. S. "Dissent Behavior and the Social Background of
    Supreme Court Justices." 32 *Journal of Politics* 580
    (1970).

————., and Stookey, H. A. "Nixon's Legacy to the Supreme
    Court: A Statistical Analysis of Judicial Behavior." 3
    Florida State University Law Review 331 (1975).

————. "Social Background as an Indicator to the Votes
    of Supreme Court Justices in Criminal Cases: 1947–1956
    Terms." 17 *American Journal of Political Science* 622
    (1973).

————. "Supreme Court Justices as Strict and Not-So-Strict
    Constructionists: Some Implications." 8 *Law & Social*

Review; the Journal of the Law & Society Ass'n 15 (1973).

———— . "Use of Power in the Supreme Court: The Opinion Assignments of Earl Warren. 1953–1960." 19 *Journal of Public Law* 49 (1970).

Van Der Veer, V. "Hugo Black and the KKK." 19 no. 3 *American Heritage* 60 (1968).

Warren, C. "The Supreme Court and Disputes Between States." An Address delivered at the College of William and Mary in Virginia. Williamsburg, Va., 1940. 366 *International Conciliation* 20 (1941).

———— . "Proposed New 'National Court of Appeals.'" 28 *The Record of the Association of the Bar of the City of York* 627 (1973).

Warren, E. "Address Delivered by Honorable Earl Warren, Chief Justice of the United States Supreme Court, Retired, at the Commencement Exercises of the Law School." 14 *Santa Clara Law Journal* 740 (1974).

———— . "Response to Recent Proposals to Dilute the Jurisdiction of the Supreme Court." 20 *Loyola Law Review* 221 (1973=74).

Wasby, S. L. "United States Supreme Court's Impact: Broadening Our Focus." 49 *Notre Dame Lawyer* 1023 (1974).

Watson, David Kemper. "Invalid Legislation: The Power of the Federal Judiciary to Declare Legislation Invalid which Conflicts with the Federal Constitution." Washington: National Association for Constitutional Government, 1937.

Wedell, H. T. "Non-Political Selection of Justices." 26 *Journal of the Bar Association of Kansas* 355 (1958).

Westin, A. F. "Ride-in." 13 no. 5 *American Heritage* 57 (1962).

Wheeler, R. "Extrajudicial Activities of the Early Supreme Court." 1973 *Supreme Court Review* 122.

"When the Supreme Court was in the Capitol." 61 *American Bar Association Journal* 949 (1975).

William O. Douglas—In Retrospect: "Introduction." B. Burleson, and J. D. Dowmer; "Bill Douglas—a portrait." T. C. Clark; "Justice Douglas and the Availability of the Federal Forum to Civil Rights Litigants." D. R. Richards; "Douglas and the First Amendment—Visiting Old Battlegrounds." M. Maverick, Jr. 28 *Baylor Law Review* 211 (1976).

Williams, R. L. "Supreme Court of the United States: The Staff
      That Keeps it Operating." 7 no. 10 *Smithsonian* 38.
      2 pts. Jan.-Feb. (1977).
Woodward, C. V. "The Birth of Jim Crow: *Plessy* v. *Ferguson.*"
      15 no. 3 *American Heritage* 52 (1964).
Wright, C. A. "The Supreme Court Today." 3 no. 3 *Trial* 10
      (1967).
Wright, J. S. "Professor Bickel, the Scholarly Tradition and the
      Supreme Court." 84 *Harvard Law Review* 769 (1971).
————— . "Role of the Supreme Court in a Democratic Society
      —Judicial Activism or Restraint?" 54 *Cornell Law
      Review* 1 (1968).
Yarbrough, T. E. "Justice Black, the First Amendment, and the
      Burger Court." 46 *Mississippi Law Journal* 203 (1975).

*Other Publications Dealing with Analysis of
Supreme Court Decisions or Pending Cases*

American Enterprise Institute for Public Policy Research.
      *Significant decisions of the Supreme Court, —————
      term.*
      1969-70 term (1970) and 1970-71 term (1971) ed. by Paul C.
      Bartholomew.
      1971-72 term (1972) to date ed. by Bruce E. Fein. (annual)
      Washington, D.C.

American Jewish Congress. Commission on Law and Social
      Action.
      *The Civil rights and civil liberties decisions of the United
      States Supreme Court for the ————— term. A sum-
      mary and analysis.* (annual) New York.

American Jewish Congress. Commission on Law, Social Action
      and Urban Affairs. (formerly Commission on Law and
      Social Action).
      *Litigation Docket of pending cases affecting freedom of
      religion and separation of church and state.* (semi-
      annual) New York.

Bureau of National Affairs.
      United States Law Week. Washington, D.C.

A review of the Supreme Court's work, weekly, each summer
during the court recess.

Harvard Law Review Association.
    Harvard Law Review. The Supreme Court, _____
    term. Cambridge, Mass.
The .first issue of each volume (November issue) is devoted to
analysis of the work of the preceding term, beginning with 63
Harvard Law Review 5 (1949).

Lawyers Cooperative Publishing Company.
    Decisions of the United States Supreme Court. 1963-64
    (annual) Rochester, N.Y.

New York University of Law.
    Annual Survey of American Law. New York: Oceana.
Chapters in each annual edition cover such topics as constitutional law and civil rights or the Supreme Court and antitrust
laws.

Supreme Court Historical Society.
    Yearbook, 1976- ed. by William F. Swindler. Washing-
    ton, D.C.

University of Chicago, Law School.
    The Supreme Court Review. 1963- ed. by Philip B. Kur-
    land. (annual) Chicago, Ill.

West Publishing Company
    *The Supreme Court of the United States. Summary of the
    _____ term.* ed. by   G. Kenneth Reiblich. (annual)
    St. Paul, Minn.

INDEX

210

ONE HUNDRED JUSTICES

Whittaker, Charles (91), 18, 20, 22,
40, 48, 49
William Mitchell College of Law,
19
Williams, George H., 75, 83
Wilson, James (4), 18, 21, 24, 26, 36,
38
Wilson, Woodrow, 11, 31, 43

Wolcott, Alexander, 74, 81-82, 83
Woodbury, Levi (30), 17, 26, 38
Woods, William B. (45), 39
Woodward, George C., 74, 81, 82
Workload, 91

Yale University Law School 19, 20,
22, 23